DATE DUE

GAYLORD			PRINTED IN U.S.A.

INCOGNITO: Bad Influences. Contains material originally published in magazine form as INCOGNITO: Bad Influences #1-5. First printing 2011.
ISBN# 978-0-7851-5155-5. Published by MARVEL WORLDWIDE, INC., a subsidiary of MARVEL ENTERTAINMENT, LLC.
OFFICE OF PUBLICATION: 135 W. 50th Street, New York, NY 10020.
 $17.99 per copy in the U.S. and $19.99 in Canada (GST #R127032852). Canadian Agreement #40668537.
Printed in the U.S.A. **Manufactured between 6/9/2011 and 6/28/2011 by QUAD/GRAPHICS, DUBUQUE, IA, USA.**

10 9 8 7 6 5 4 3 2 1

ED BRUBAKER SEAN PHILLIPS

INCOGNITO

Bad Influences

Colors by Val Staples

I hate it when comic creators get bitching and moaning about how their art form doesn't get the respect it deserves, isn't honored the way theater or painting or mainstream literature is honored, and all that blah-de-blah-de-fucking-blah.

Oh go cry a river somewhere over your twenty-year-old copies of **Maus** and leave me alone.

Then there are these card-carrying members of Fanboy Nation who want to establish a "read-comics-in-public" day, to make funny books seem more socially normative.

Fuck that.

I don't want comics to be respectable. I don't want everyone proudly looking at them in public. I want the act of reading comic books to feel dirty and unhealthy and transgressive, to feel like sin, like a visit to a whorehouse, or a secret fight club, or maybe both at the same time. I don't read comics, I do comics, like shots, four-color grain alcohol slurped right out of the White Queen's dainty navel; afterwards she can slap me around a little and tell me how she's going to punish my wrongdoer. I didn't put down my money for a moving literary epiphany. I dropped that cash to see badass women cavort in fetish costumes while fighting evil, to watch brutal men strangle monsters with their bare hands, to see a city block leveled (if not a whole city), and to have a front-row seat as malformed masters of evil are sliced in half by their own death ray machines.

Don't get me wrong. I am often engaged, enthralled, and moved by the redemptive experience of high art, as it is found in a film like "Rules of the Game," a book like Malamud's "A New Life," or a comic like "Fun Home." It's just that I don't seem to be compulsively drawn to that kind of thing. What really gets my pulse jacked are stories of grime and punishment, lawlessness and disorder, the bad and the ugly (hold the good).

Stories of this ilk grab me like a magnet grabs iron shavings. The creators of such work are blood-slicked MMA fighters, in a world where to fight at all is increasingly seen as both barbaric, and embarrassingly out of step with the times. If I was a more sensible man, governed by more sensible, forward-looking notions, I'm sure I would invest my time in better mannered, more tasteful art forms. But my deepest enthusiasm has always been reserved for the creators of stories that speak to my nerve-endings.

I suppose it's a failing; I have always had compassion for the wrong people.

Speaking of the wrong people, let's talk about Ed Brubaker and Sean Phillips.

INCOGNITO: BAD INFLUENCES is their latest crime of passion, but is only one outrage in a five-year crime spree that dates back to their first creator-owned book together, CRIMINAL: COWARD. I recommend the entire CRIMINAL and INCOGNITO library without reservation.

Under the Influence

CRIMINAL and INCOGNITO are to comics what the albums of the Black Keys are to rock and the pictures of Quentin Tarantino are to film. That is to say, they are willful efforts to explore a given medium in its most primal, most unthought state; to get down to the id of a particular kind of art. The id of film is, no doubt about it, the American grindhouse cinema of the 70s; the id of rock is Muddy roaring that he's got his mojo working; the id of comic books may be viewed in the blood-spattered crime comics and horror books of the early fifties, and is here again, unadulterated and pure, in the work of Brubaker and Phillips.

I hasten to add that these are not coy, artificial, wink-wink attempts at homage. INCOGNITO is not the kind of work that operates from homage, a parasite living on nostalgia and borrowed time; it is the kind of elemental work other people pay homage to twenty years on down the road.

BAD INFLUENCES is the second book in the story of Zack Overkill, a nearly indestructible man who spent years using his powers to get rich, get laid, and lay waste (Didn't read the first book yet? Stop where you are. It's not that you can't read this book if you didn't bother with book one. It's that you shouldn't. Go and get it, read it and come back).

Only one thing could endanger our (anti-)hero: growing a conscience. Zack is never going to be on the side of the angels, but in the course of his two-fisted travels, he catches a bad case of humanity, and is never quite able to shake it. While searching for Simon Slaughter, a former hero, who went deep undercover among the bad guys, and who has apparently gone native, Zack finds his own soul... and isn't very happy about it. It was, frankly, a whole lot more fun whoring and kicking-ass, in the days before he learned how to think. In this way, Zack's inner struggle is a perfect analogy for the comic business as a whole: is it better to work for a noble, elevating, occasionally boring goal... or to get away with murder?

Ed Brubaker's answer to that important, even necessary question is right here in this book. I don't want to give anything away, or speak for him, but it's probably worth noting: Ed **didn't** name his protagonist Zack Over**think**.

At a pivotal moment in the story, Zack catches himself feeling bad for all the outlaws he's crossed and destroyed, and ruminates: **Maybe my problem is I have compassion for the wrong people**. Caring about, rooting for, and getting off on the dirty, dirty lives of the bad guys... that's just sick.

Oh, you too?

Joe Hill
New Hampshire, April, 2011

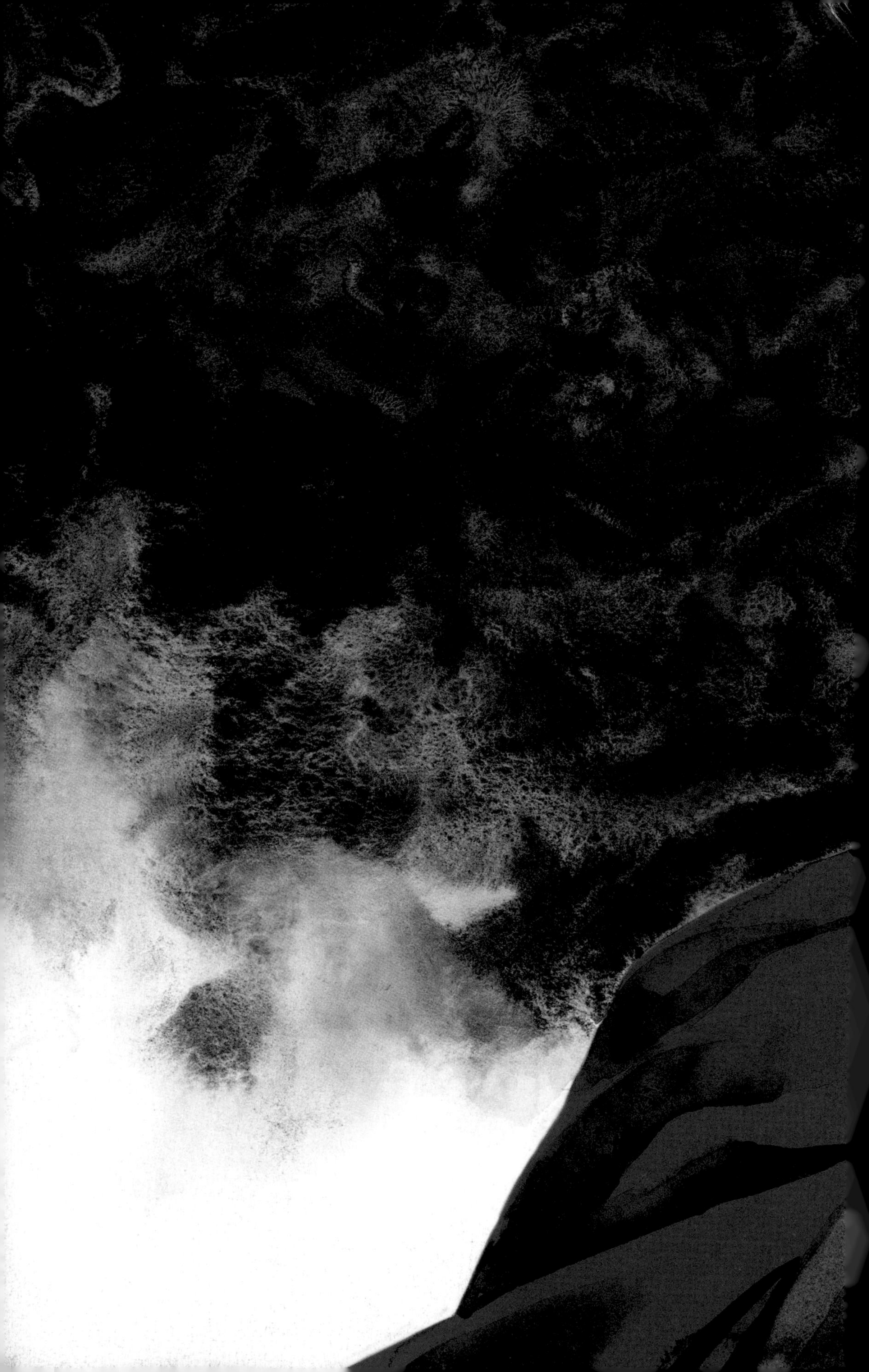

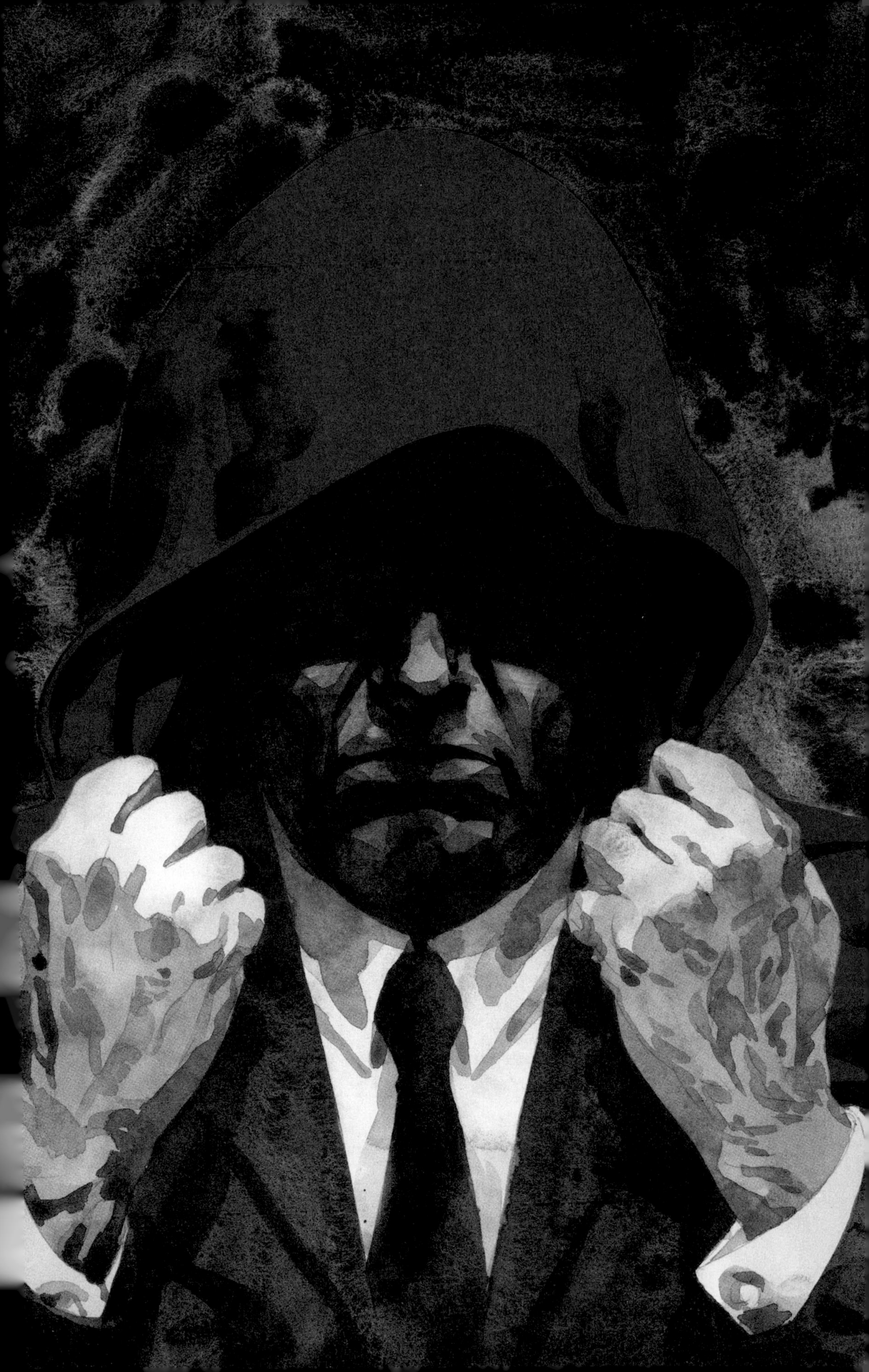

Chapter One

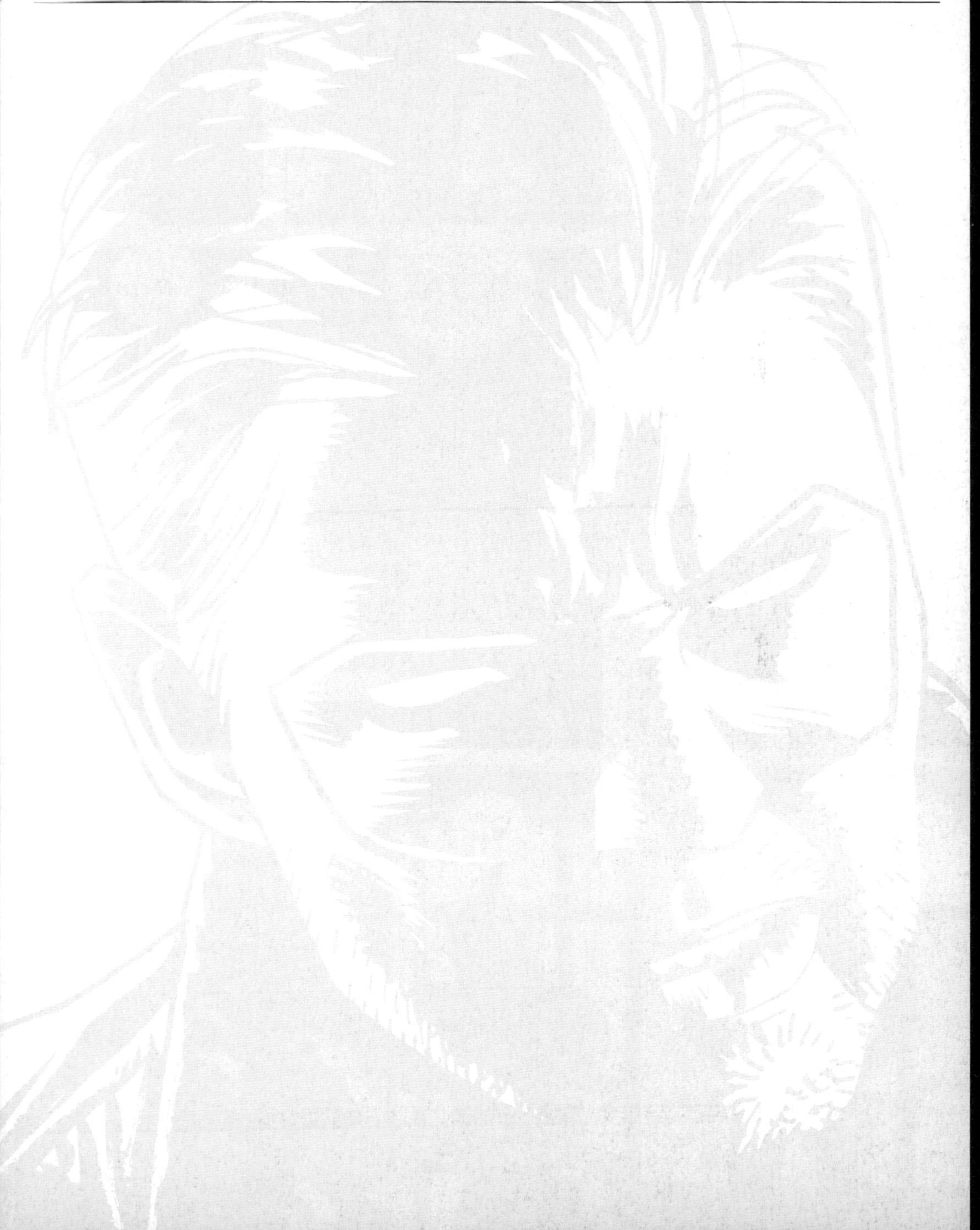

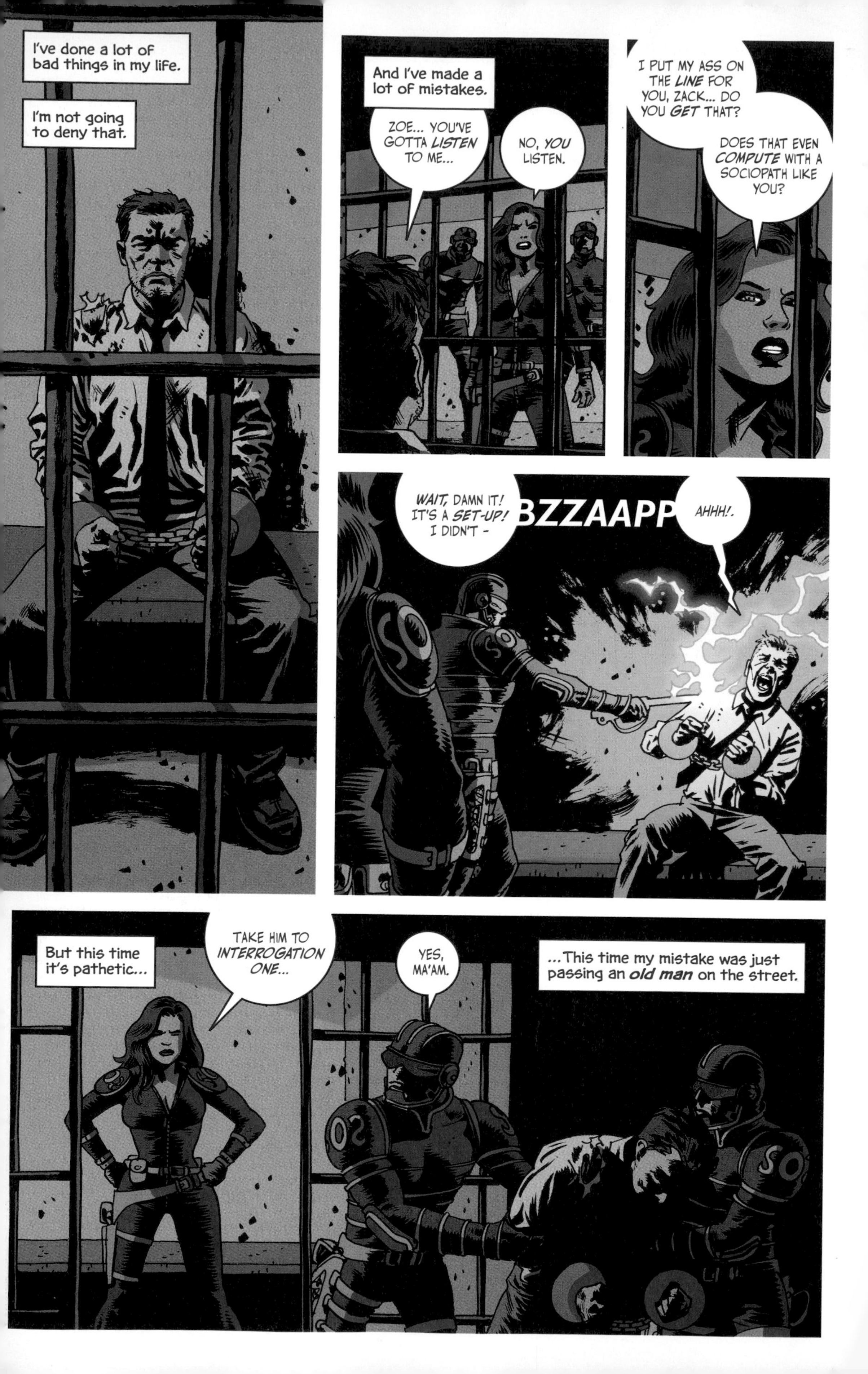
I've done a lot of bad things in my life.
I'm not going to deny that.
And I've made a lot of mistakes.
ZOE... YOU'VE GOTTA LISTEN TO ME...
NO, YOU LISTEN.
I PUT MY ASS ON THE LINE FOR YOU, ZACK... DO YOU GET THAT?
DOES THAT EVEN COMPUTE WITH A SOCIOPATH LIKE YOU?
WAIT, DAMN IT! IT'S A SET-UP! I DIDN'T -
BZZAAPP
AHHH!.
But this time it's pathetic...
TAKE HIM TO INTERROGATION ONE...
YES, MA'AM.
...This time my mistake was just passing an old man on the street.

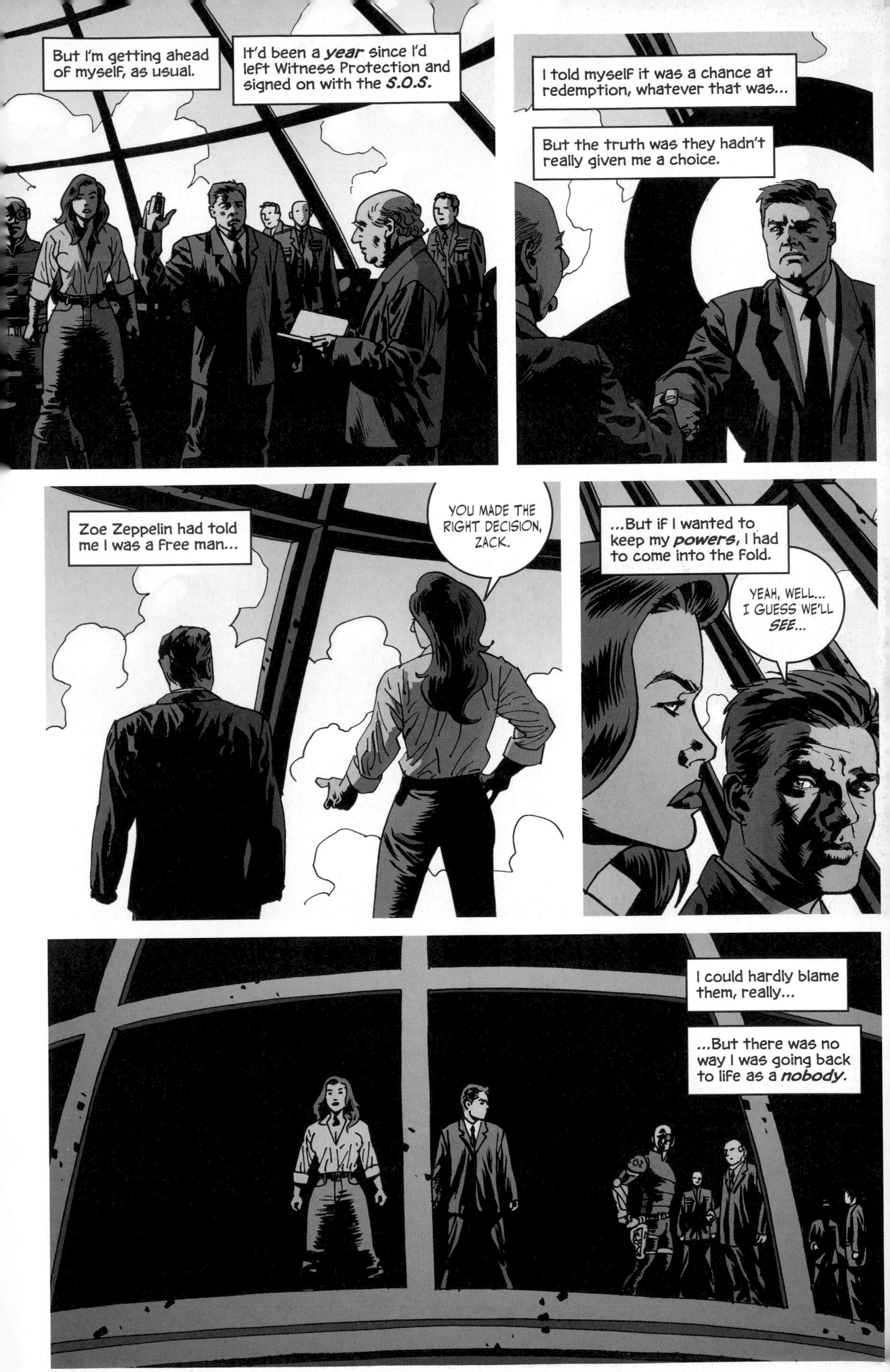
But I'm getting ahead of myself, as usual.
It'd been a *year* since I'd left Witness Protection and signed on with the *S.O.S.*
I told myself it was a chance at redemption, whatever that was...
But the truth was they hadn't really given me a choice.
Zoe Zeppelin had told me I was a free man...
YOU MADE THE RIGHT DECISION, ZACK.
...But if I wanted to keep my *powers*, I had to come into the fold.
YEAH, WELL... I GUESS WE'LL *SEE*...
I could hardly blame them, really...
...But there was no way I was going back to life as a *nobody*.

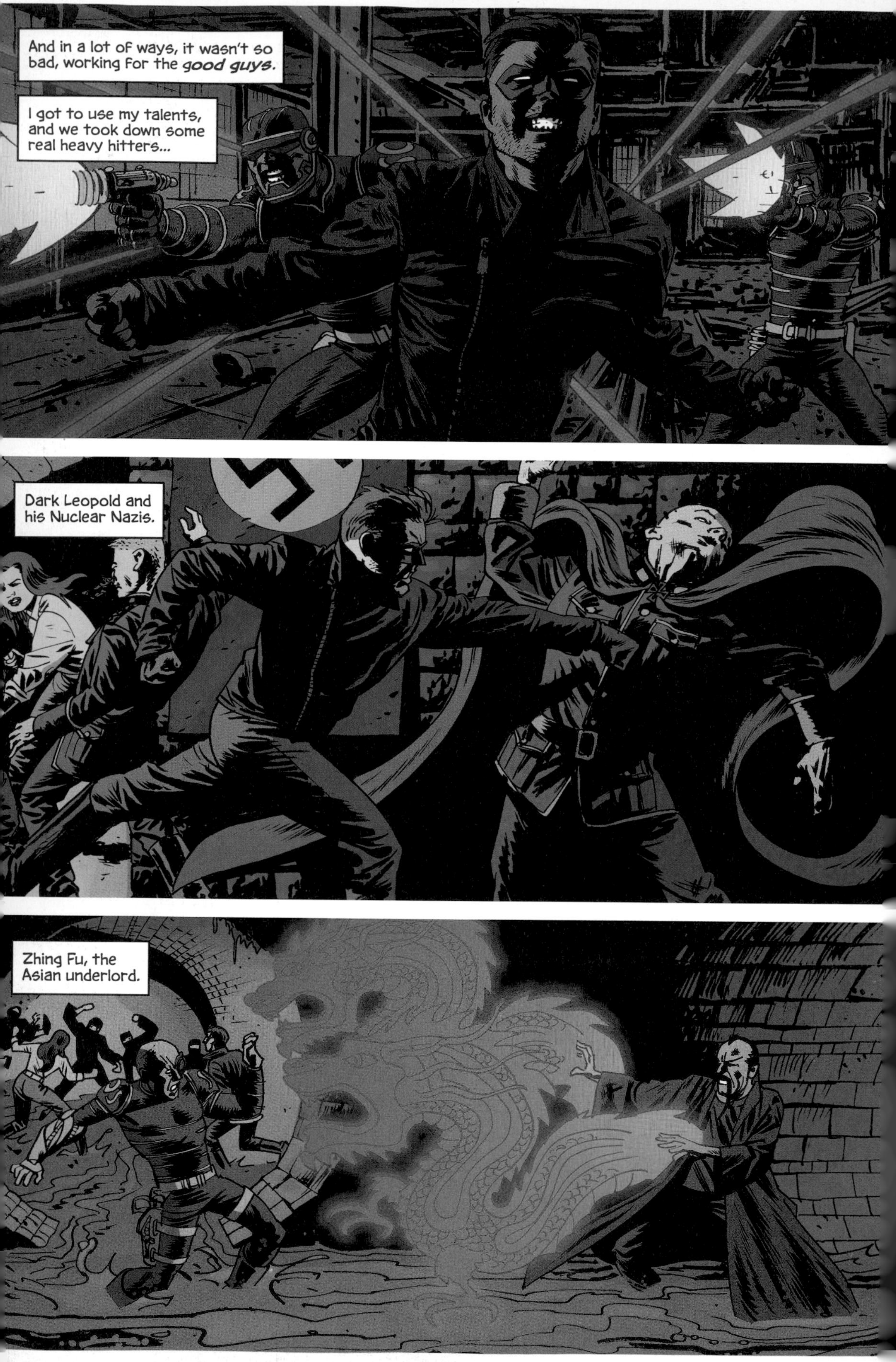
And in a lot of ways, it wasn't so bad, working for the *good guys.*
I got to use my talents, and we took down some real heavy hitters...
Dark Leopold and his Nuclear Nazis.
Zhing Fu, the Asian underlord.

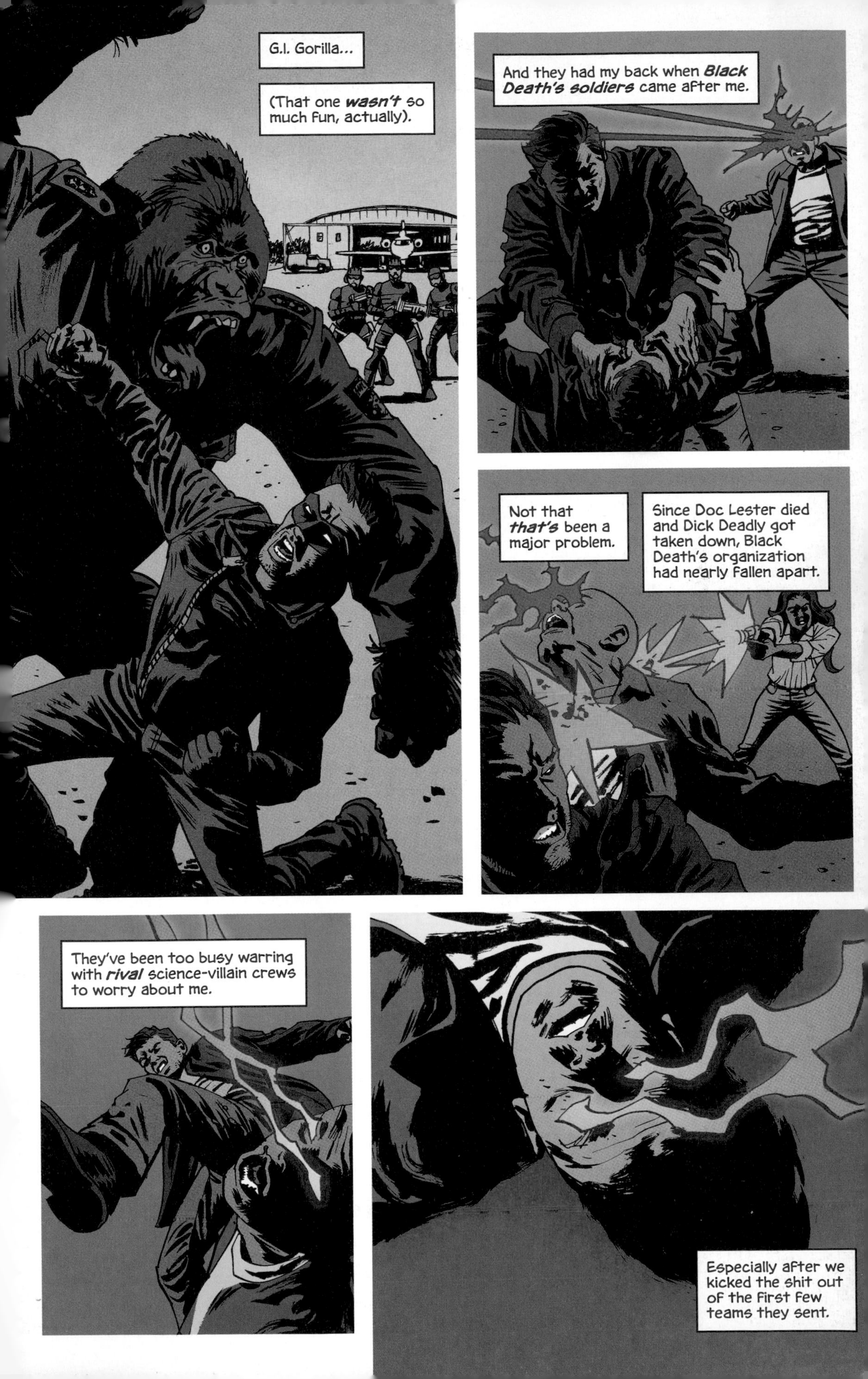
G.I. Gorilla...
(That one wasn't so much fun, actually).
And they had my back when Black Death's soldiers came after me.
Not that that's been a major problem.
Since Doc Lester died and Dick Deadly got taken down, Black Death's organization had nearly fallen apart.
They've been too busy warring with rival science-villain crews to worry about me.
Especially after we kicked the shit out of the first few teams they sent.

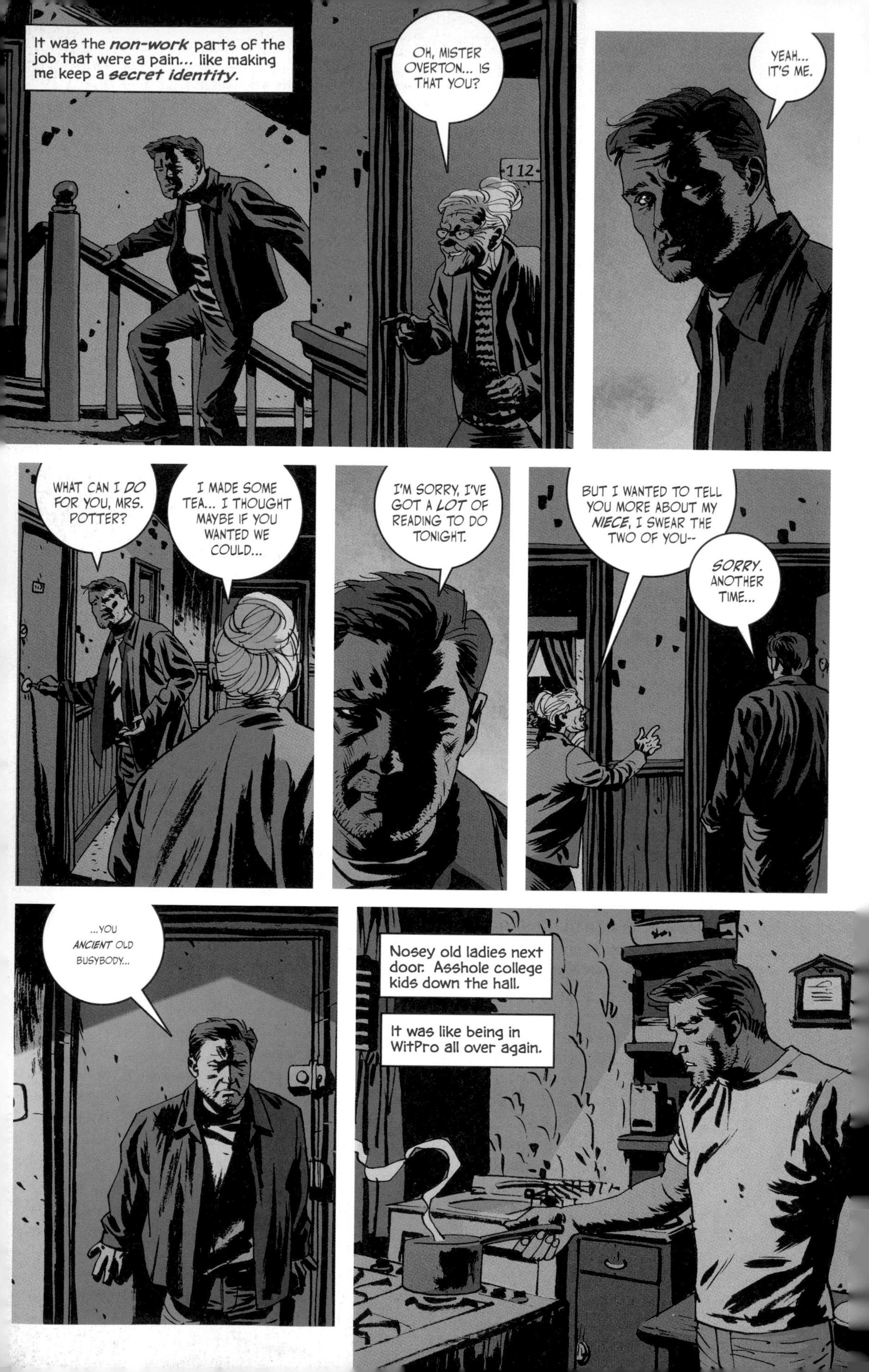
It was the non-work parts of the job that were a pain... like making me keep a secret identity.
OH, MISTER OVERTON... IS THAT YOU?
112
YEAH... IT'S ME.
WHAT CAN I DO FOR YOU, MRS. POTTER?
I MADE SOME TEA... I THOUGHT MAYBE IF YOU WANTED WE COULD...
I'M SORRY, I'VE GOT A LOT OF READING TO DO TONIGHT.
BUT I WANTED TO TELL YOU MORE ABOUT MY NIECE, I SWEAR THE TWO OF YOU--
SORRY. ANOTHER TIME...
...YOU ANCIENT OLD BUSYBODY...
Nosey old ladies next door. Asshole college kids down the hall.
It was like being in WitPro all over again.

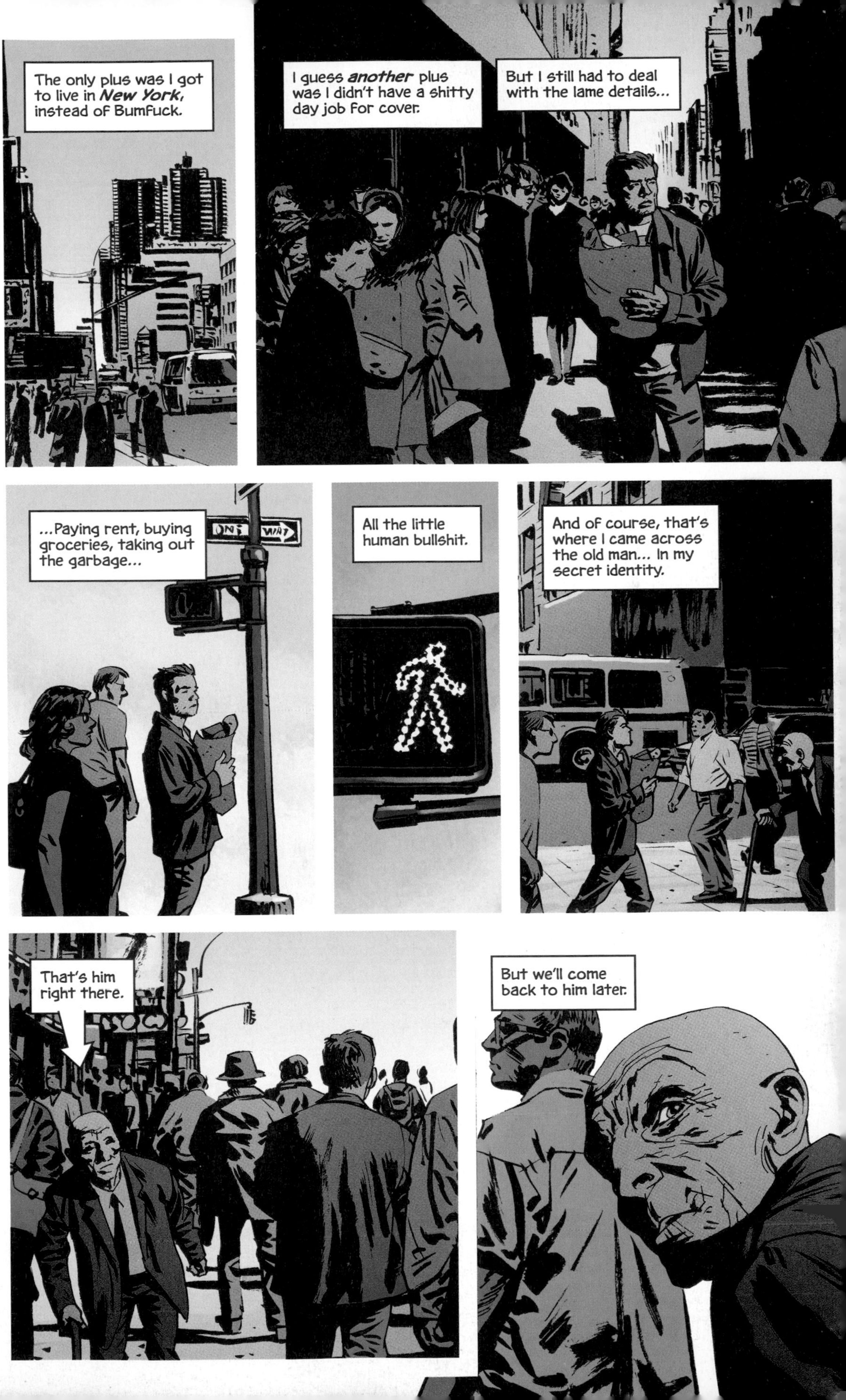
The only plus was I got to live in *New York*, instead of Bumfuck.
I guess *another* plus was I didn't have a shitty day job for cover.
But I still had to deal with the lame details...
...Paying rent, buying groceries, taking out the garbage...
All the little human bullshit.
And of course, that's where I came across the old man... In my secret identity.
That's him right there.
But we'll come back to him later.

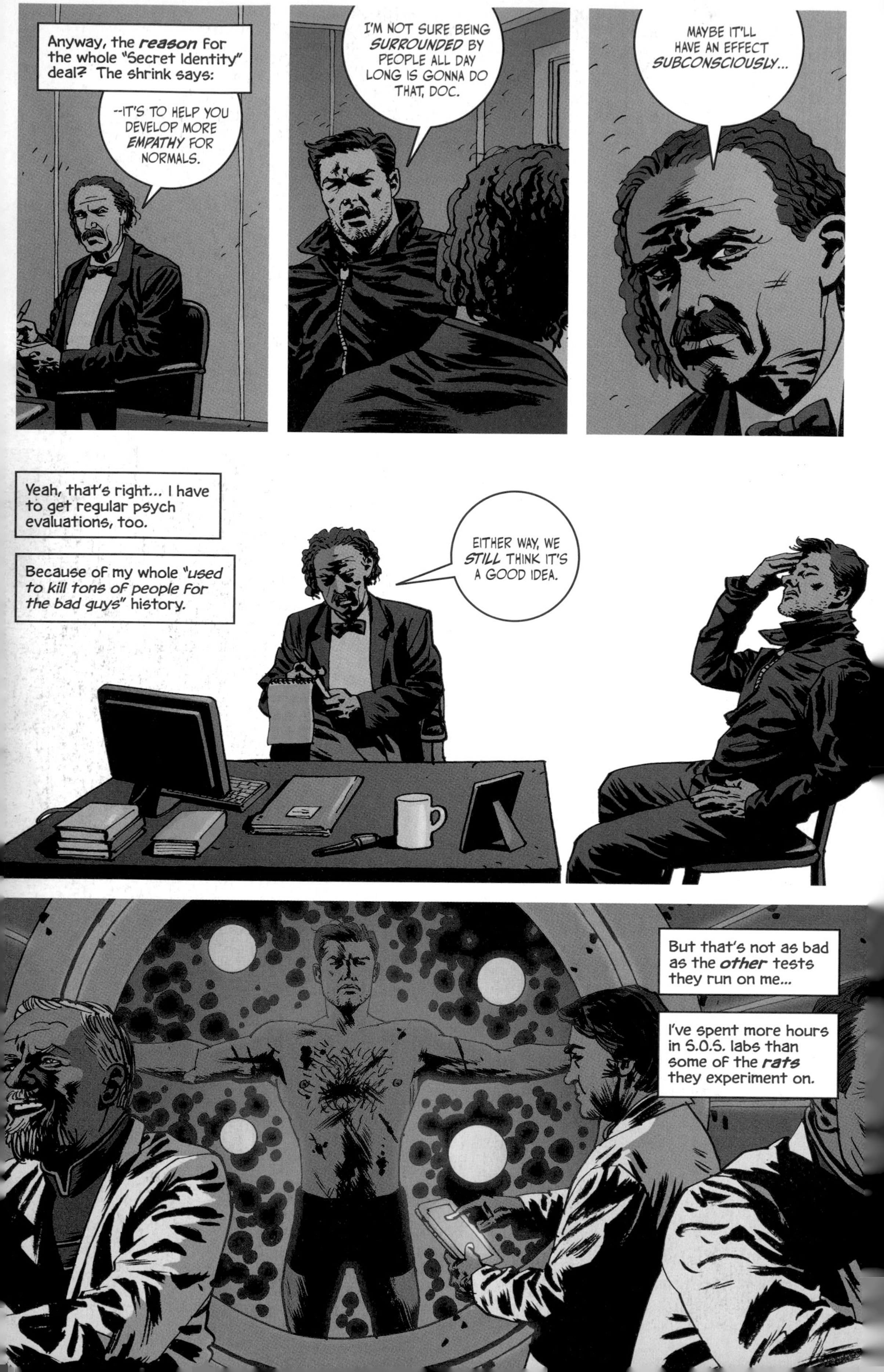

Anyway, the *reason* for the whole "Secret Identity" deal? The shrink says:
--IT'S TO HELP YOU DEVELOP MORE *EMPATHY* FOR NORMALS.
I'M NOT SURE BEING *SURROUNDED* BY PEOPLE ALL DAY LONG IS GONNA DO THAT, DOC.
MAYBE IT'LL HAVE AN EFFECT *SUBCONSCIOUSLY*...
Yeah, that's right... I have to get regular psych evaluations, too.
Because of my whole "*used to kill tons of people for the bad guys*" history.
EITHER WAY, WE *STILL* THINK IT'S A GOOD IDEA.
But that's not as bad as the *other* tests they run on me...
I've spent more hours in S.O.S. labs than some of the *rats* they experiment on.

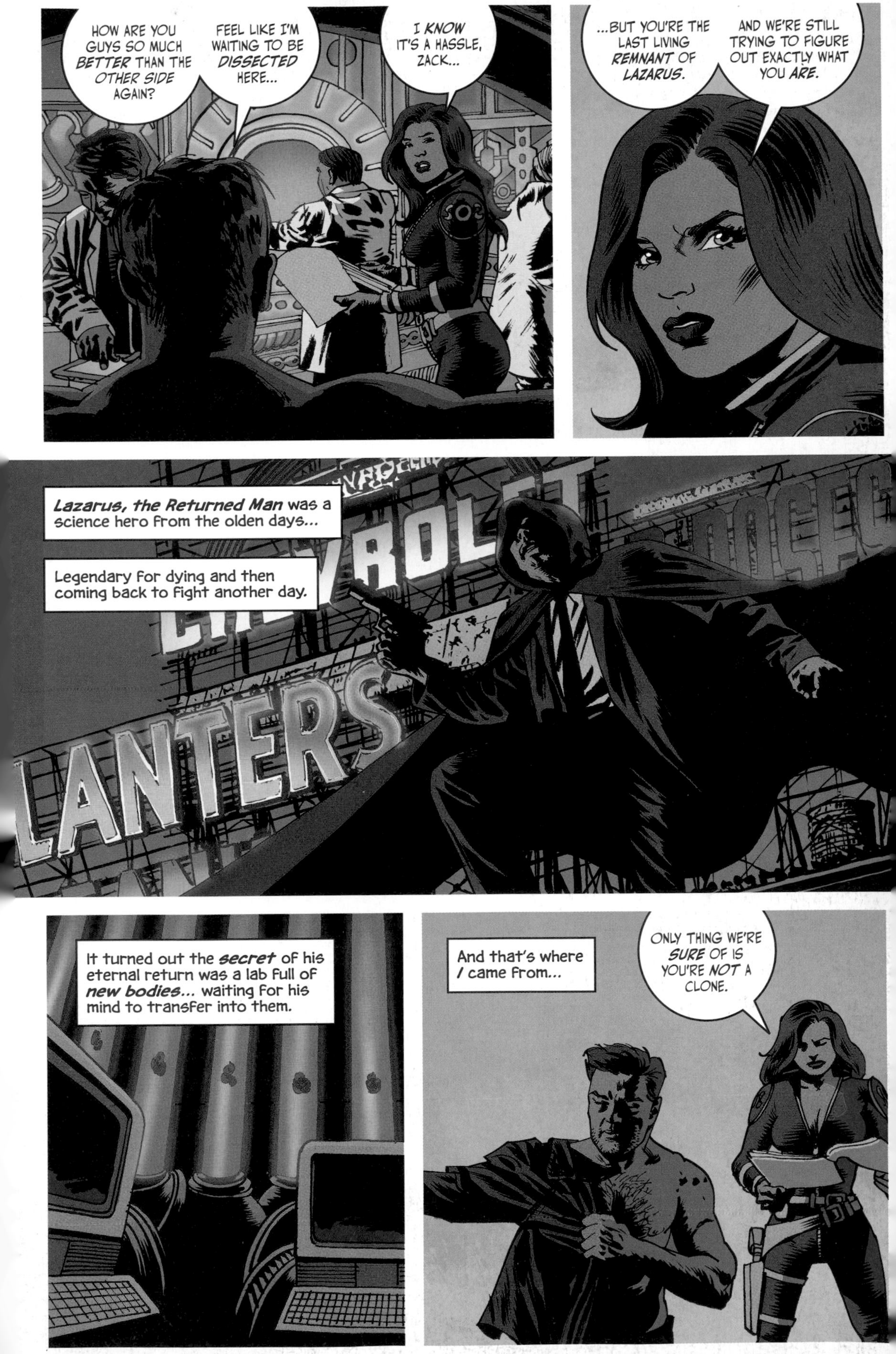
HOW ARE YOU GUYS SO MUCH BETTER THAN THE OTHER SIDE AGAIN?
FEEL LIKE I'M WAITING TO BE DISSECTED HERE...
I KNOW IT'S A HASSLE, ZACK...
...BUT YOU'RE THE LAST LIVING REMNANT OF LAZARUS.
AND WE'RE STILL TRYING TO FIGURE OUT EXACTLY WHAT YOU ARE.
Lazarus, the Returned Man was a science hero from the olden days...
Legendary for dying and then coming back to fight another day.
LANTERS
It turned out the secret of his eternal return was a lab full of new bodies... waiting for his mind to transfer into them.
And that's where I came from...
ONLY THING WE'RE SURE OF IS YOU'RE NOT A CLONE.

YOUR DNA STRUCTURE SHOWS *NO EVIDENCE* OF COPIED CELLS *OR* PREMATURE AGING...

IT'S *REALLY* FASCINATING.

I'M SURE...

...BUT Y'KNOW WHAT?

I DON'T NEED CONSTANT *REMINDERS* I WAS GROWN IN A *TEST TUBE*.

MS. ZEPPELIN SAYS YOU'RE *UNCOMFORTABLE* WITH YOUR ORIGINS?

CHRIST... DO WE *REALLY* HAVE TO TALK ABOUT THAT?

ACCEPTING THE *TRUTH* IS PART OF YOUR *GROWTH PROCESS,* ZACK.

BUT WE CAN TALK ABOUT YOUR *ACTING OUT* INSTEAD, IF YOU'D PREFER...

MY *WHAT*?

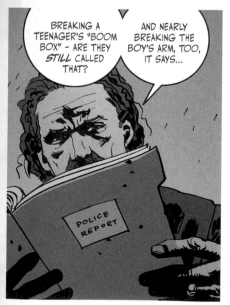

BREAKING A TEENAGER'S "BOOM BOX" – ARE THEY *STILL* CALLED THAT?

AND NEARLY BREAKING THE BOY'S ARM, TOO, IT SAYS...

C'MON... I WAS HAVING *EMPATHY* FOR EVERYONE THAT ASSHOLE WAS DISTURBING...

UH HUNH... I SEE.

And *that* was my life... my new life...

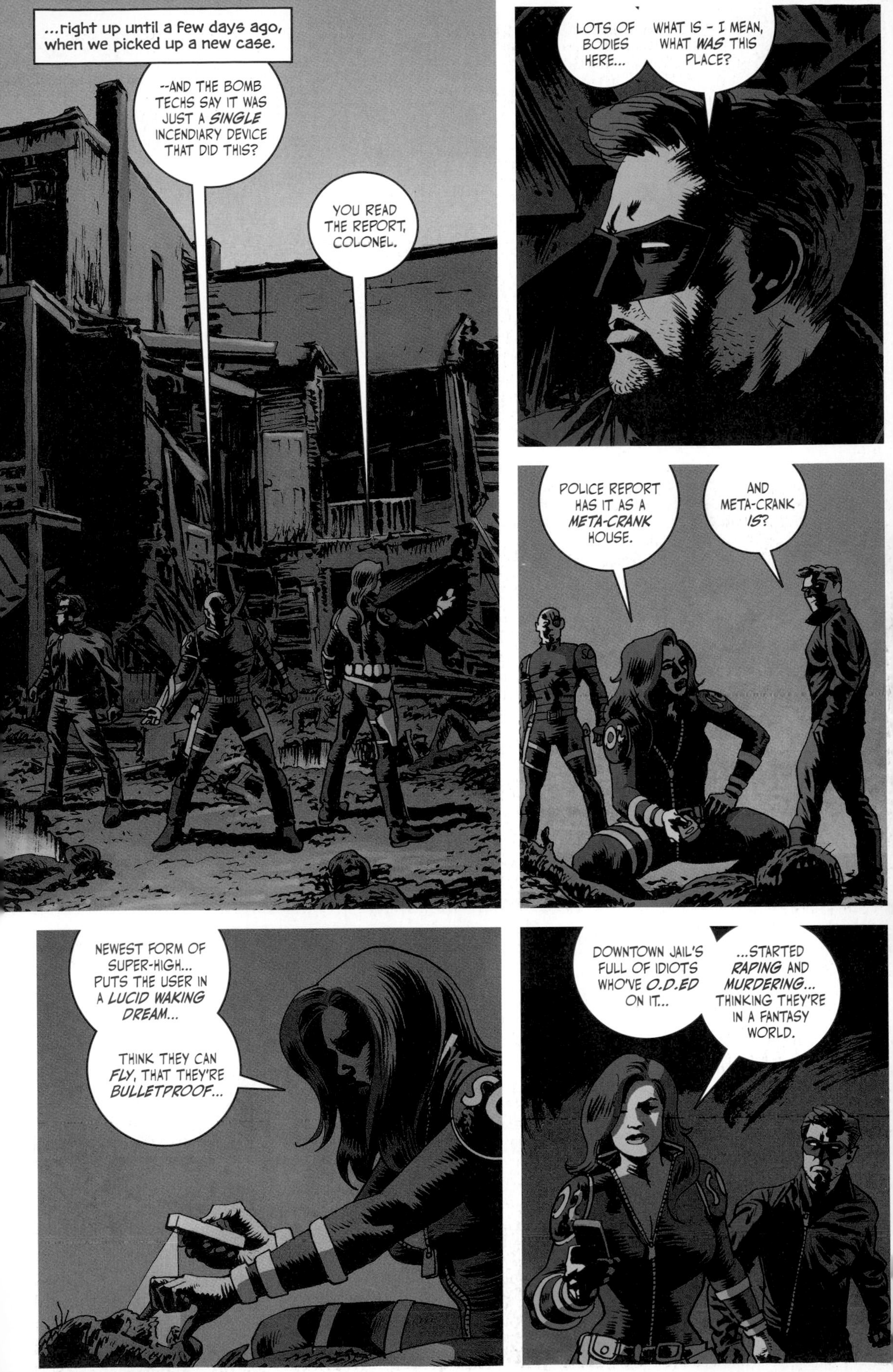
...right up until a few days ago, when we picked up a new case.
--AND THE BOMB TECHS SAY IT WAS JUST A *SINGLE* INCENDIARY DEVICE THAT DID THIS?
YOU READ THE REPORT, COLONEL.
LOTS OF BODIES HERE...
WHAT IS - I MEAN, WHAT *WAS* THIS PLACE?
POLICE REPORT HAS IT AS A *META-CRANK* HOUSE.
AND META-CRANK *IS*?
NEWEST FORM OF SUPER-HIGH... PUTS THE USER IN A *LUCID WAKING DREAM*...
THINK THEY CAN *FLY*, THAT THEY'RE *BULLETPROOF*...
DOWNTOWN JAIL'S FULL OF IDIOTS WHO'VE *O.D.ED* ON IT...
...STARTED *RAPING* AND *MURDERING*... THINKING THEY'RE IN A FANTASY WORLD.

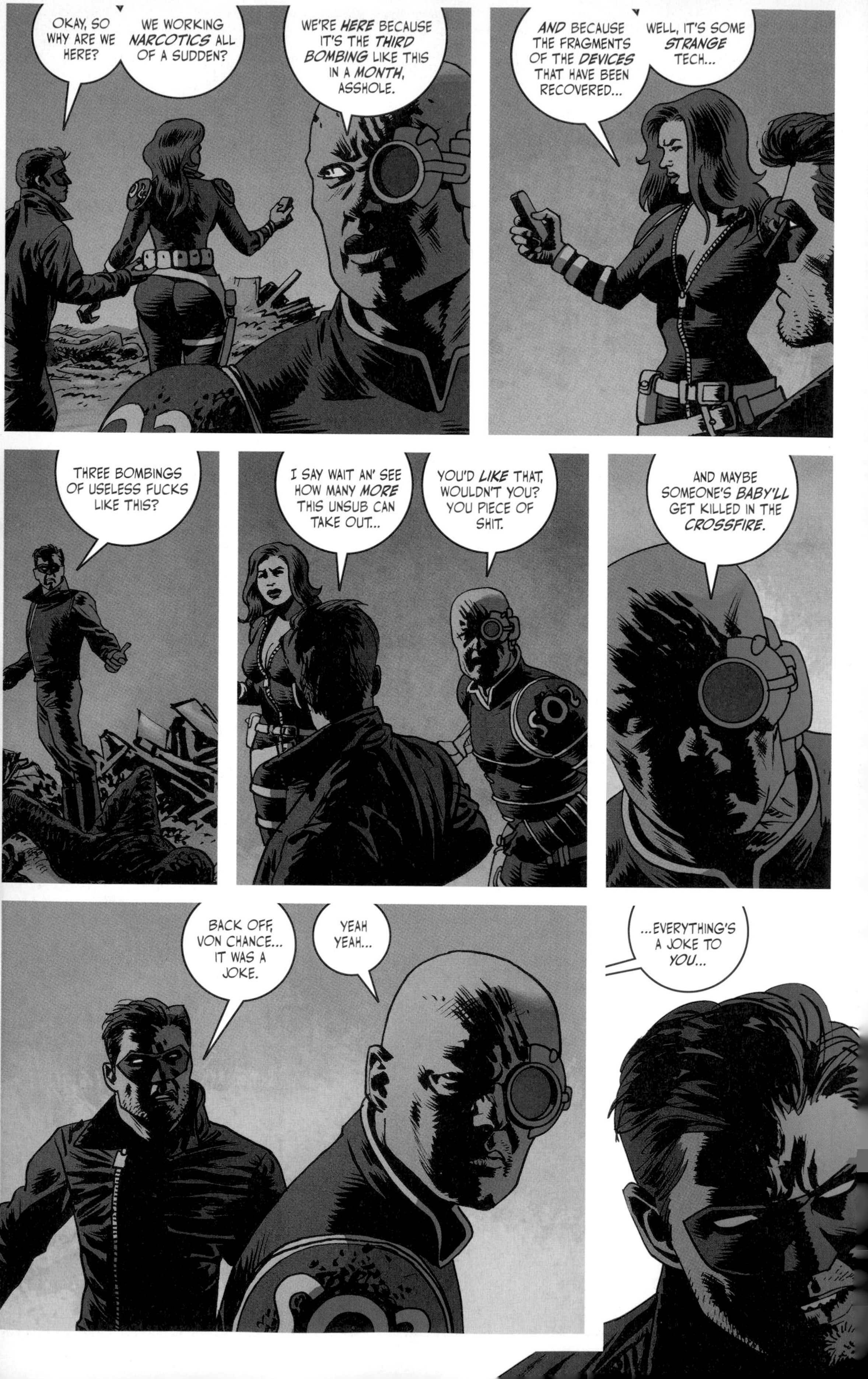
OKAY, SO WHY ARE WE HERE?
WE WORKING NARCOTICS ALL OF A SUDDEN?
WE'RE HERE BECAUSE IT'S THE THIRD BOMBING LIKE THIS IN A MONTH, ASSHOLE.
AND BECAUSE THE FRAGMENTS OF THE DEVICES THAT HAVE BEEN RECOVERED...
WELL, IT'S SOME STRANGE TECH...
THREE BOMBINGS OF USELESS FUCKS LIKE THIS?
I SAY WAIT AN' SEE HOW MANY MORE THIS UNSUB CAN TAKE OUT...
YOU'D LIKE THAT, WOULDN'T YOU? YOU PIECE OF SHIT.
AND MAYBE SOMEONE'S BABY'LL GET KILLED IN THE CROSSFIRE.
BACK OFF, VON CHANCE... IT WAS A JOKE.
YEAH YEAH...
...EVERYTHING'S A JOKE TO YOU...

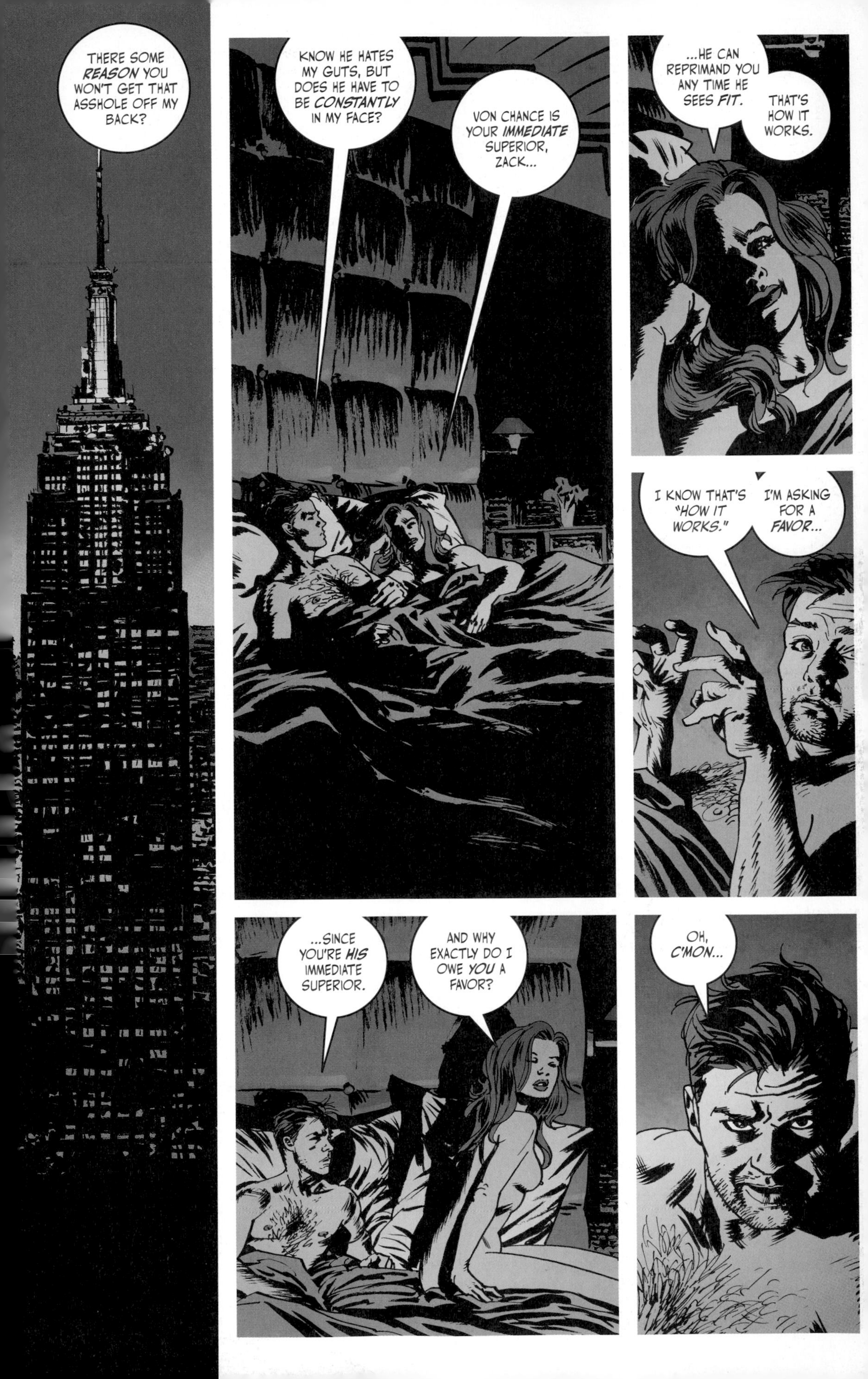
THERE SOME *REASON* YOU WON'T GET THAT ASSHOLE OFF MY BACK?
KNOW HE HATES MY GUTS, BUT DOES HE HAVE TO BE *CONSTANTLY* IN MY FACE?
VON CHANCE IS YOUR *IMMEDIATE* SUPERIOR, ZACK...
...HE CAN REPRIMAND YOU ANY TIME HE SEES *FIT*.
THAT'S HOW IT WORKS.
I KNOW THAT'S "*HOW IT WORKS.*"
I'M ASKING FOR A *FAVOR*...
...SINCE YOU'RE *HIS* IMMEDIATE SUPERIOR.
AND WHY EXACTLY DO I OWE *YOU* A FAVOR?
OH, *C'MON*...

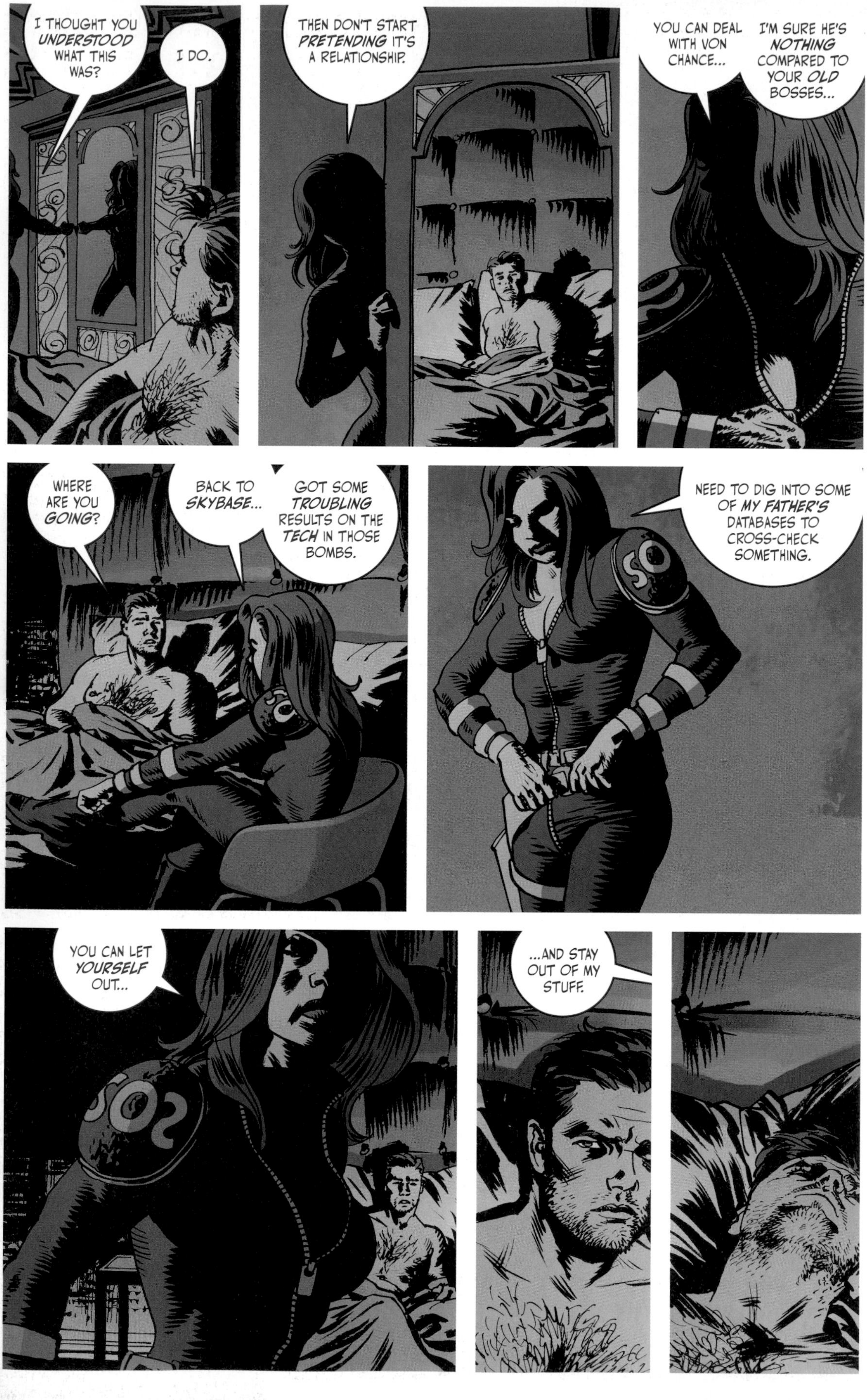

I THOUGHT YOU UNDERSTOOD WHAT THIS WAS?
I DO.
THEN DON'T START PRETENDING IT'S A RELATIONSHIP.
YOU CAN DEAL WITH VON CHANCE...
I'M SURE HE'S NOTHING COMPARED TO YOUR OLD BOSSES...
WHERE ARE YOU GOING?
BACK TO SKYBASE...
GOT SOME TROUBLING RESULTS ON THE TECH IN THOSE BOMBS.
NEED TO DIG INTO SOME OF MY FATHER'S DATABASES TO CROSS-CHECK SOMETHING.
YOU CAN LET YOURSELF OUT...
...AND STAY OUT OF MY STUFF.

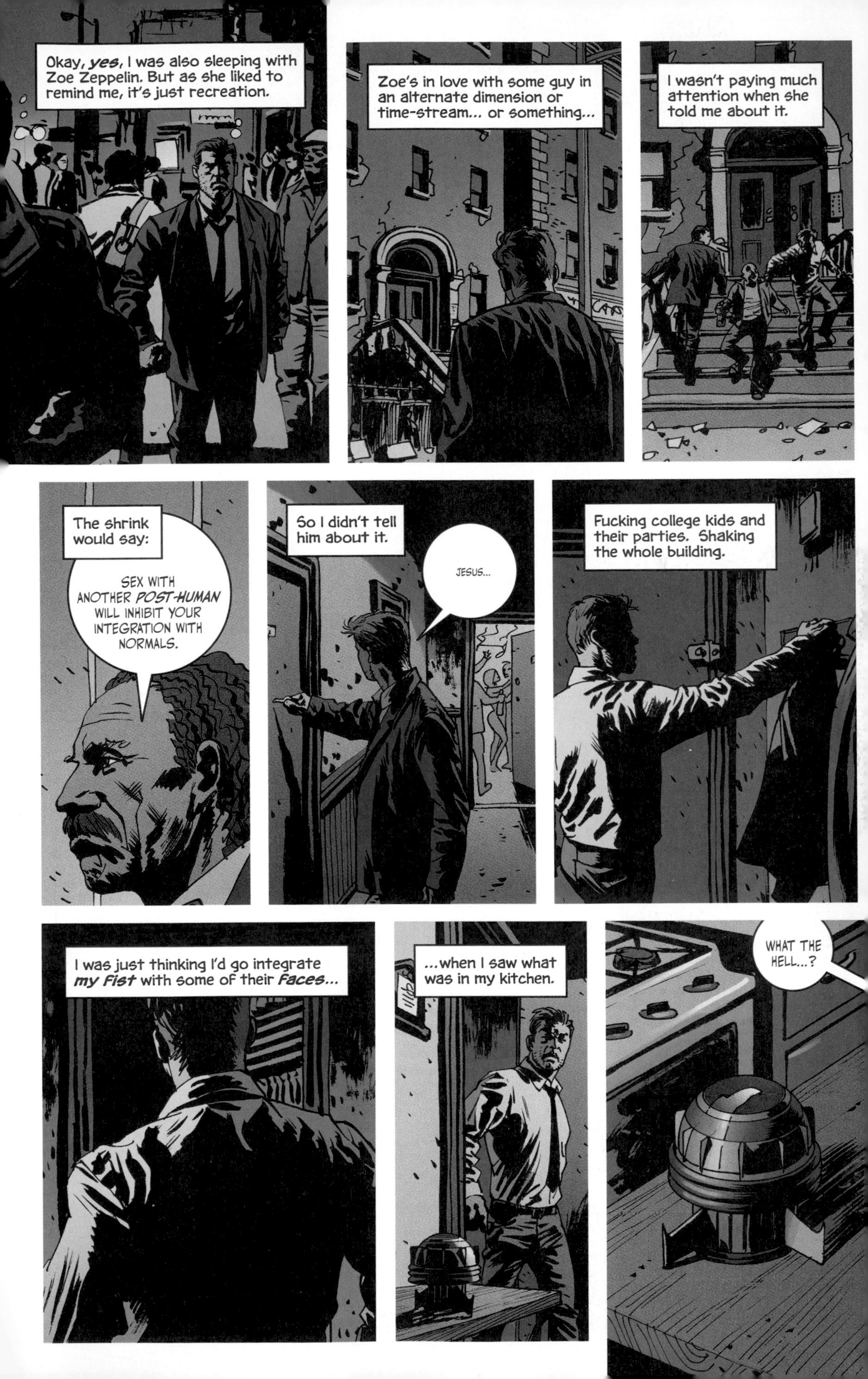
Okay, *yes*, I was also sleeping with Zoe Zeppelin. But as she liked to remind me, it's just recreation.
Zoe's in love with some guy in an alternate dimension or time-stream... or something...
I wasn't paying much attention when she told me about it.
The shrink would say:
SEX WITH ANOTHER *POST-HUMAN* WILL INHIBIT YOUR INTEGRATION WITH NORMALS.
So I didn't tell him about it.
JESUS...
Fucking college kids and their parties. Shaking the whole building.
I was just thinking I'd go integrate *my fist* with some of their *faces*...
...when I saw what was in my kitchen.
WHAT THE HELL...?

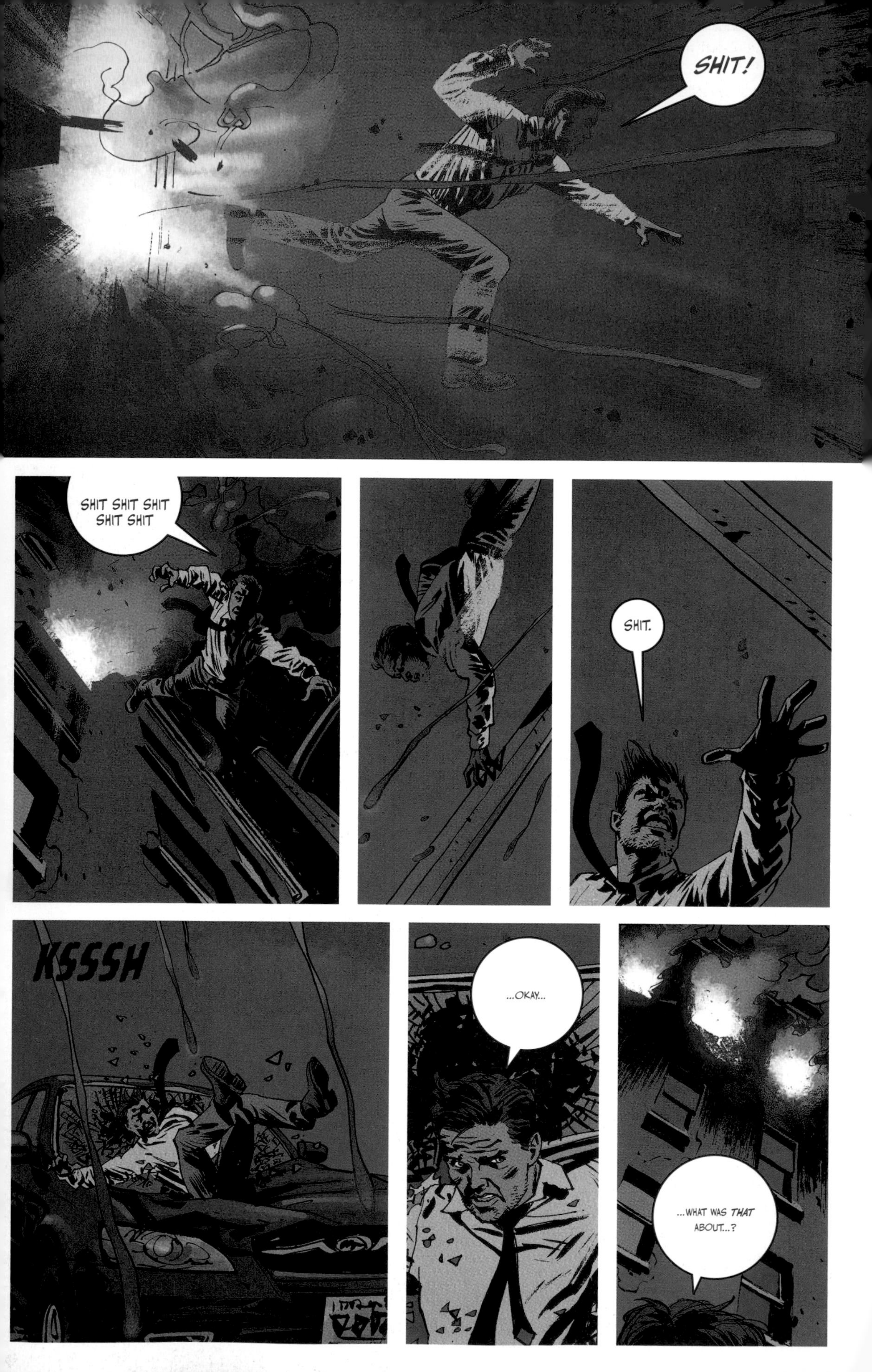
SHIT!
SHIT SHIT SHIT SHIT SHIT
SHIT.
KSSSH
...OKAY...
...WHAT WAS *THAT* ABOUT...?

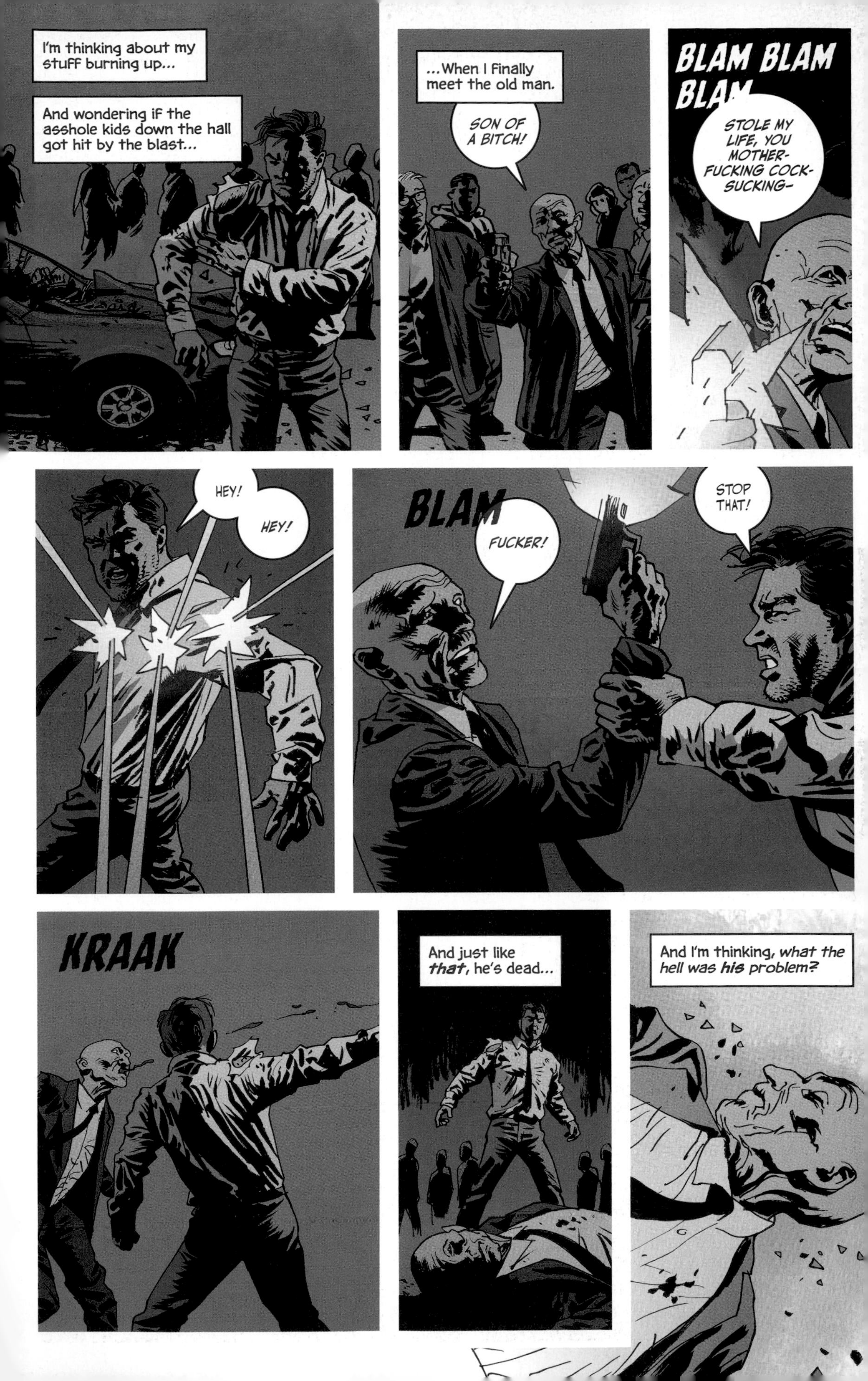
I'm thinking about my stuff burning up...
And wondering if the asshole kids down the hall got hit by the blast...
...When I finally meet the old man.
SON OF A BITCH!
BLAM BLAM BLAM
STOLE MY LIFE, YOU MOTHER-FUCKING COCK-SUCKING-
HEY!
HEY!
BLAM
FUCKER!
STOP THAT!
KRAAK
And just like *that*, he's dead...
And I'm thinking, *what the hell was **his** problem?*

The Old Man's Problem

THE OLD MAN WAS *IGNATIUS BEEKMAN*, KNOWN MOSTLY AS IG. BACK IN THE 1940S, IG WAS A MINOR LEAGUE CROOK...

... WHO WAS UNLUCKY ENOUGH TO CROSS PATHS WITH *LAZARUS*.

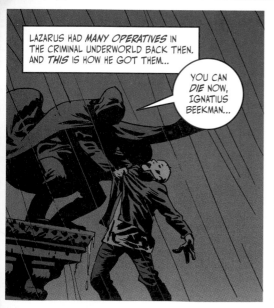

LAZARUS HAD *MANY OPERATIVES* IN THE CRIMINAL UNDERWORLD BACK THEN. AND *THIS* IS HOW HE GOT THEM...

YOU CAN *DIE* NOW, IGNATIUS BEEKMAN...

...OR YOU CAN BE MY *EYES* AND *EARS*.

IT'S *YOUR* CHOICE.

...OH GOD... *PLEASE* DON'T KILL ME... *PLEASE*...

I'M *NO ONE*... I'M NOTHING...

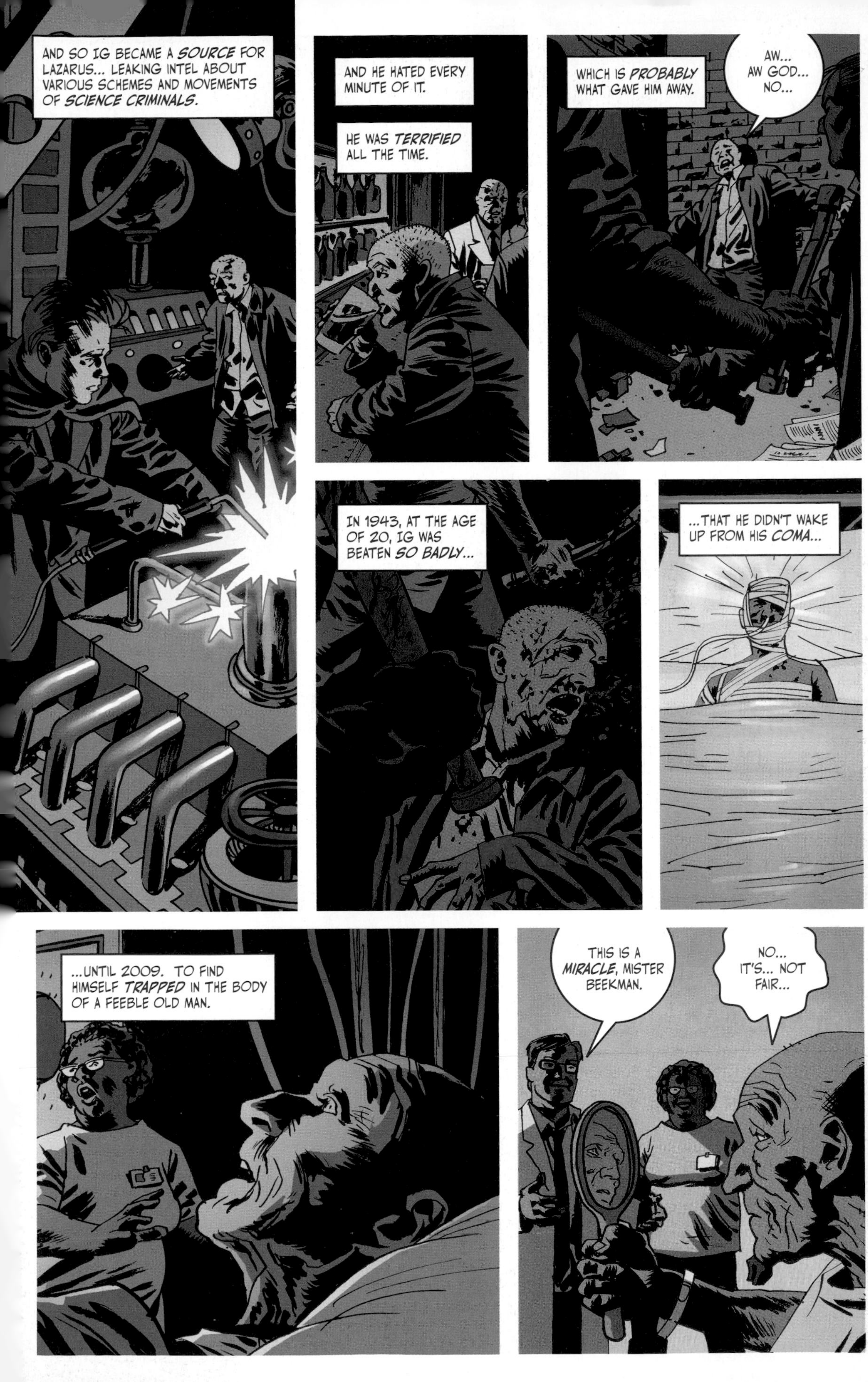
AND SO IG BECAME A SOURCE FOR LAZARUS... LEAKING INTEL ABOUT VARIOUS SCHEMES AND MOVEMENTS OF SCIENCE CRIMINALS.
AND HE HATED EVERY MINUTE OF IT.
HE WAS TERRIFIED ALL THE TIME.
WHICH IS PROBABLY WHAT GAVE HIM AWAY.
AW... AW GOD... NO...
IN 1943, AT THE AGE OF 20, IG WAS BEATEN SO BADLY...
...THAT HE DIDN'T WAKE UP FROM HIS COMA...
...UNTIL 2009. TO FIND HIMSELF TRAPPED IN THE BODY OF A FEEBLE OLD MAN.
THIS IS A MIRACLE, MISTER BEEKMAN.
NO... IT'S... NOT FAIR...

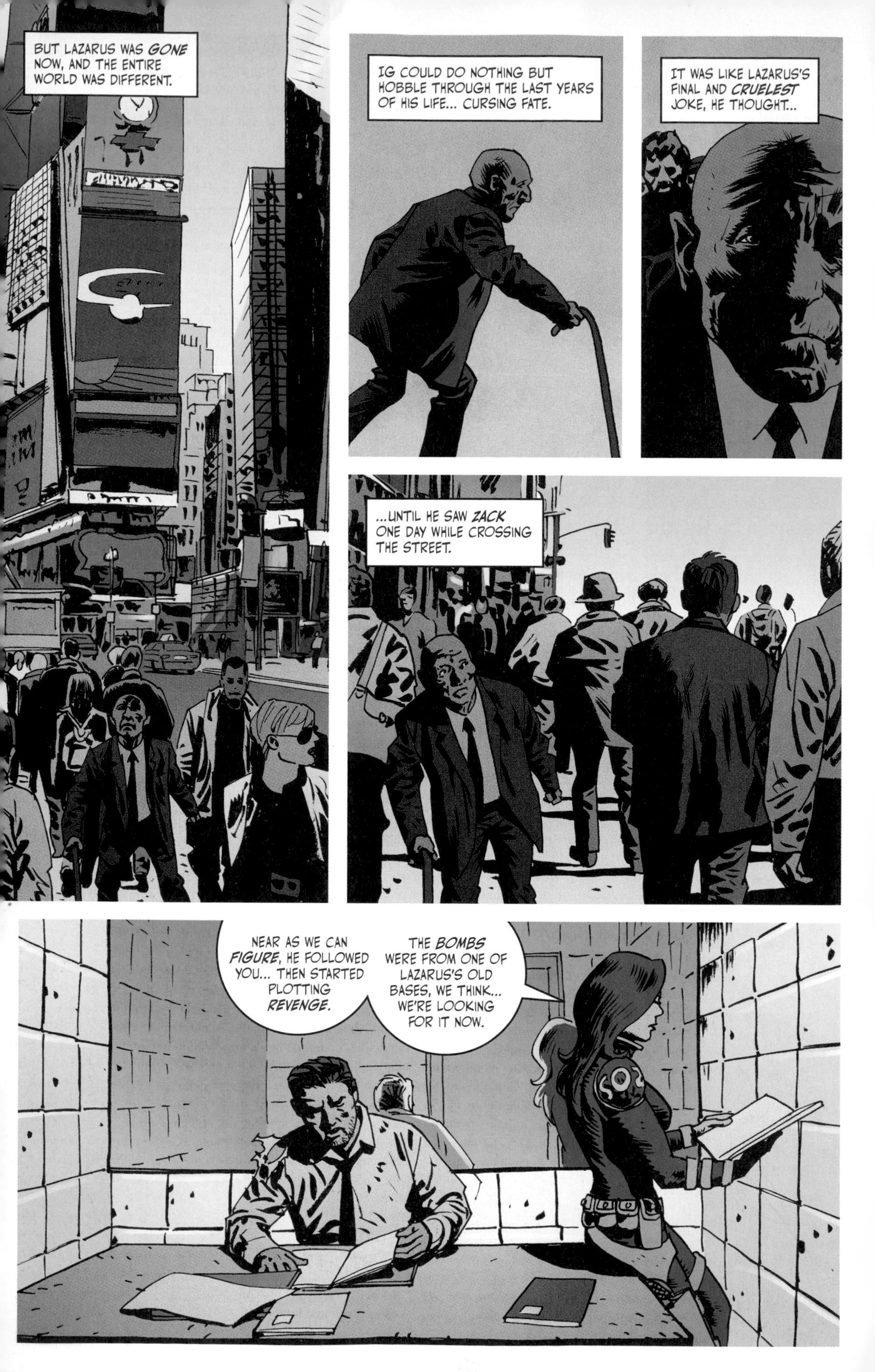
BUT LAZARUS WAS GONE NOW, AND THE ENTIRE WORLD WAS DIFFERENT.
IG COULD DO NOTHING BUT HOBBLE THROUGH THE LAST YEARS OF HIS LIFE... CURSING FATE.
IT WAS LIKE LAZARUS'S FINAL AND CRUELEST JOKE, HE THOUGHT...
...UNTIL HE SAW ZACK ONE DAY WHILE CROSSING THE STREET.
NEAR AS WE CAN FIGURE, HE FOLLOWED YOU... THEN STARTED PLOTTING REVENGE.
THE BOMBS WERE FROM ONE OF LAZARUS'S OLD BASES, WE THINK... WE'RE LOOKING FOR IT NOW.

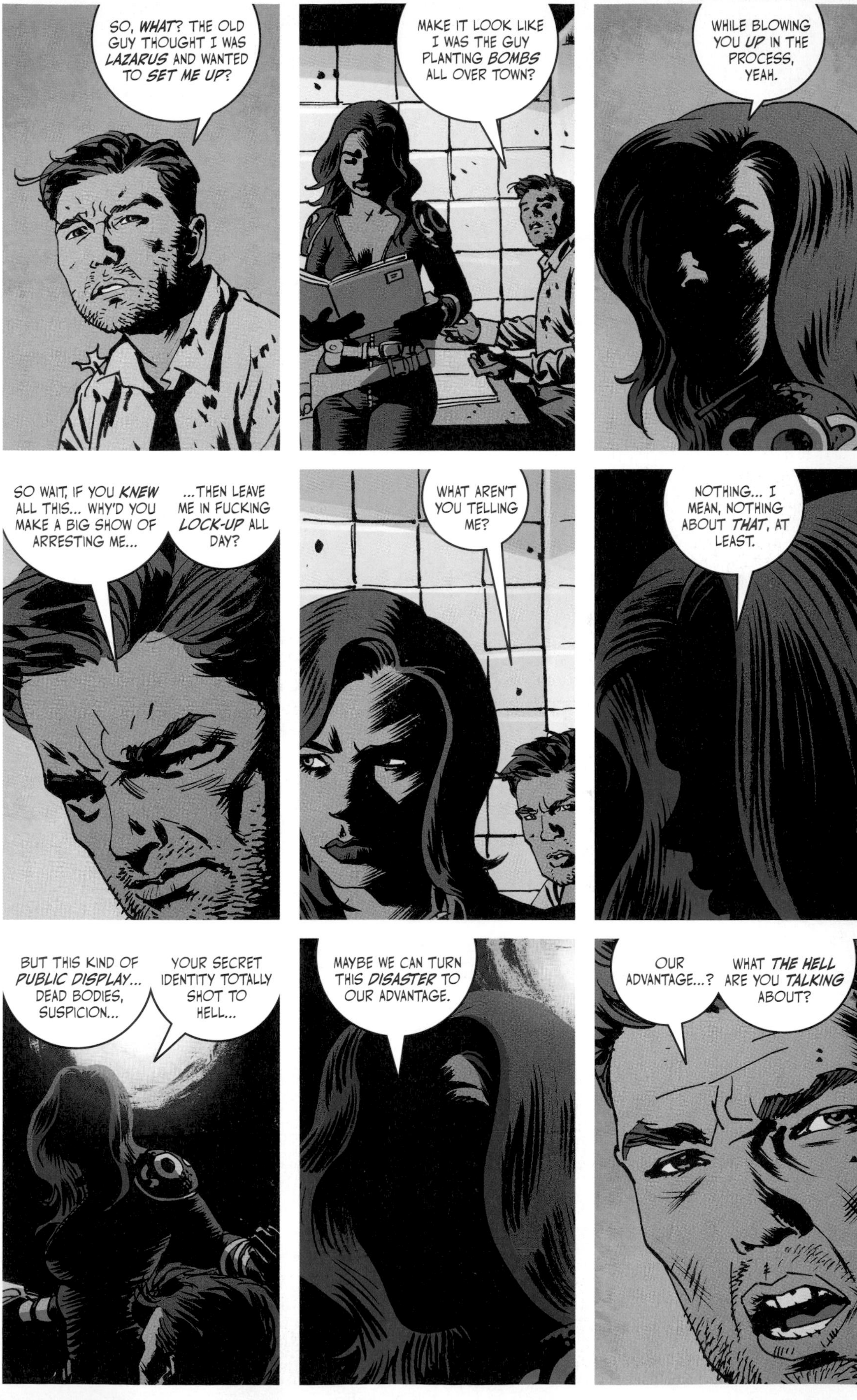
SO, WHAT? THE OLD GUY THOUGHT I WAS LAZARUS AND WANTED TO SET ME UP?
MAKE IT LOOK LIKE I WAS THE GUY PLANTING BOMBS ALL OVER TOWN?
WHILE BLOWING YOU UP IN THE PROCESS, YEAH.
SO WAIT, IF YOU KNEW ALL THIS... WHY'D YOU MAKE A BIG SHOW OF ARRESTING ME...
...THEN LEAVE ME IN FUCKING LOCK-UP ALL DAY?
WHAT AREN'T YOU TELLING ME?
NOTHING... I MEAN, NOTHING ABOUT THAT, AT LEAST.
BUT THIS KIND OF PUBLIC DISPLAY... DEAD BODIES, SUSPICION...
YOUR SECRET IDENTITY TOTALLY SHOT TO HELL...
MAYBE WE CAN TURN THIS DISASTER TO OUR ADVANTAGE.
OUR ADVANTAGE...?
WHAT THE HELL ARE YOU TALKING ABOUT?

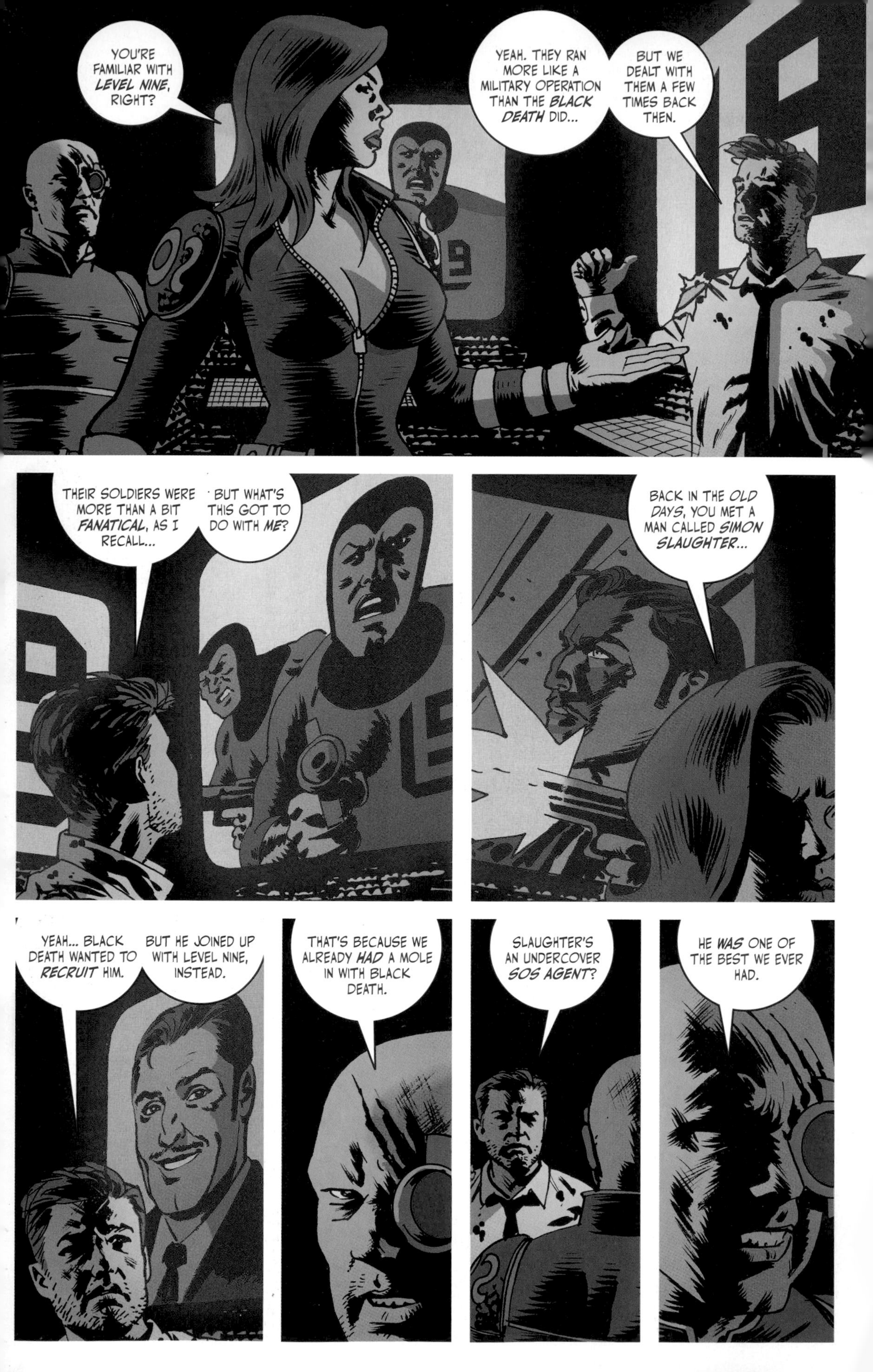
YOU'RE FAMILIAR WITH LEVEL NINE, RIGHT?
YEAH. THEY RAN MORE LIKE A MILITARY OPERATION THAN THE BLACK DEATH DID...
BUT WE DEALT WITH THEM A FEW TIMES BACK THEN.
THEIR SOLDIERS WERE MORE THAN A BIT FANATICAL, AS I RECALL...
BUT WHAT'S THIS GOT TO DO WITH ME?
BACK IN THE OLD DAYS, YOU MET A MAN CALLED SIMON SLAUGHTER...
YEAH... BLACK DEATH WANTED TO RECRUIT HIM.
BUT HE JOINED UP WITH LEVEL NINE, INSTEAD.
THAT'S BECAUSE WE ALREADY HAD A MOLE IN WITH BLACK DEATH.
SLAUGHTER'S AN UNDERCOVER SOS AGENT?
HE WAS ONE OF THE BEST WE EVER HAD.

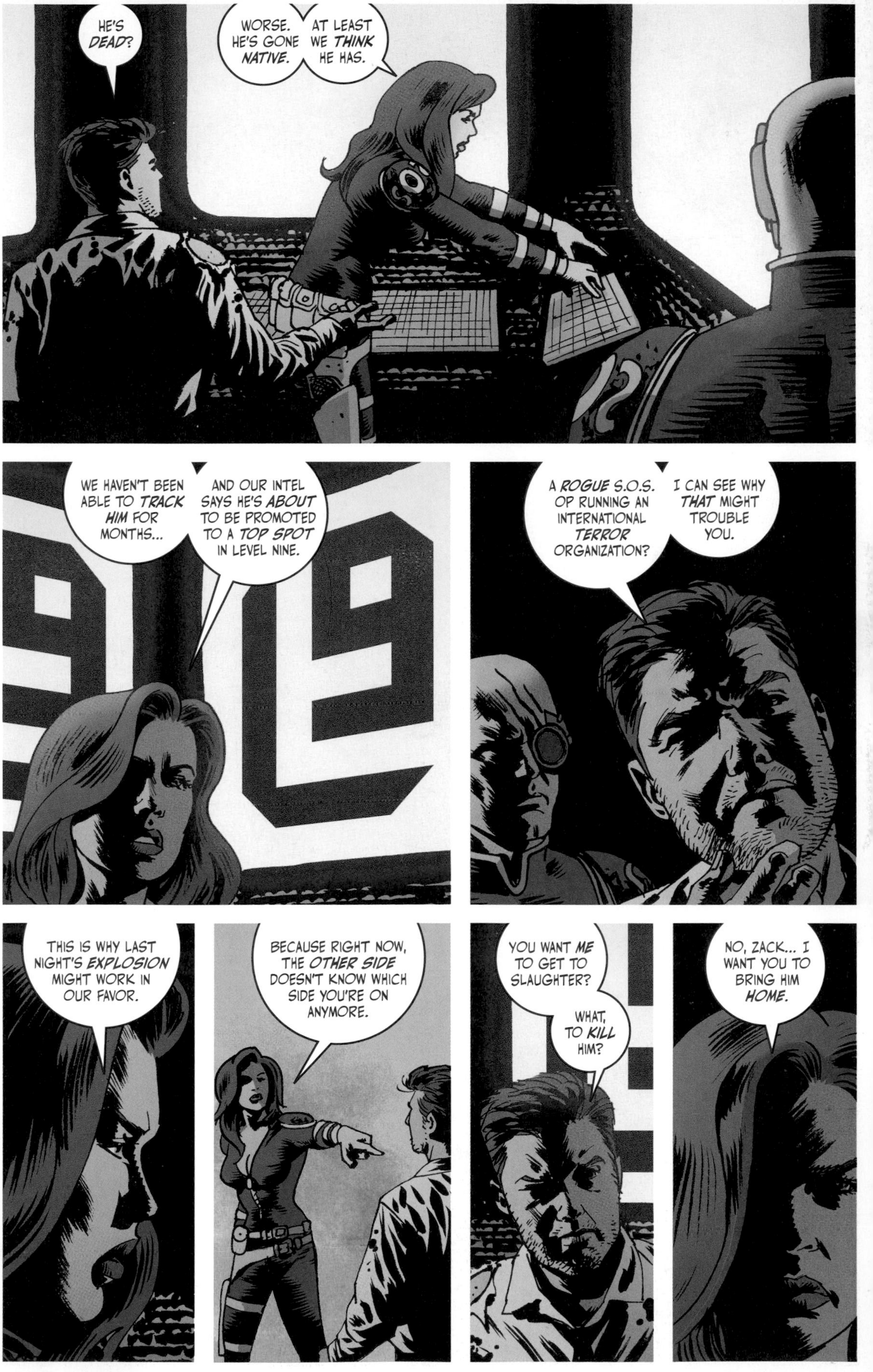
HE'S *DEAD?*
WORSE. HE'S GONE *NATIVE.*
AT LEAST WE *THINK* HE HAS.
WE HAVEN'T BEEN ABLE TO *TRACK HIM* FOR MONTHS...
AND OUR INTEL SAYS HE'S *ABOUT* TO BE PROMOTED TO A *TOP SPOT* IN LEVEL NINE.
A *ROGUE* S.O.S. OP RUNNING AN INTERNATIONAL *TERROR* ORGANIZATION?
I CAN SEE WHY *THAT* MIGHT TROUBLE YOU.
THIS IS WHY LAST NIGHT'S *EXPLOSION* MIGHT WORK IN OUR FAVOR.
BECAUSE RIGHT NOW, THE *OTHER SIDE* DOESN'T KNOW WHICH SIDE YOU'RE ON ANYMORE.
YOU WANT *ME* TO GET TO SLAUGHTER?
WHAT, TO *KILL* HIM?
NO, ZACK... I WANT YOU TO BRING HIM *HOME.*

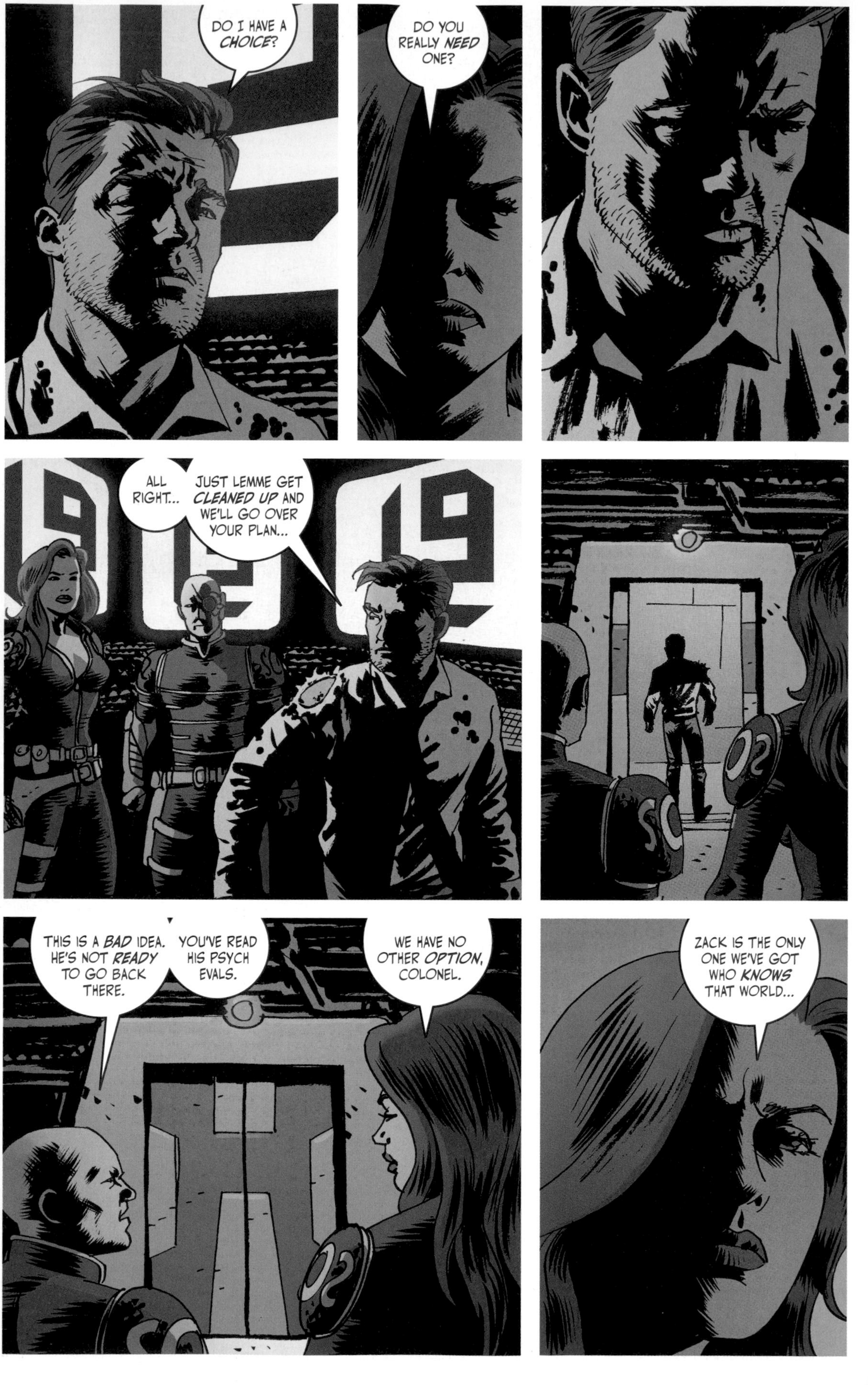

DO I HAVE A CHOICE?
DO YOU REALLY NEED ONE?
ALL RIGHT...
JUST LEMME GET CLEANED UP AND WE'LL GO OVER YOUR PLAN...
THIS IS A BAD IDEA. HE'S NOT READY TO GO BACK THERE.
YOU'VE READ HIS PSYCH EVALS.
WE HAVE NO OTHER OPTION, COLONEL.
ZACK IS THE ONLY ONE WE'VE GOT WHO KNOWS THAT WORLD...

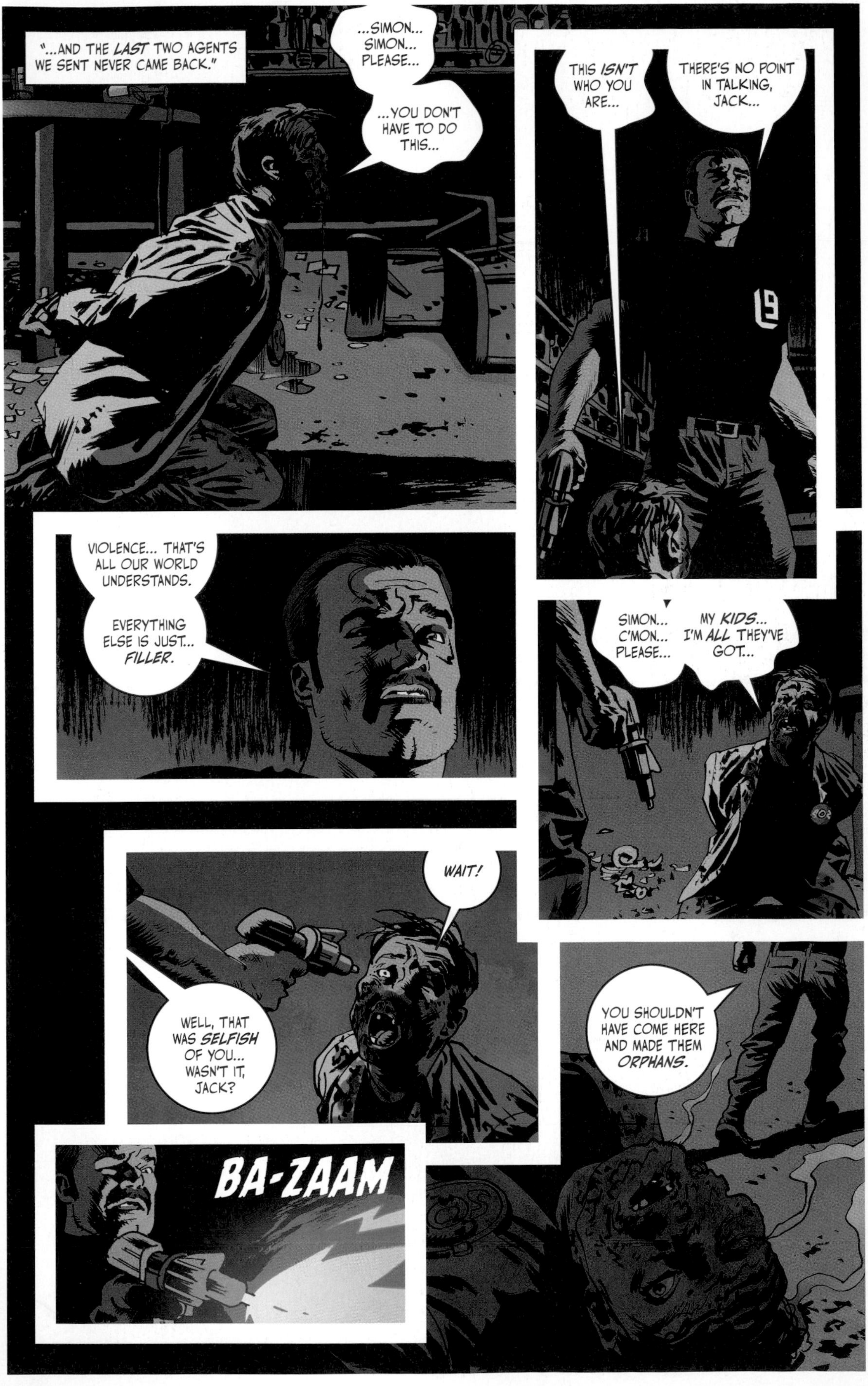
"...AND THE *LAST* TWO AGENTS WE SENT NEVER CAME BACK."
...SIMON... SIMON... PLEASE...
...YOU DON'T HAVE TO DO THIS...
THIS *ISN'T* WHO YOU ARE...
THERE'S NO POINT IN TALKING, JACK...
VIOLENCE... THAT'S ALL OUR WORLD UNDERSTANDS.
EVERYTHING ELSE IS JUST... *FILLER*.
SIMON... C'MON... PLEASE...
MY *KIDS*... I'M *ALL* THEY'VE GOT...
WAIT!
WELL, THAT WAS *SELFISH* OF YOU... WASN'T IT, JACK?
YOU SHOULDN'T HAVE COME HERE AND MADE THEM *ORPHANS*.
BA-ZAAM

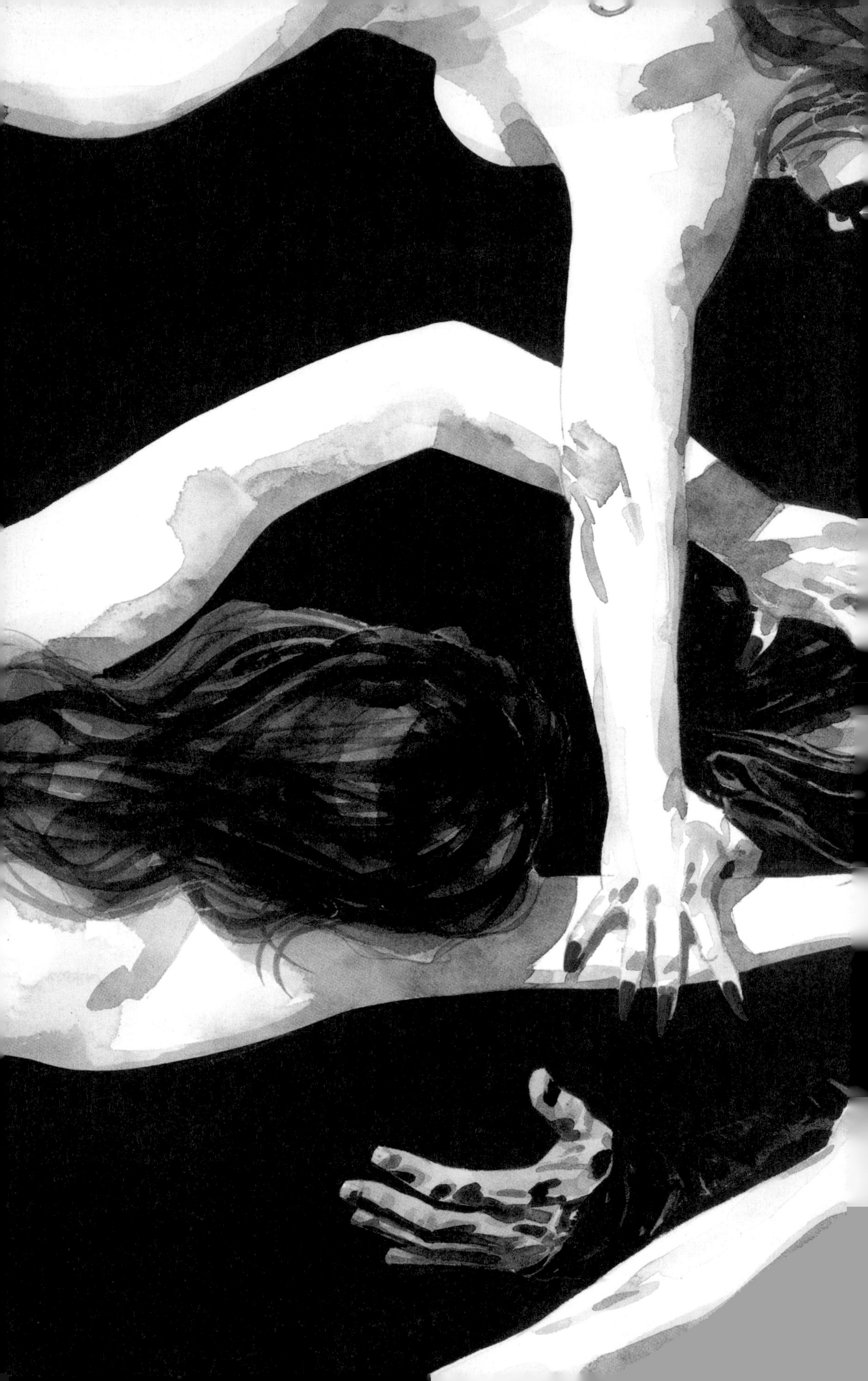

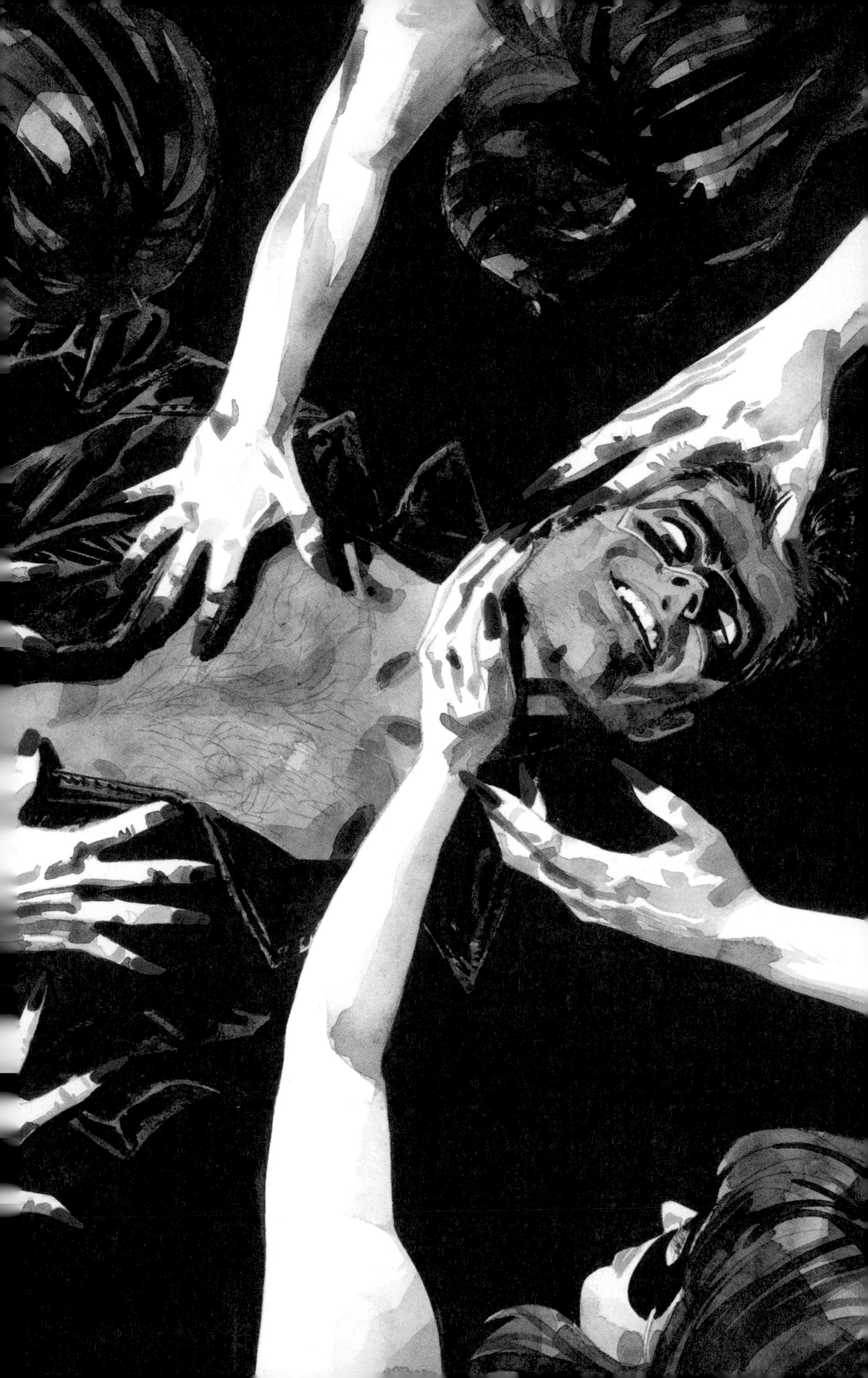

Chapter Two

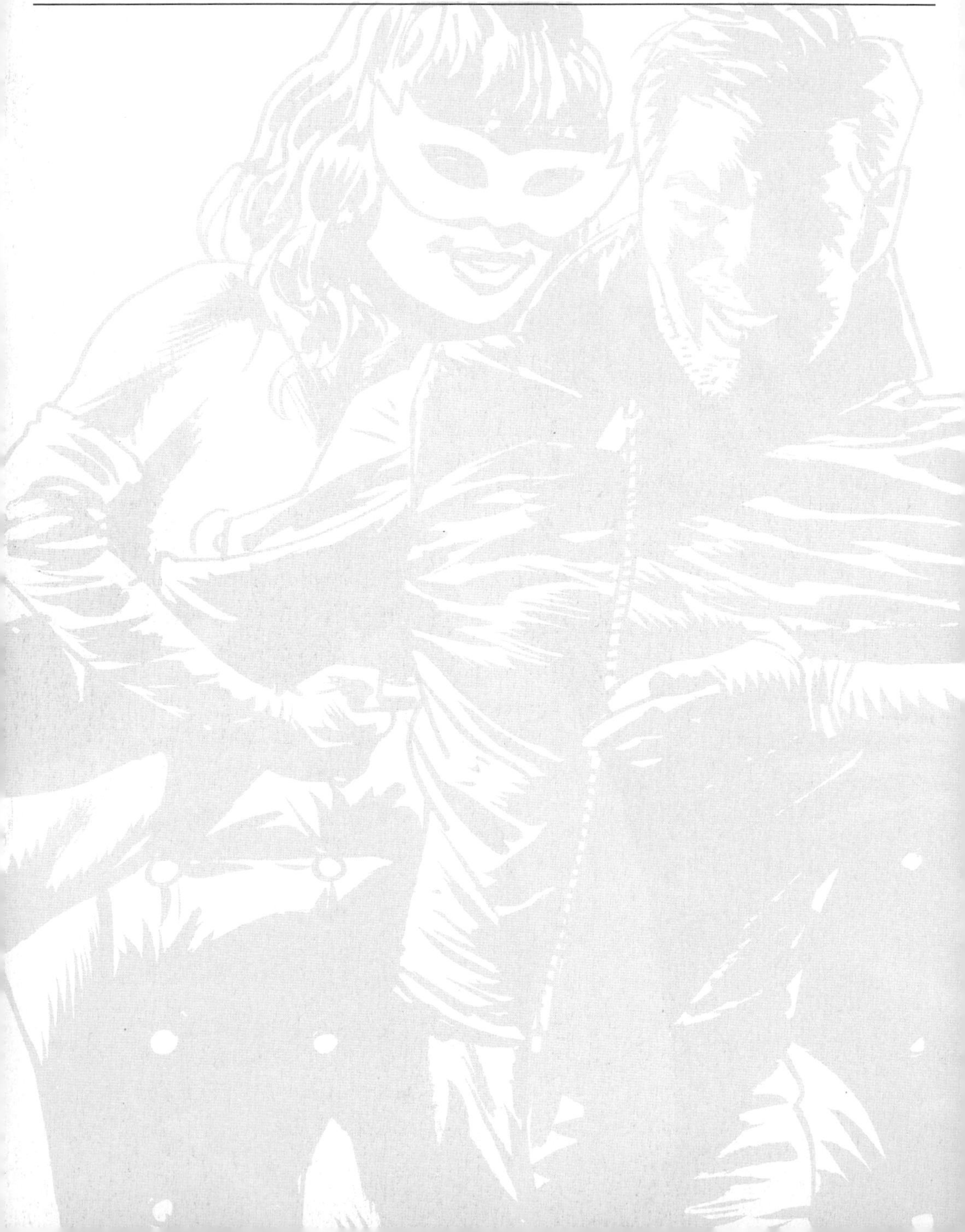

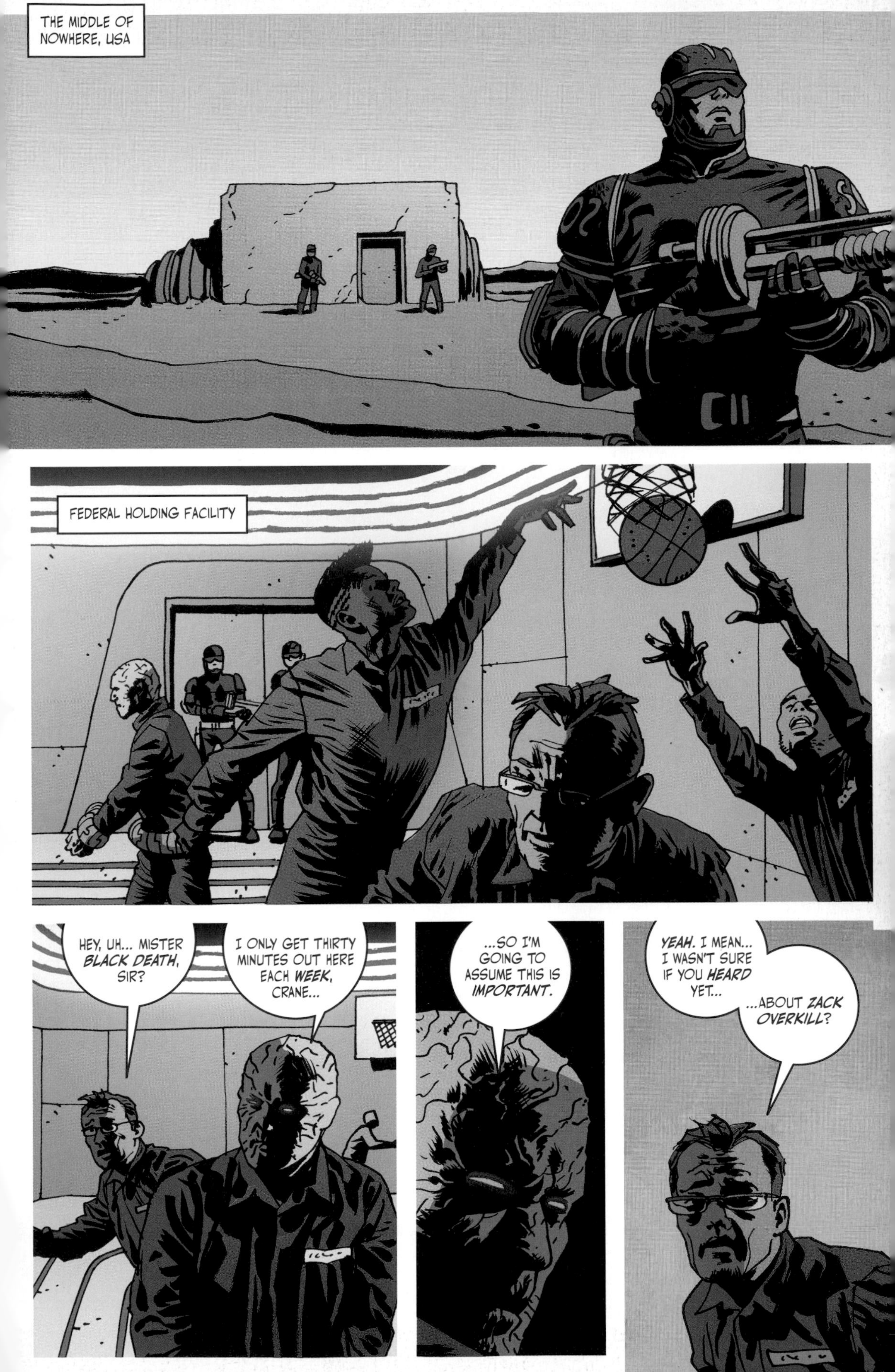
THE MIDDLE OF NOWHERE, USA
FEDERAL HOLDING FACILITY
HEY, UH... MISTER BLACK DEATH, SIR?
I ONLY GET THIRTY MINUTES OUT HERE EACH WEEK, CRANE...
...SO I'M GOING TO ASSUME THIS IS IMPORTANT.
YEAH. I MEAN... I WASN'T SURE IF YOU HEARD YET...
...ABOUT ZACK OVERKILL?

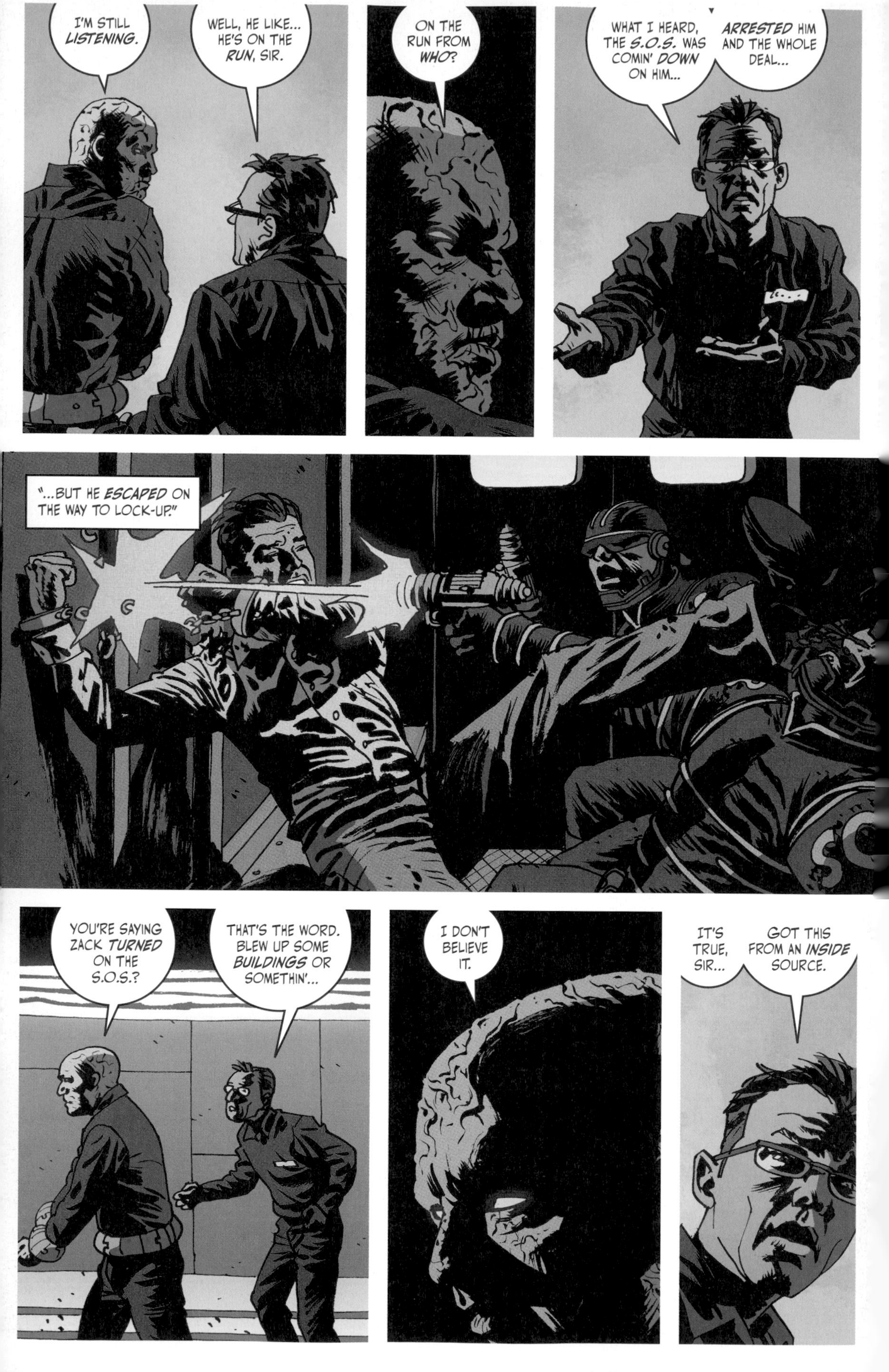

I'M STILL LISTENING.
WELL, HE LIKE... HE'S ON THE RUN, SIR.
ON THE RUN FROM WHO?
WHAT I HEARD, THE S.O.S. WAS COMIN' DOWN ON HIM...
ARRESTED HIM AND THE WHOLE DEAL...
"...BUT HE ESCAPED ON THE WAY TO LOCK-UP."
YOU'RE SAYING ZACK TURNED ON THE S.O.S.?
THAT'S THE WORD. BLEW UP SOME BUILDINGS OR SOMETHIN'...
I DON'T BELIEVE IT.
IT'S TRUE, SIR...
GOT THIS FROM AN INSIDE SOURCE.

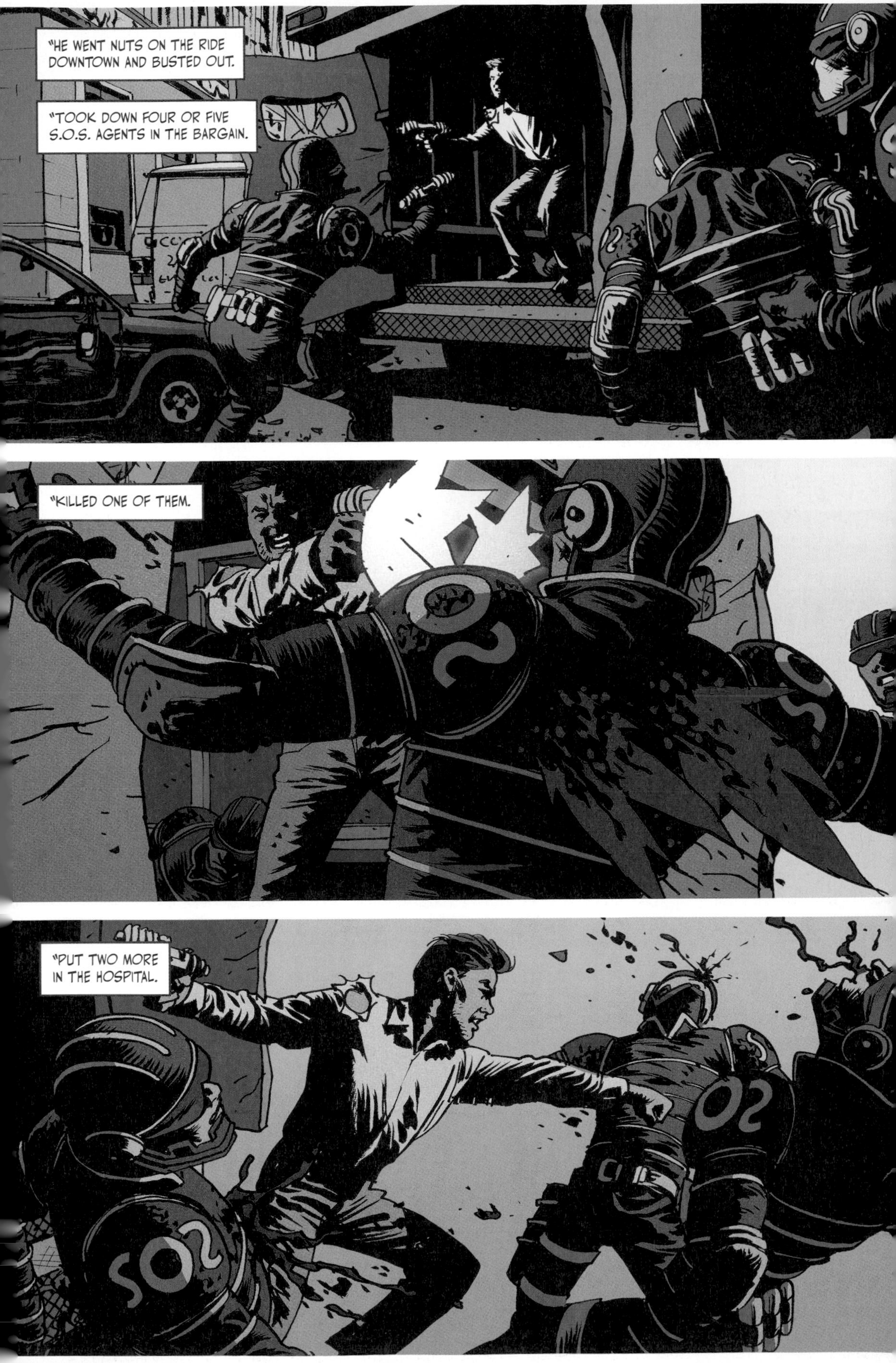
"HE WENT NUTS ON THE RIDE DOWNTOWN AND BUSTED OUT.
"TOOK DOWN FOUR OR FIVE S.O.S. AGENTS IN THE BARGAIN.
"KILLED ONE OF THEM.
"PUT TWO MORE IN THE HOSPITAL.

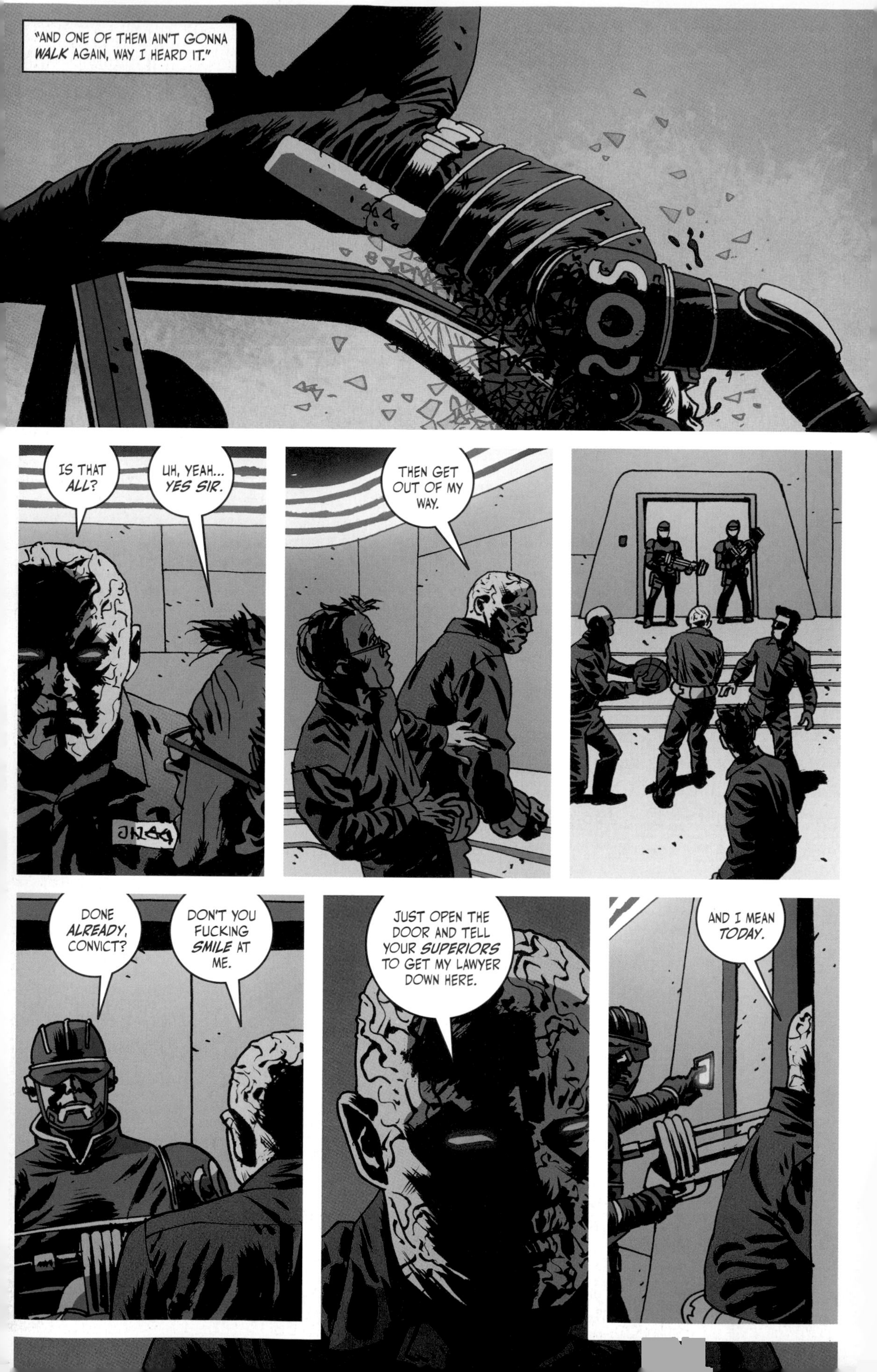
"AND ONE OF THEM AIN'T GONNA WALK AGAIN, WAY I HEARD IT."
IS THAT ALL?
UH, YEAH... YES SIR.
THEN GET OUT OF MY WAY.
JN144
DONE ALREADY, CONVICT?
DON'T YOU FUCKING SMILE AT ME.
JUST OPEN THE DOOR AND TELL YOUR SUPERIORS TO GET MY LAWYER DOWN HERE.
AND I MEAN TODAY.

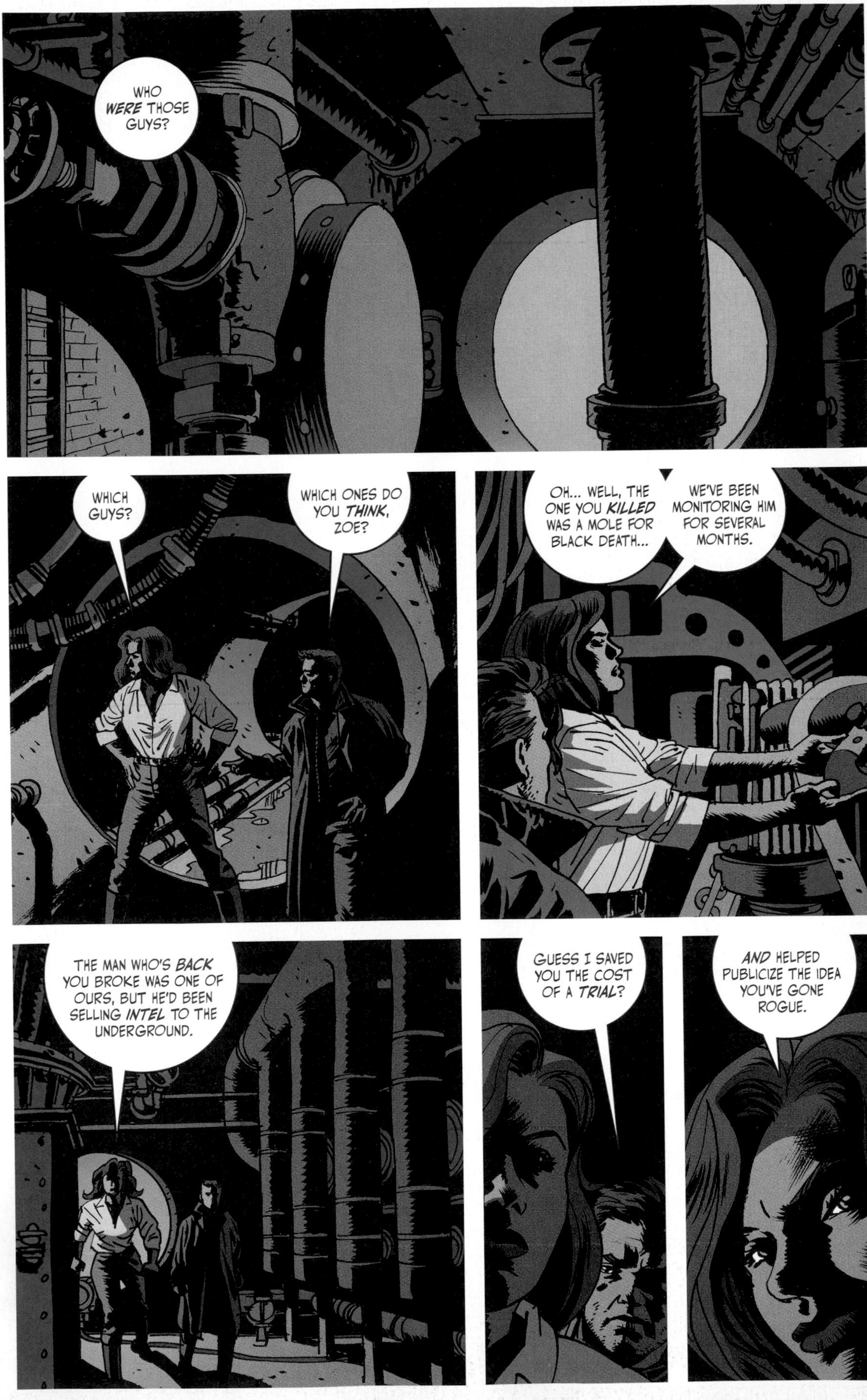
WHO *WERE* THOSE GUYS?
WHICH GUYS?
WHICH ONES DO YOU *THINK*, ZOE?
OH... WELL, THE ONE YOU *KILLED* WAS A MOLE FOR BLACK DEATH...
WE'VE BEEN MONITORING HIM FOR SEVERAL MONTHS.
THE MAN WHO'S *BACK* YOU BROKE WAS ONE OF OURS, BUT HE'D BEEN SELLING *INTEL* TO THE UNDERGROUND.
GUESS I SAVED YOU THE COST OF A *TRIAL*?
AND HELPED PUBLICIZE THE IDEA YOU'VE GONE ROGUE.

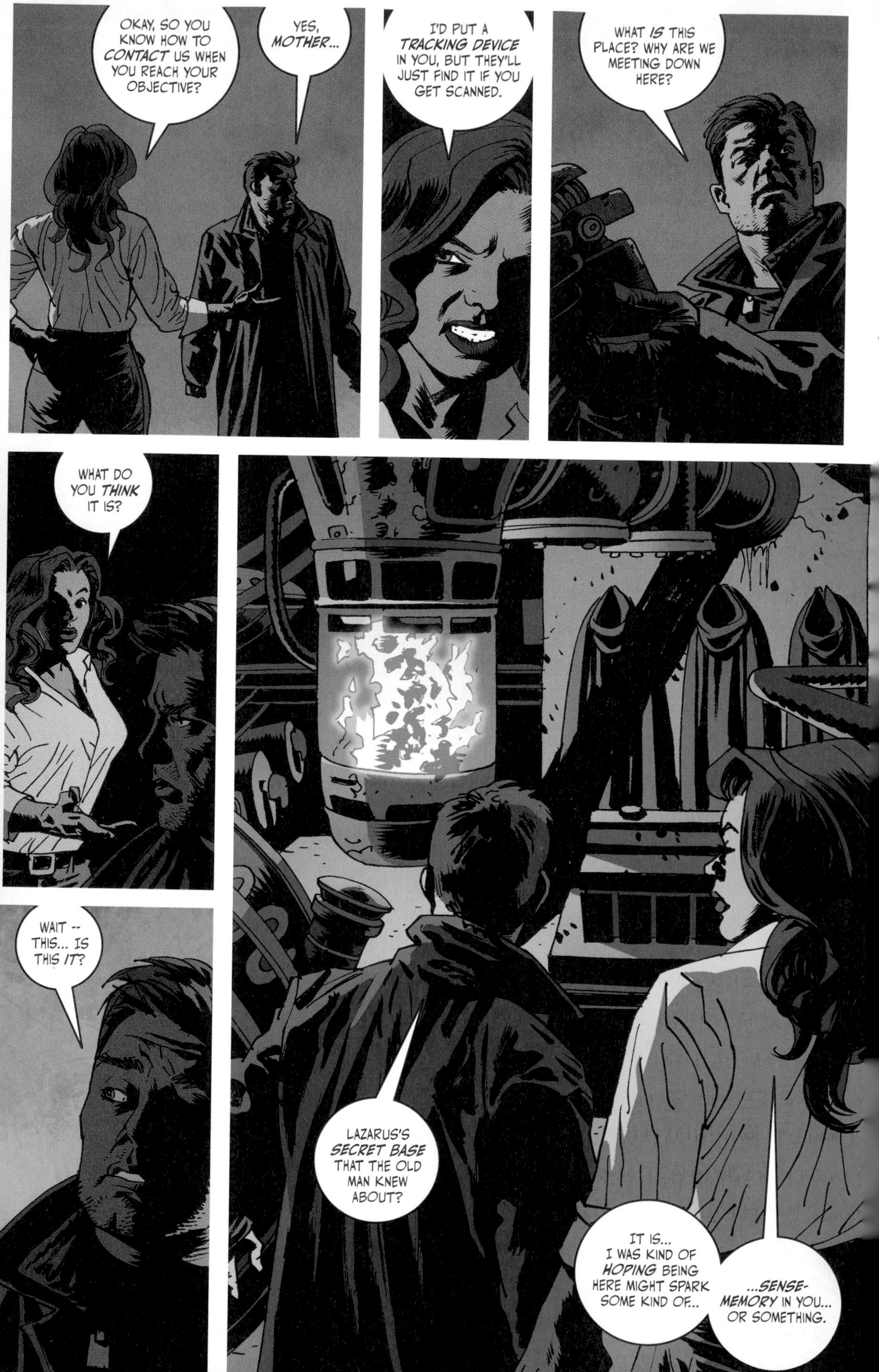
OKAY, SO YOU KNOW HOW TO CONTACT US WHEN YOU REACH YOUR OBJECTIVE?
YES, MOTHER...
I'D PUT A TRACKING DEVICE IN YOU, BUT THEY'LL JUST FIND IT IF YOU GET SCANNED.
WHAT IS THIS PLACE? WHY ARE WE MEETING DOWN HERE?
WHAT DO YOU THINK IT IS?
WAIT -- THIS... IS THIS IT?
LAZARUS'S SECRET BASE THAT THE OLD MAN KNEW ABOUT?
IT IS... I WAS KIND OF HOPING BEING HERE MIGHT SPARK SOME KIND OF...
...SENSE-MEMORY IN YOU... OR SOMETHING.

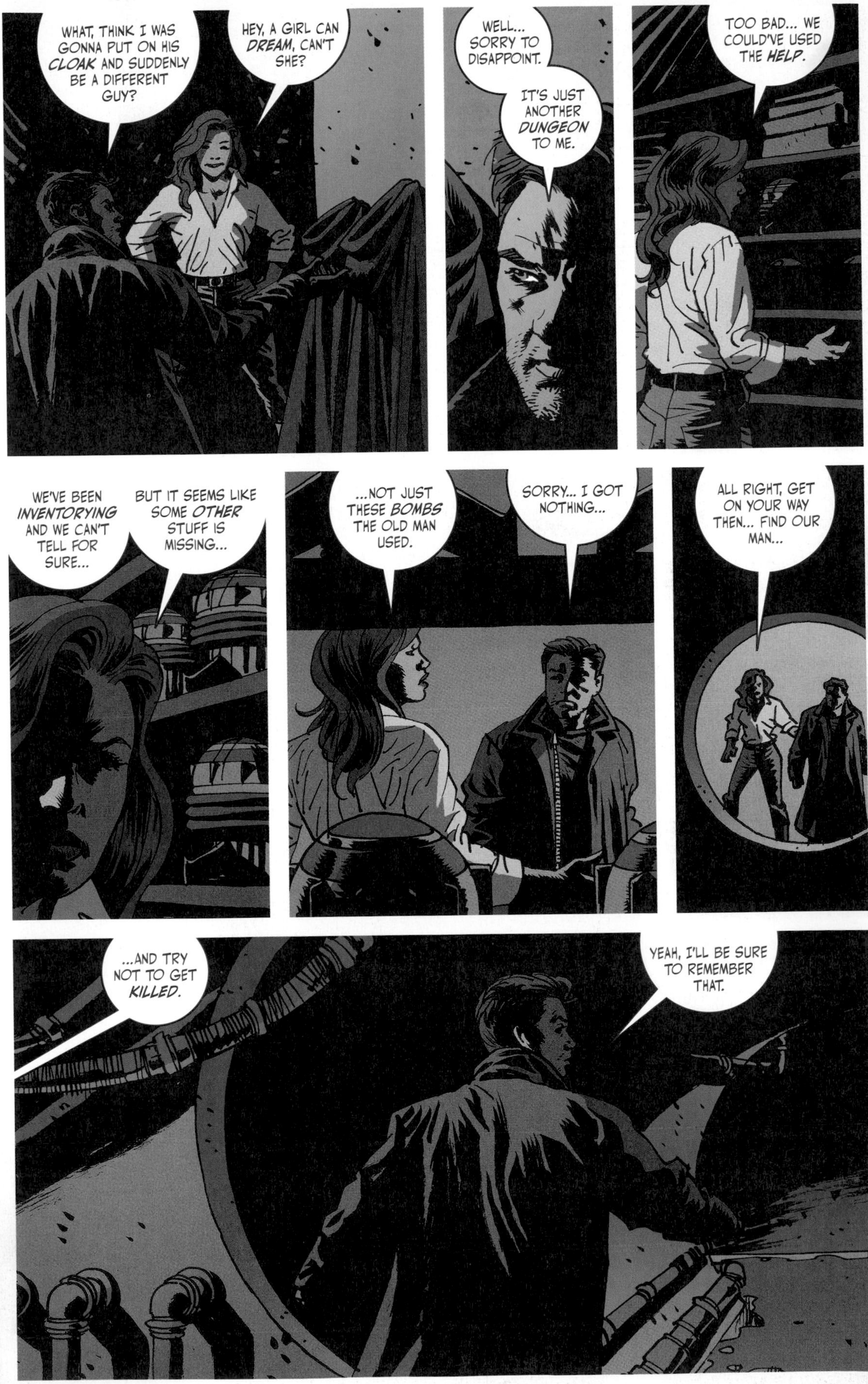
WHAT, THINK I WAS GONNA PUT ON HIS CLOAK AND SUDDENLY BE A DIFFERENT GUY?
HEY, A GIRL CAN DREAM, CAN'T SHE?
WELL... SORRY TO DISAPPOINT.
IT'S JUST ANOTHER DUNGEON TO ME.
TOO BAD... WE COULD'VE USED THE HELP.
WE'VE BEEN INVENTORYING AND WE CAN'T TELL FOR SURE...
BUT IT SEEMS LIKE SOME OTHER STUFF IS MISSING...
...NOT JUST THESE BOMBS THE OLD MAN USED.
SORRY... I GOT NOTHING...
ALL RIGHT, GET ON YOUR WAY THEN... FIND OUR MAN...
...AND TRY NOT TO GET KILLED.
YEAH, I'LL BE SURE TO REMEMBER THAT.

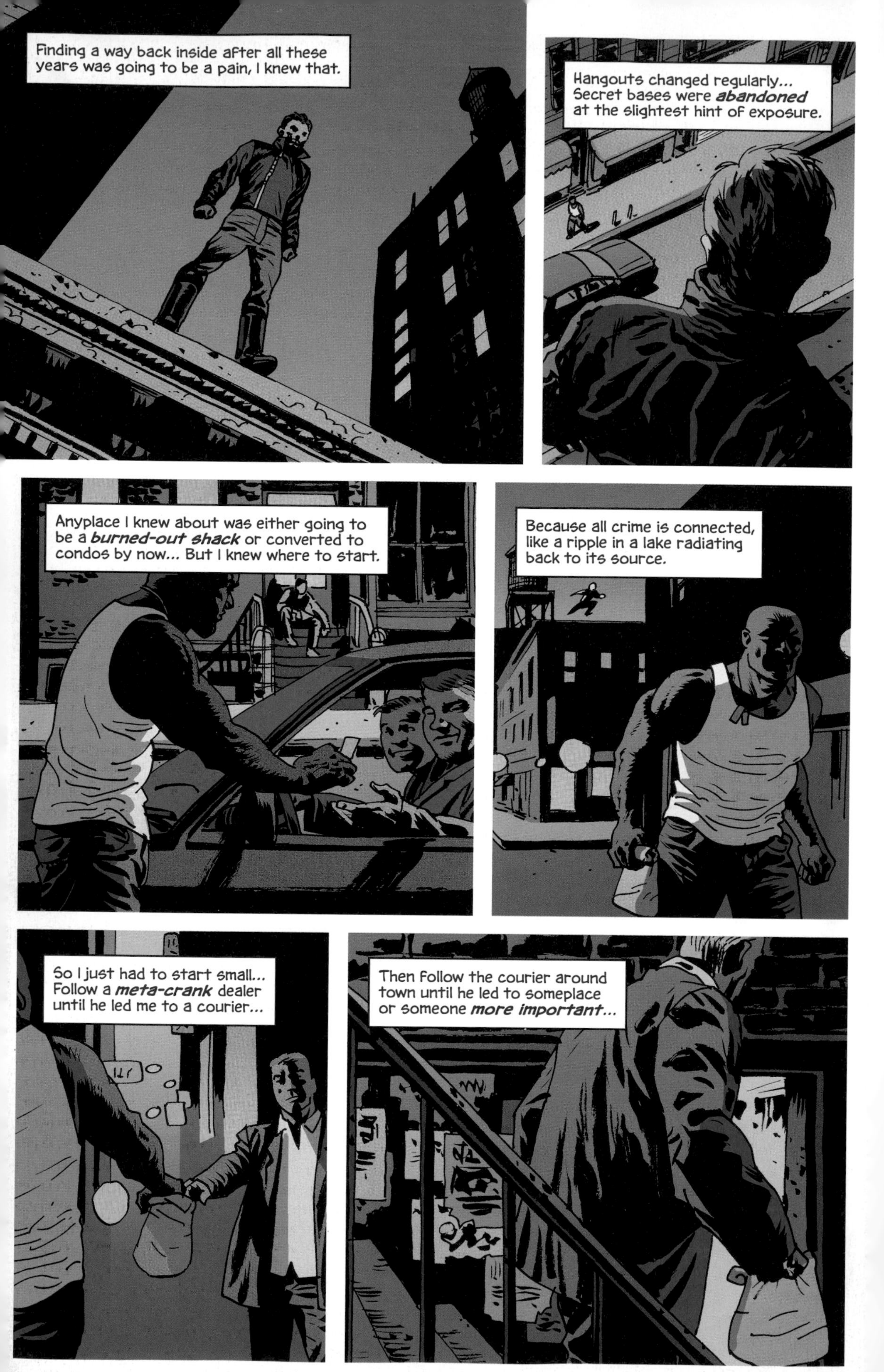
Finding a way back inside after all these years was going to be a pain, I knew that.
Hangouts changed regularly... Secret bases were *abandoned* at the slightest hint of exposure.
Anyplace I knew about was either going to be a *burned-out shack* or converted to condos by now... But I knew where to start.
Because all crime is connected, like a ripple in a lake radiating back to its source.
So I just had to start small... Follow a *meta-crank* dealer until he led me to a courier...
Then follow the courier around town until he led to someplace or someone *more important*...

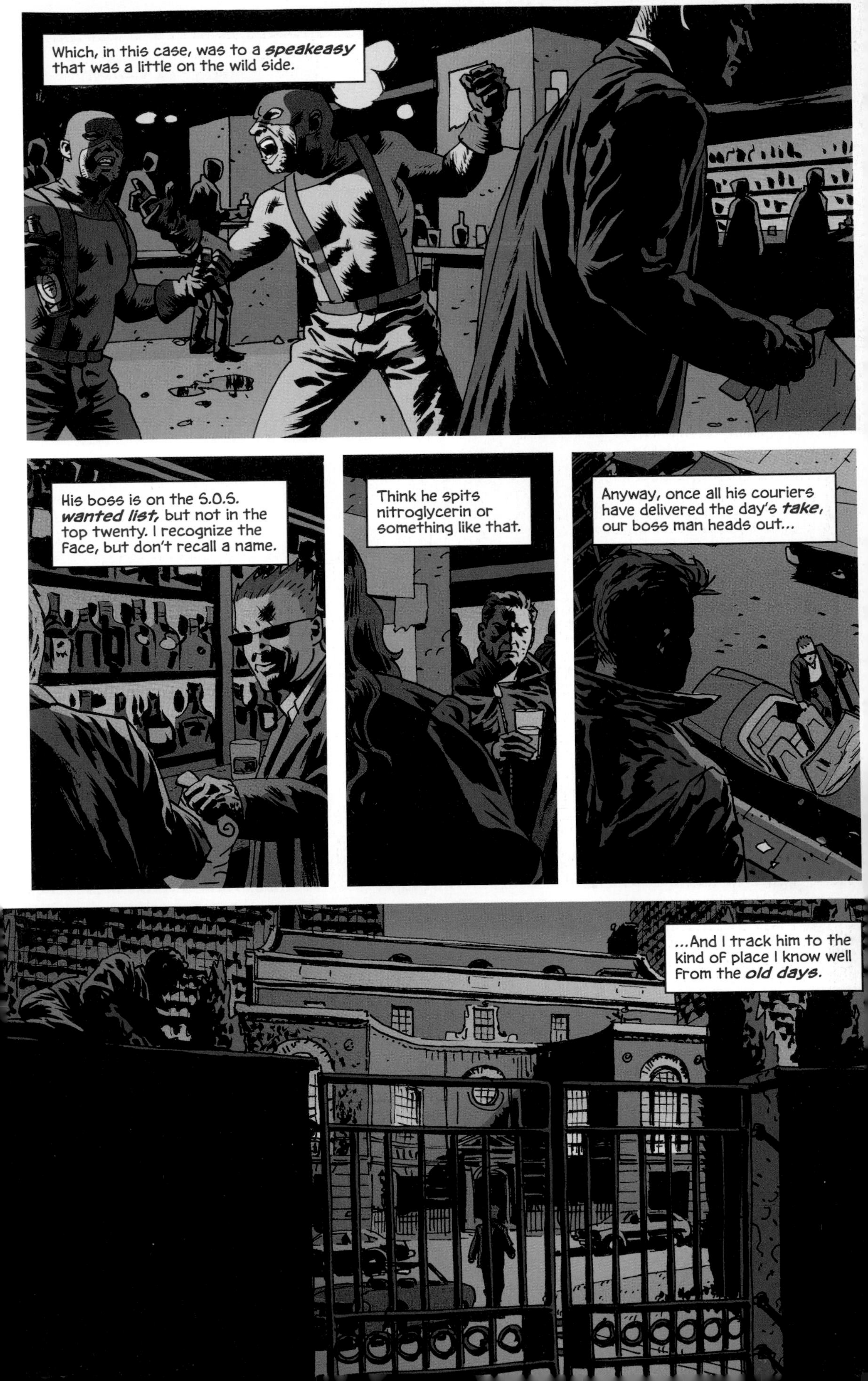
Which, in this case, was to a *speakeasy* that was a little on the wild side.
His boss is on the S.O.S. *wanted list,* but not in the top twenty. I recognize the face, but don't recall a name.
Think he spits nitroglycerin or something like that.
Anyway, once all his couriers have delivered the day's *take,* our boss man heads out...
...And I track him to the kind of place I know well from the *old days.*

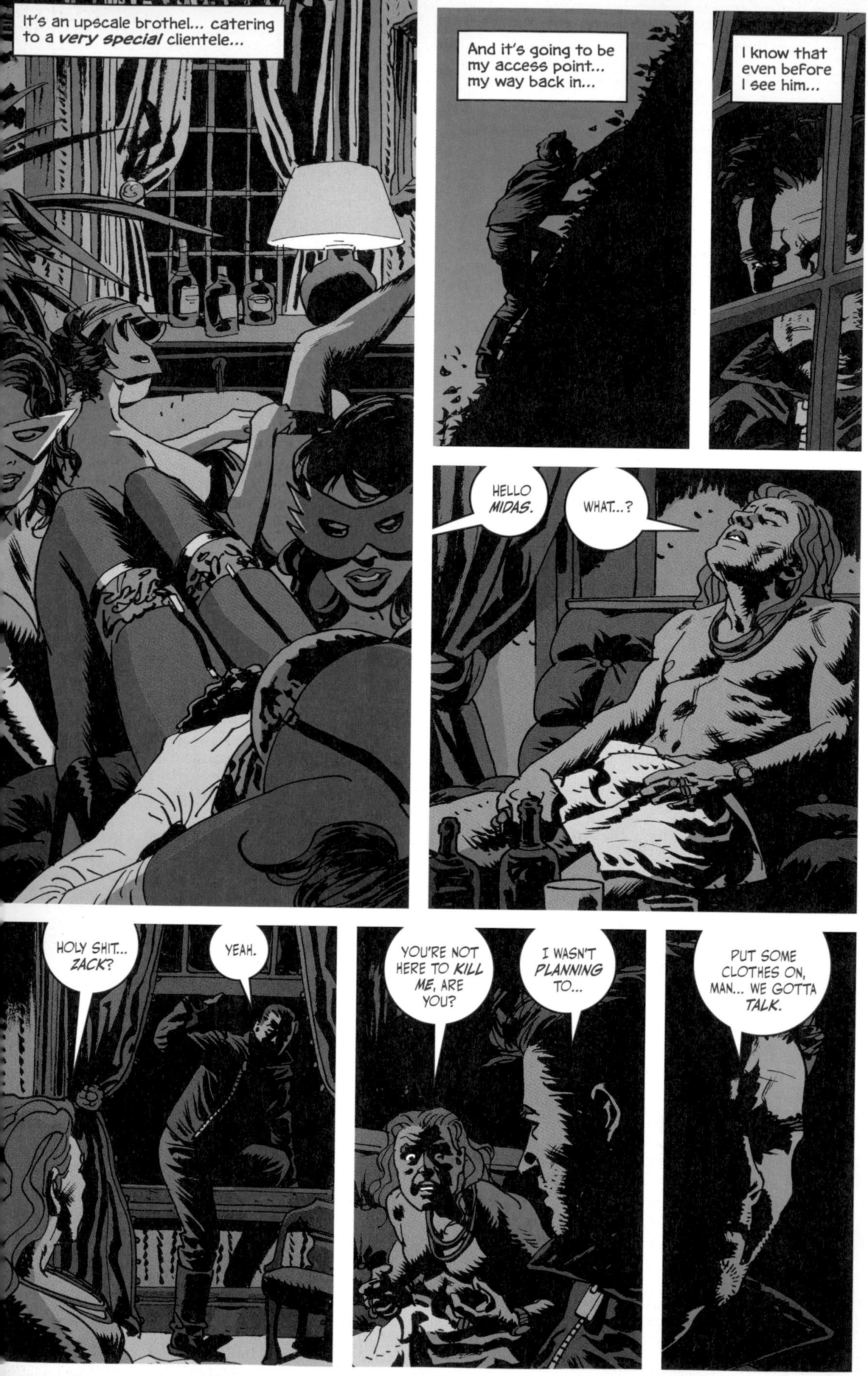
It's an upscale brothel... catering to a *very special* clientele...
And it's going to be my access point... my way back in...
I know that even before I see him...
HELLO *MIDAS.*
WHAT...?
HOLY SHIT... *ZACK?*
YEAH.
YOU'RE NOT HERE TO *KILL ME*, ARE YOU?
I WASN'T *PLANNING* TO...
PUT SOME CLOTHES ON, MAN... WE GOTTA *TALK.*

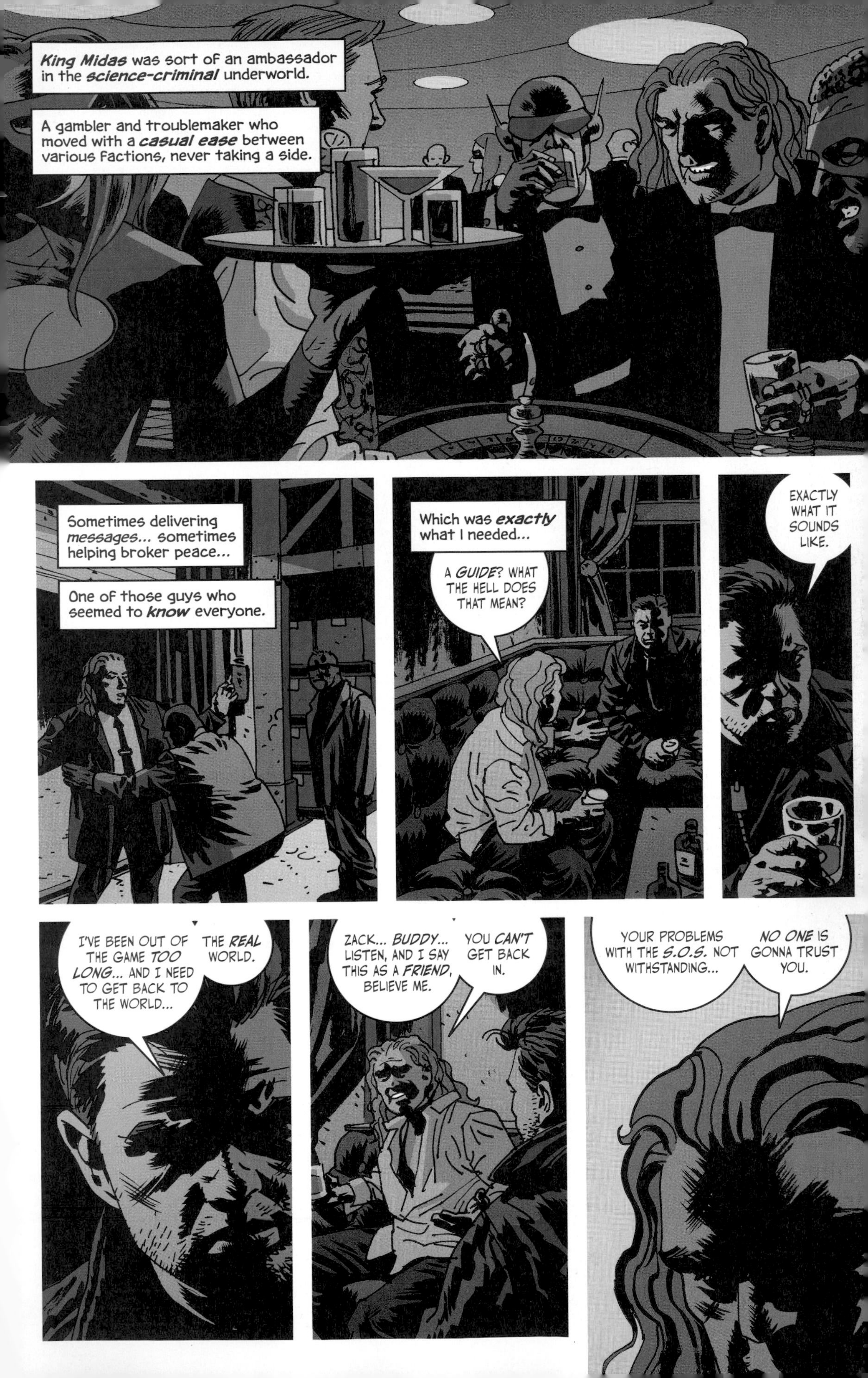
King Midas was sort of an ambassador in the science-criminal underworld.
A gambler and troublemaker who moved with a casual ease between various factions, never taking a side.
Sometimes delivering messages... sometimes helping broker peace...
One of those guys who seemed to know everyone.
Which was exactly what I needed...
A GUIDE? WHAT THE HELL DOES THAT MEAN?
EXACTLY WHAT IT SOUNDS LIKE.
I'VE BEEN OUT OF THE GAME TOO LONG... AND I NEED TO GET BACK TO THE WORLD...
THE REAL WORLD.
ZACK... BUDDY... LISTEN, AND I SAY THIS AS A FRIEND, BELIEVE ME.
YOU CAN'T GET BACK IN.
YOUR PROBLEMS WITH THE S.O.S. NOT WITHSTANDING...
NO ONE IS GONNA TRUST YOU.

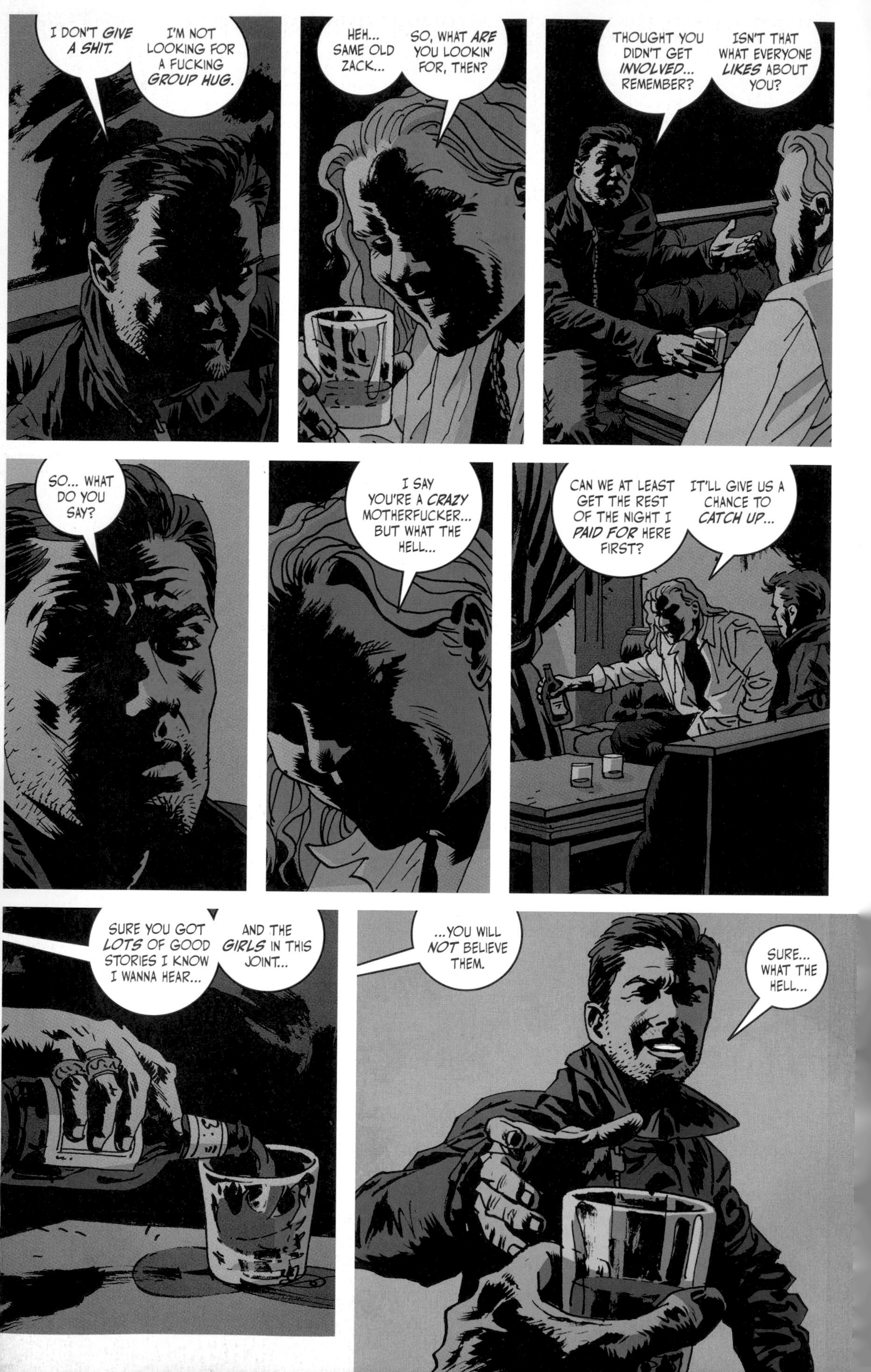
I DON'T GIVE A SHIT.
I'M NOT LOOKING FOR A FUCKING GROUP HUG.
HEH... SAME OLD ZACK...
SO, WHAT ARE YOU LOOKIN' FOR, THEN?
THOUGHT YOU DIDN'T GET INVOLVED... REMEMBER?
ISN'T THAT WHAT EVERYONE LIKES ABOUT YOU?
SO... WHAT DO YOU SAY?
I SAY YOU'RE A CRAZY MOTHERFUCKER... BUT WHAT THE HELL...
CAN WE AT LEAST GET THE REST OF THE NIGHT I PAID FOR HERE FIRST?
IT'LL GIVE US A CHANCE TO CATCH UP...
SURE YOU GOT LOTS OF GOOD STORIES I KNOW I WANNA HEAR...
AND THE GIRLS IN THIS JOINT...
...YOU WILL NOT BELIEVE THEM.
SURE... WHAT THE HELL...

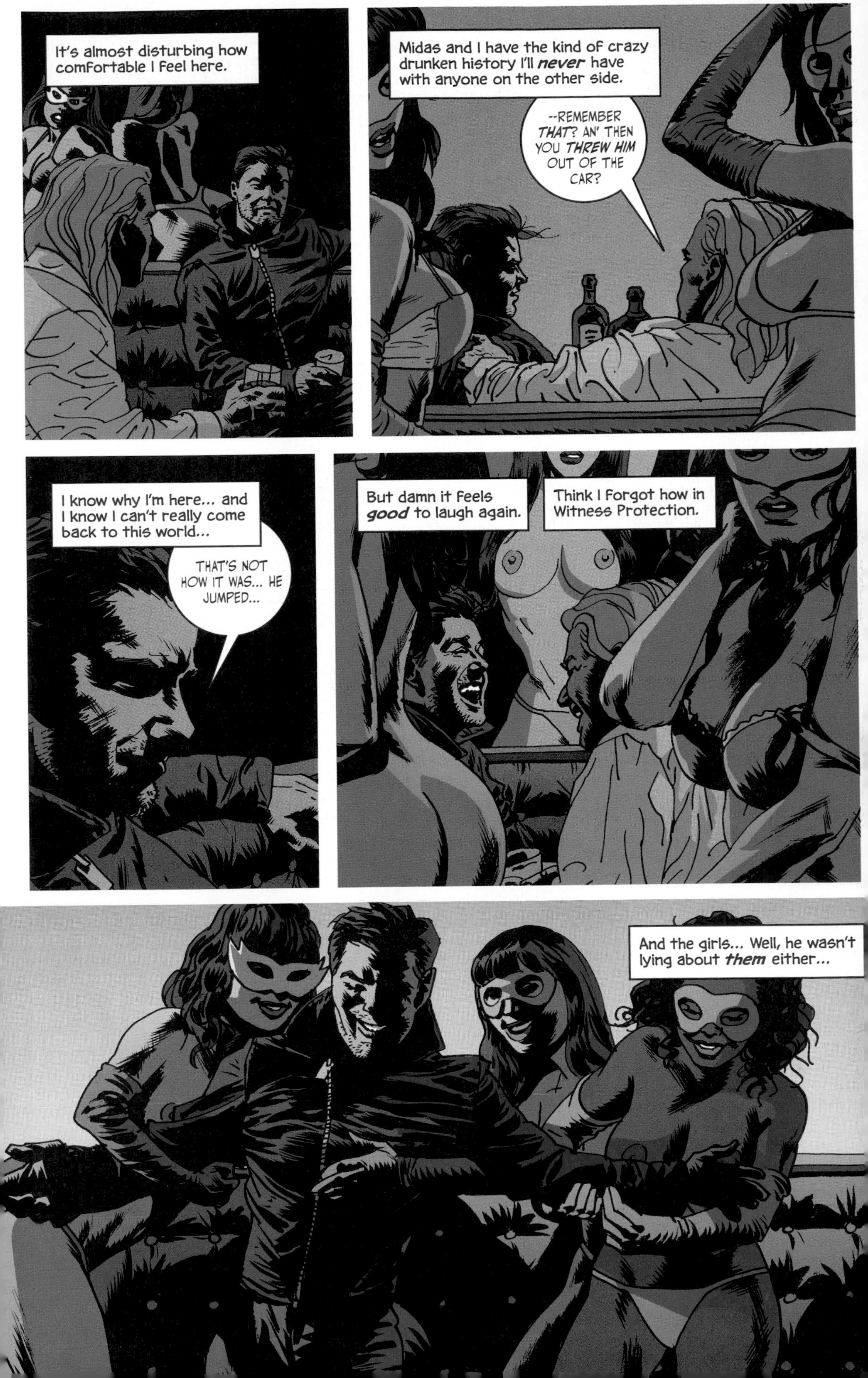

It's almost disturbing how comfortable I feel here.
Midas and I have the kind of crazy drunken history I'll *never* have with anyone on the other side.
--REMEMBER *THAT*? AN' THEN YOU *THREW HIM* OUT OF THE CAR?
I know why I'm here... and I know I can't really come back to this world...
THAT'S NOT HOW IT WAS... HE JUMPED...
But damn it feels *good* to laugh again.
Think I forgot how in Witness Protection.
And the girls... Well, he wasn't lying about *them* either...

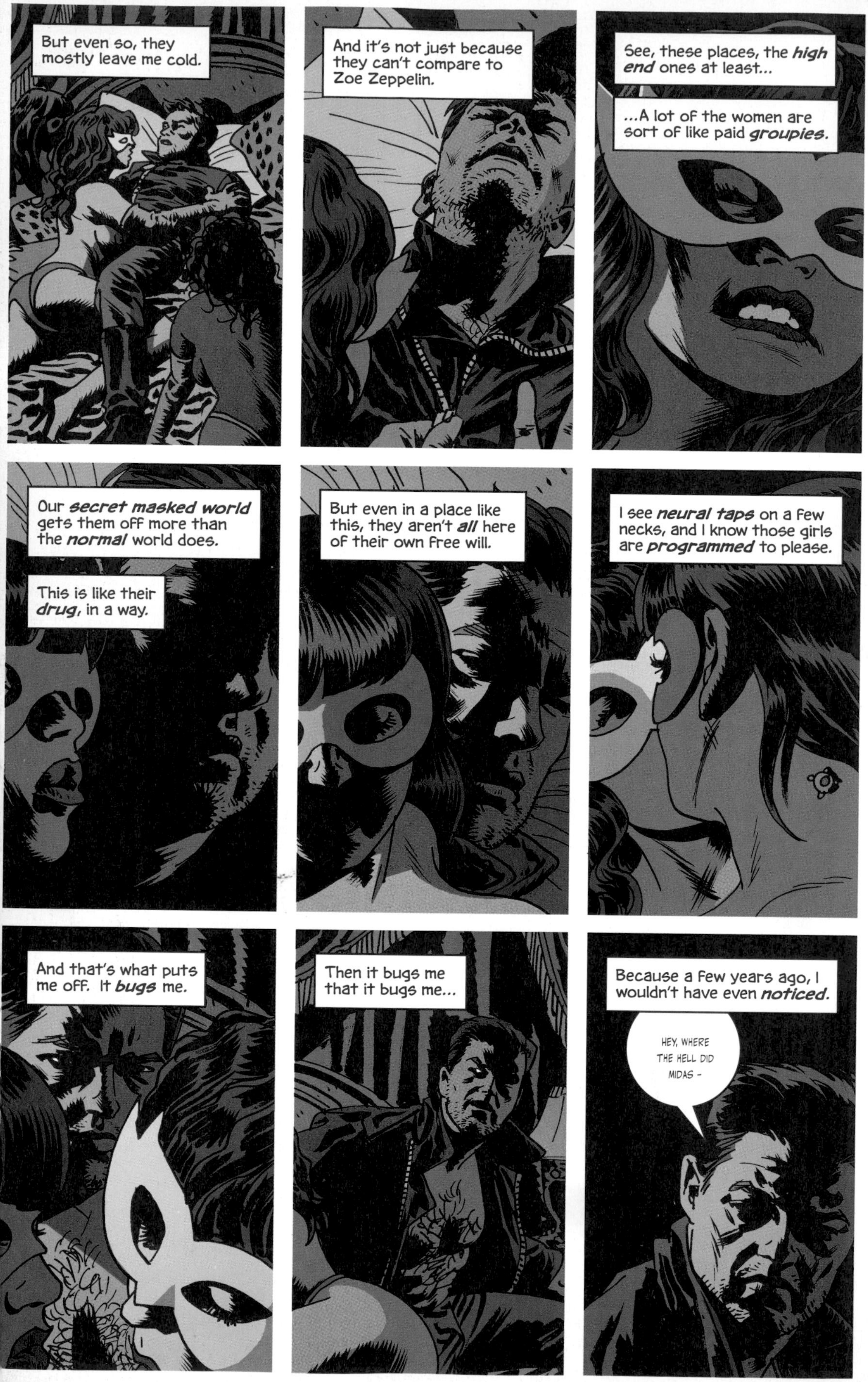
But even so, they mostly leave me cold.
And it's not just because they can't compare to Zoe Zeppelin.
See, these places, the *high end* ones at least...
...A lot of the women are sort of like paid *groupies.*
Our *secret masked world* gets them off more than the *normal* world does.
This is like their *drug*, in a way.
But even in a place like this, they aren't *all* here of their own free will.
I see *neural taps* on a few necks, and I know those girls are *programmed* to please.
And that's what puts me off. It *bugs* me.
Then it bugs me that it bugs me...
Because a few years ago, I wouldn't have even *noticed.*
HEY, WHERE THE HELL DID MIDAS -

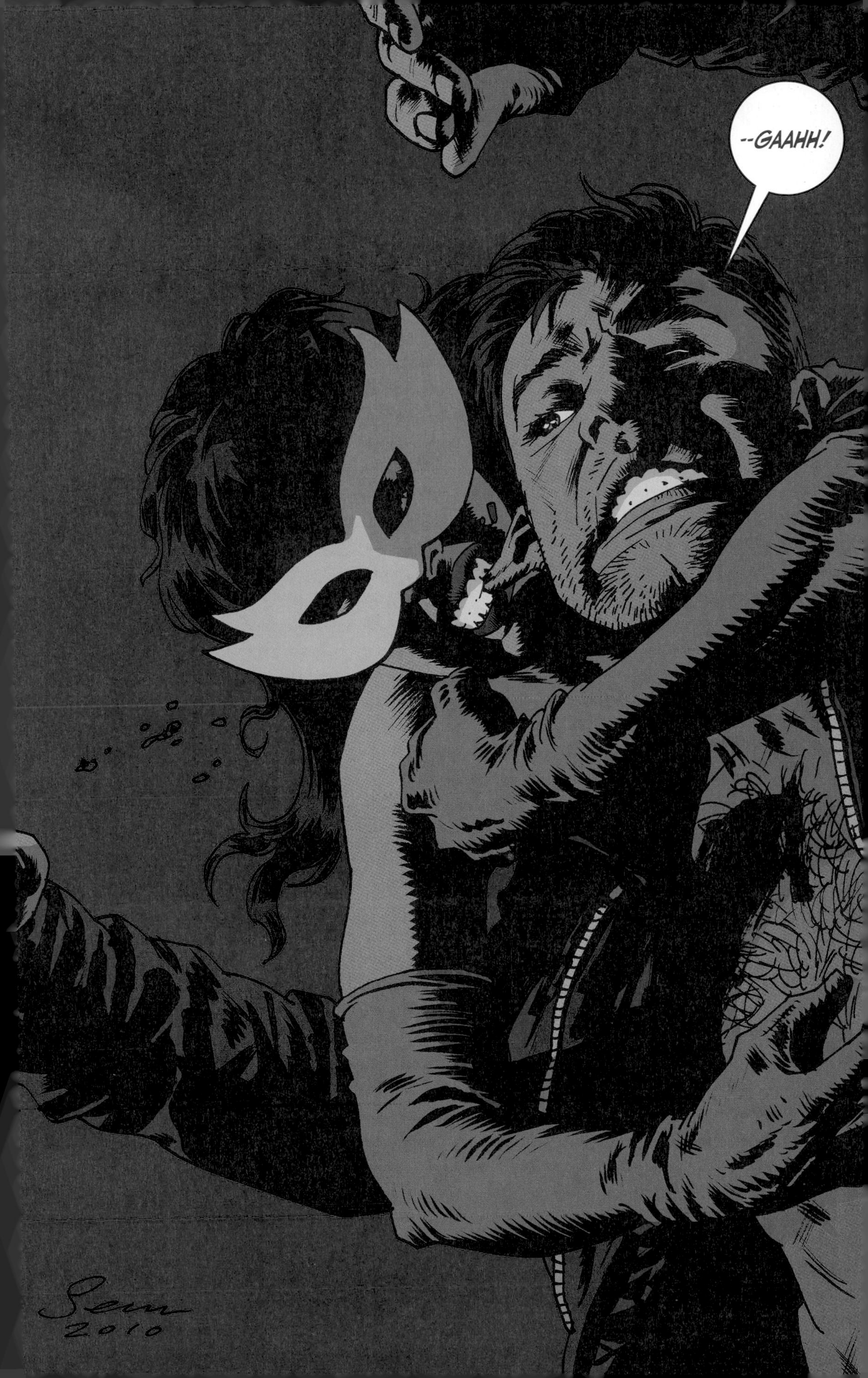
--GAAHH!
Sean
2010

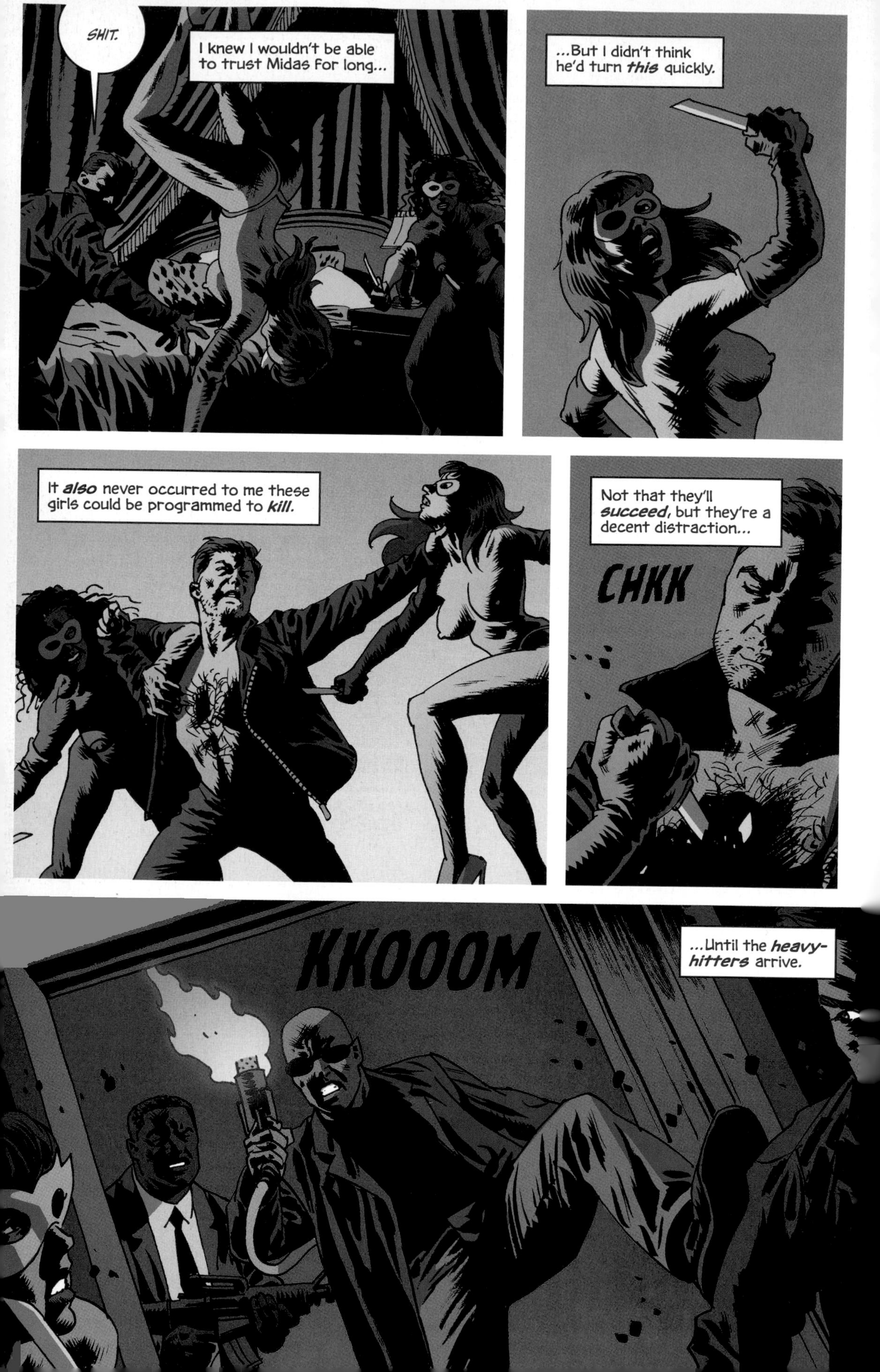
SHIT.
I knew I wouldn't be able to trust Midas for long...
...But I didn't think he'd turn *this* quickly.
It *also* never occurred to me these girls could be programmed to *kill.*
Not that they'll *succeed*, but they're a decent distraction...
CHKK
KKOOOM
...Until the *heavy-hitters* arrive.

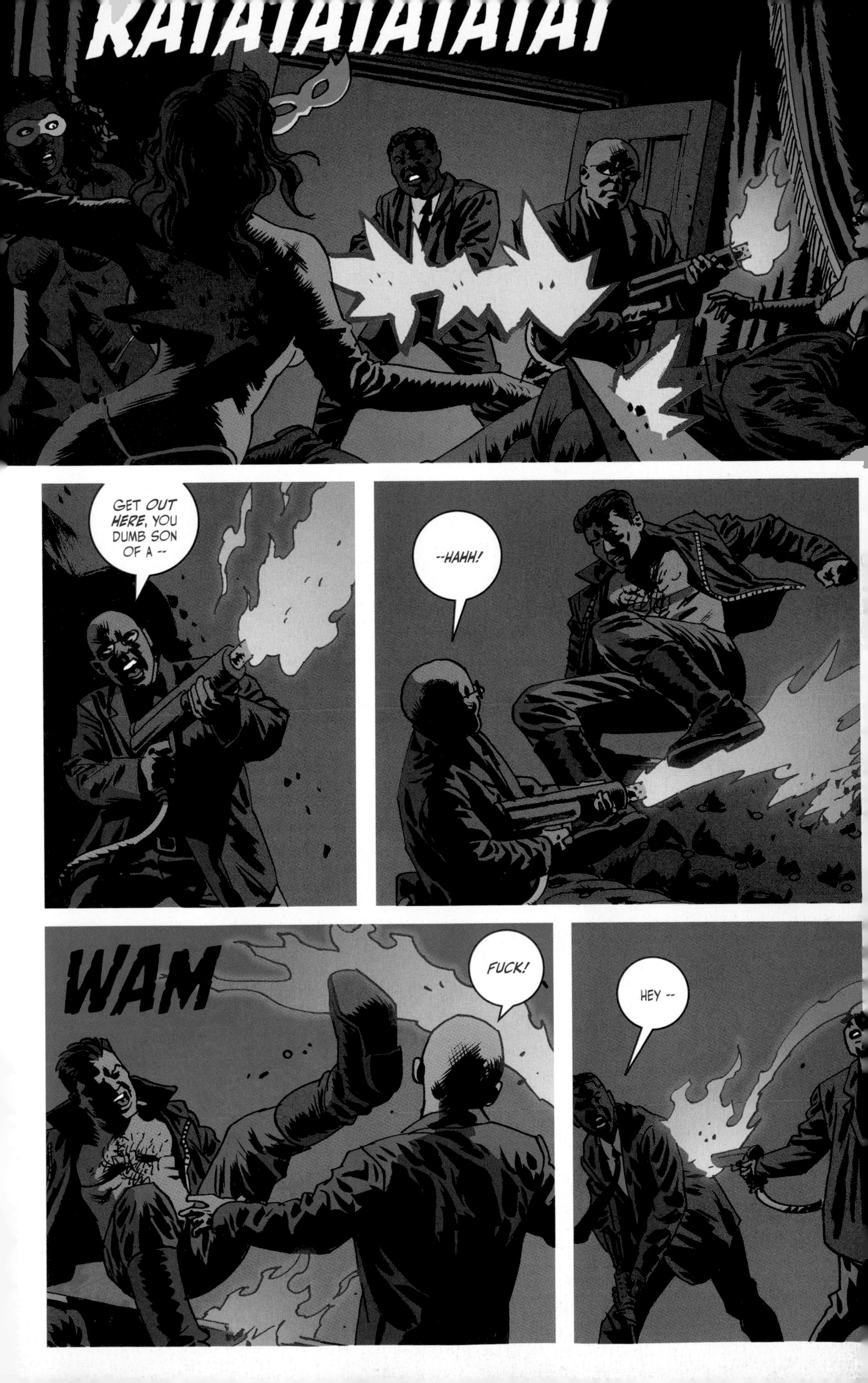
RATATATATATATAT
GET OUT HERE, YOU DUMB SON OF A --
--HAHH!
WAM
FUCK!
HEY --

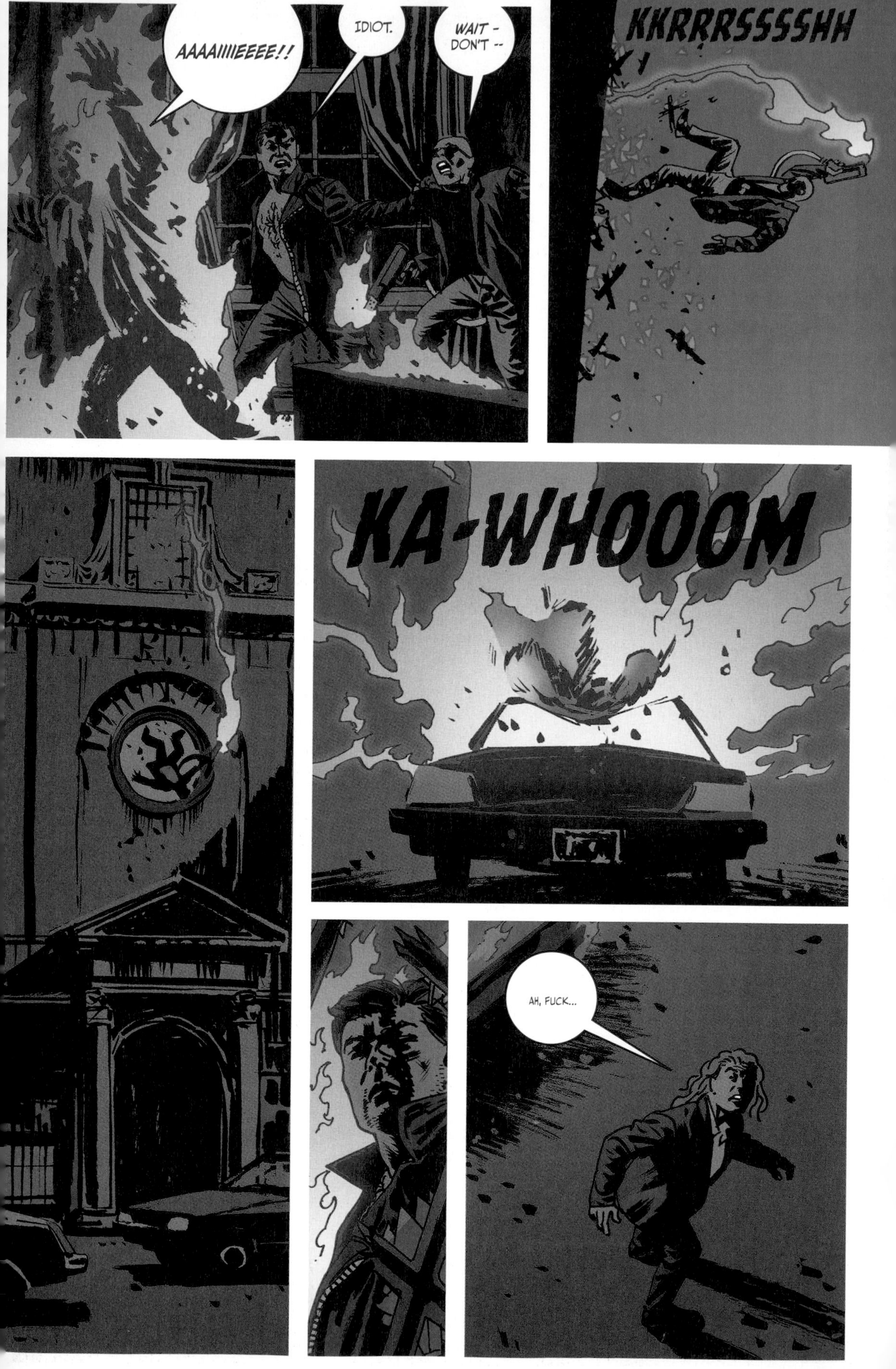
AAAAIIIIEEEE!!
IDIOT.
WAIT - DON'T --
KKRRRRSSSSHH
KA-WHOOOM
AH, FUCK...

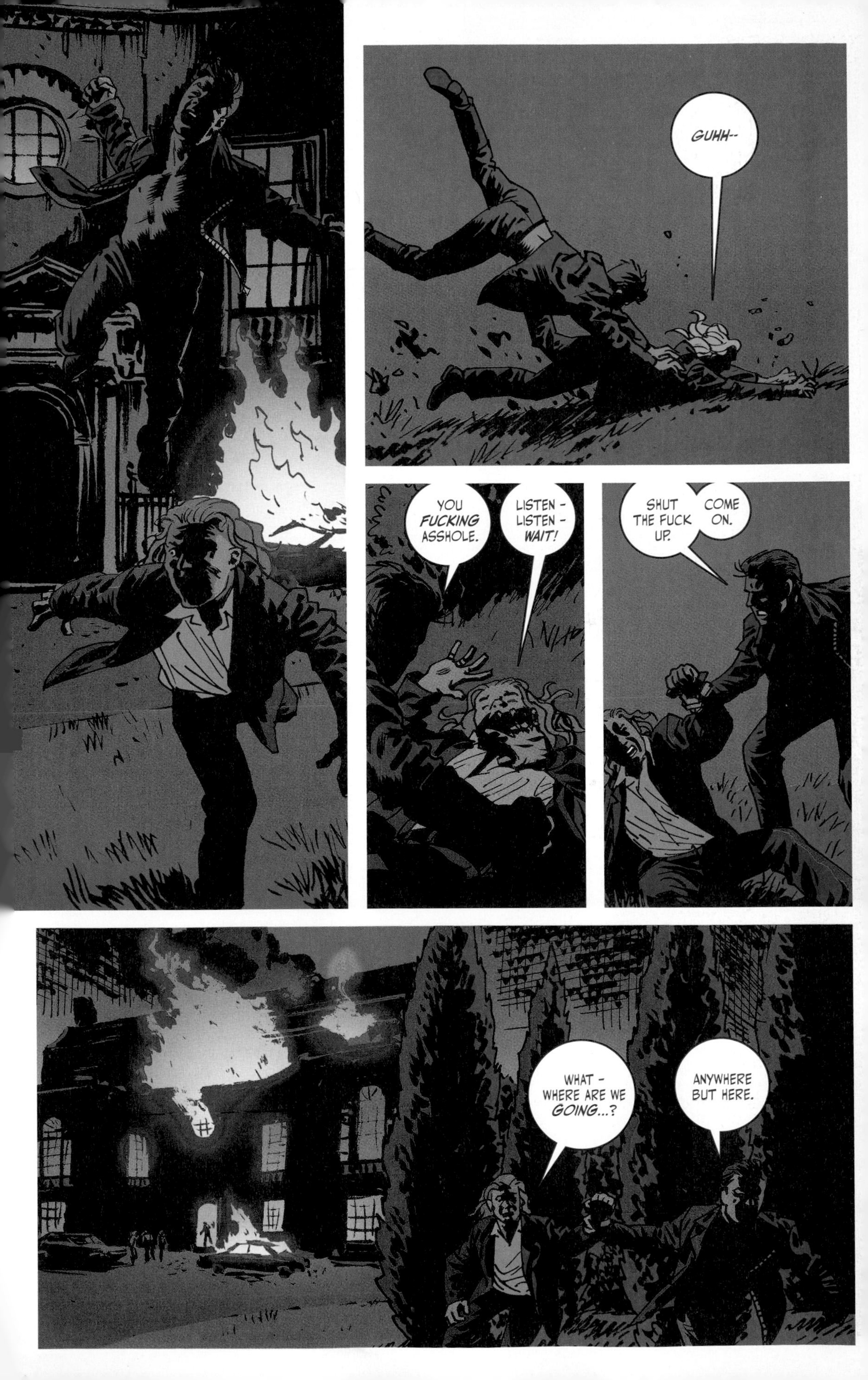
GUHH--
YOU FUCKING ASSHOLE.
LISTEN - LISTEN - WAIT!
SHUT THE FUCK UP.
COME ON.
WHAT - WHERE ARE WE GOING...?
ANYWHERE BUT HERE.

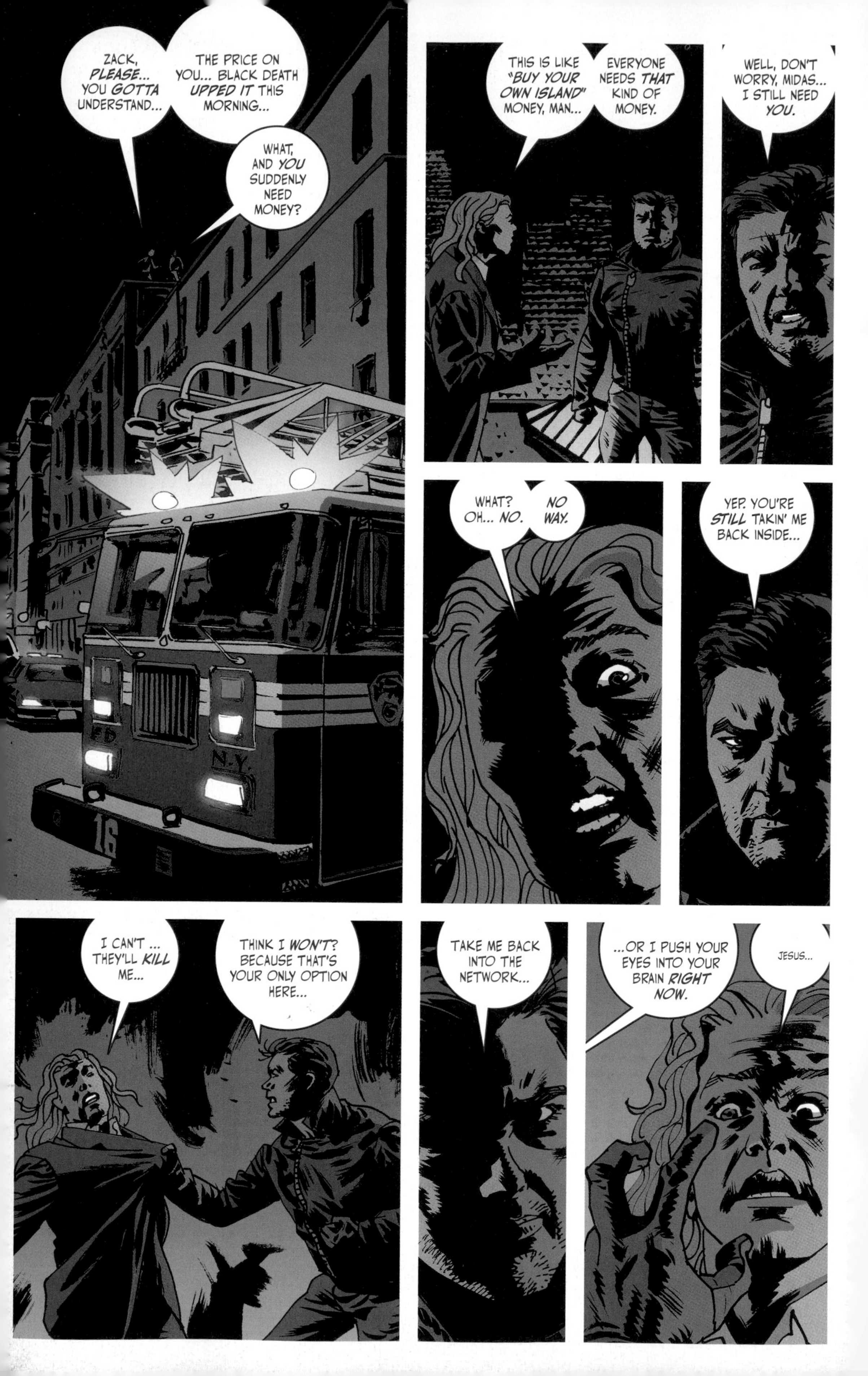
ZACK, PLEASE... YOU GOTTA UNDERSTAND...
THE PRICE ON YOU... BLACK DEATH UPPED IT THIS MORNING...
WHAT, AND YOU SUDDENLY NEED MONEY?
THIS IS LIKE "BUY YOUR OWN ISLAND" MONEY, MAN...
EVERYONE NEEDS THAT KIND OF MONEY.
WELL, DON'T WORRY, MIDAS... I STILL NEED YOU.
WHAT? OH... NO.
NO WAY.
YEP. YOU'RE STILL TAKIN' ME BACK INSIDE...
I CAN'T ... THEY'LL KILL ME...
THINK I WON'T? BECAUSE THAT'S YOUR ONLY OPTION HERE...
TAKE ME BACK INTO THE NETWORK...
...OR I PUSH YOUR EYES INTO YOUR BRAIN RIGHT NOW.
JESUS...
16
N.Y.
F.D.

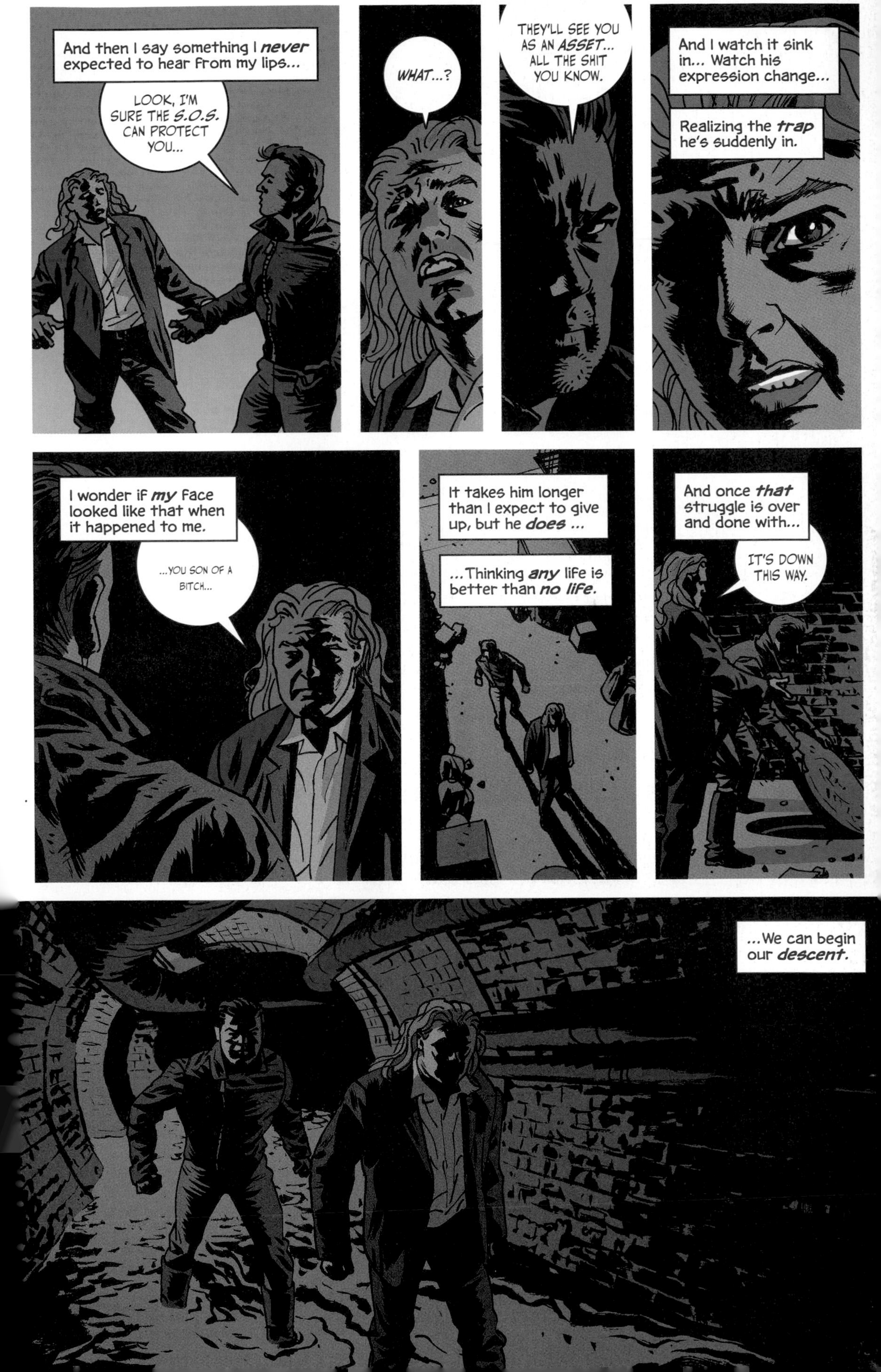

And then I say something I never expected to hear from my lips...
LOOK, I'M SURE THE S.O.S. CAN PROTECT YOU...
WHAT...?
THEY'LL SEE YOU AS AN ASSET... ALL THE SHIT YOU KNOW.
And I watch it sink in... Watch his expression change...
Realizing the trap he's suddenly in.
I wonder if my face looked like that when it happened to me.
...YOU SON OF A BITCH...
It takes him longer than I expect to give up, but he does ...
...Thinking any life is better than no life.
And once that struggle is over and done with...
IT'S DOWN THIS WAY.
...We can begin our descent.

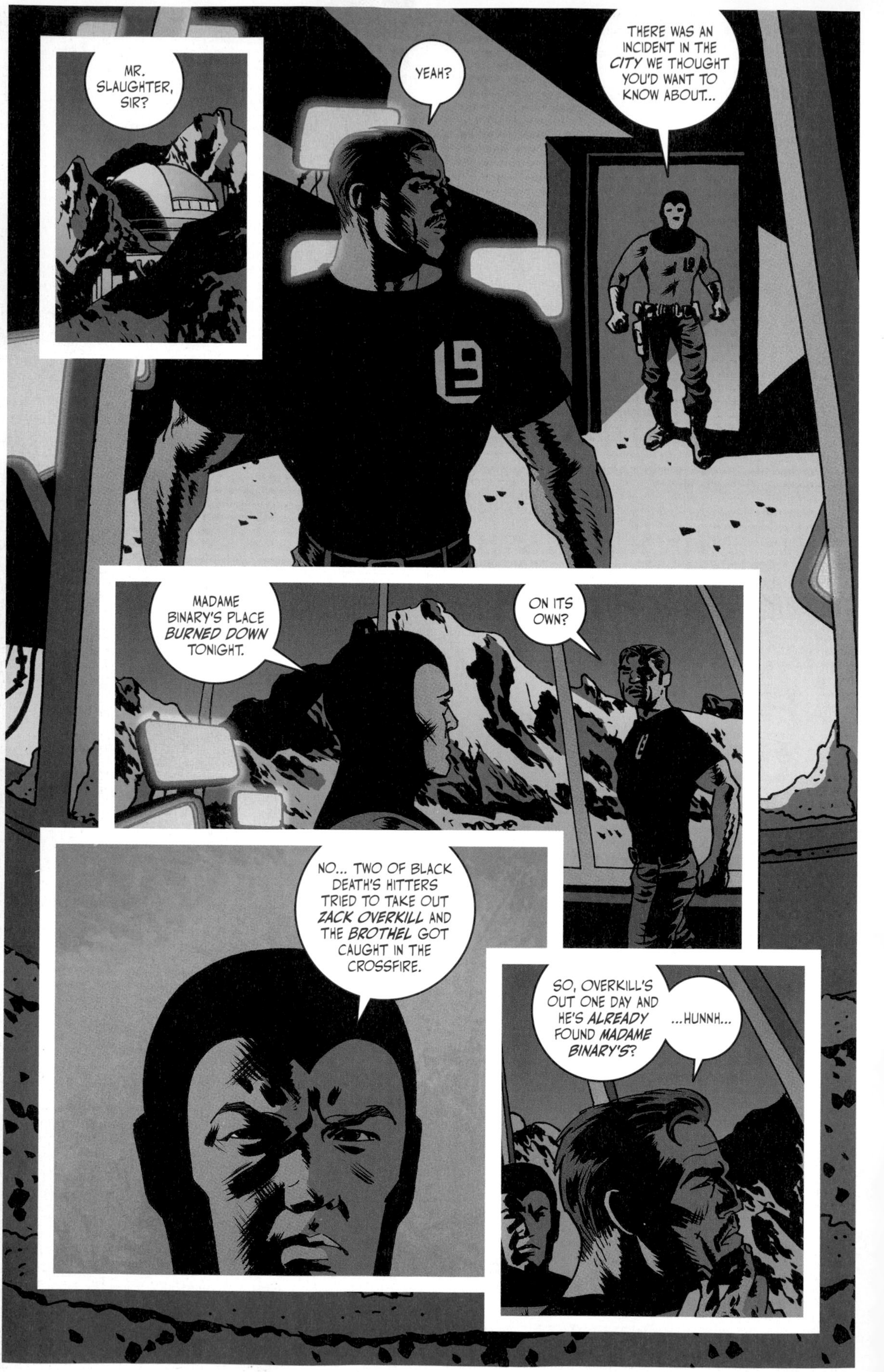
MR. SLAUGHTER, SIR?
YEAH?
THERE WAS AN INCIDENT IN THE CITY WE THOUGHT YOU'D WANT TO KNOW ABOUT...
MADAME BINARY'S PLACE BURNED DOWN TONIGHT.
ON ITS OWN?
NO... TWO OF BLACK DEATH'S HITTERS TRIED TO TAKE OUT ZACK OVERKILL AND THE BROTHEL GOT CAUGHT IN THE CROSSFIRE.
SO, OVERKILL'S OUT ONE DAY AND HE'S ALREADY FOUND MADAME BINARY'S?
...HUNNH...

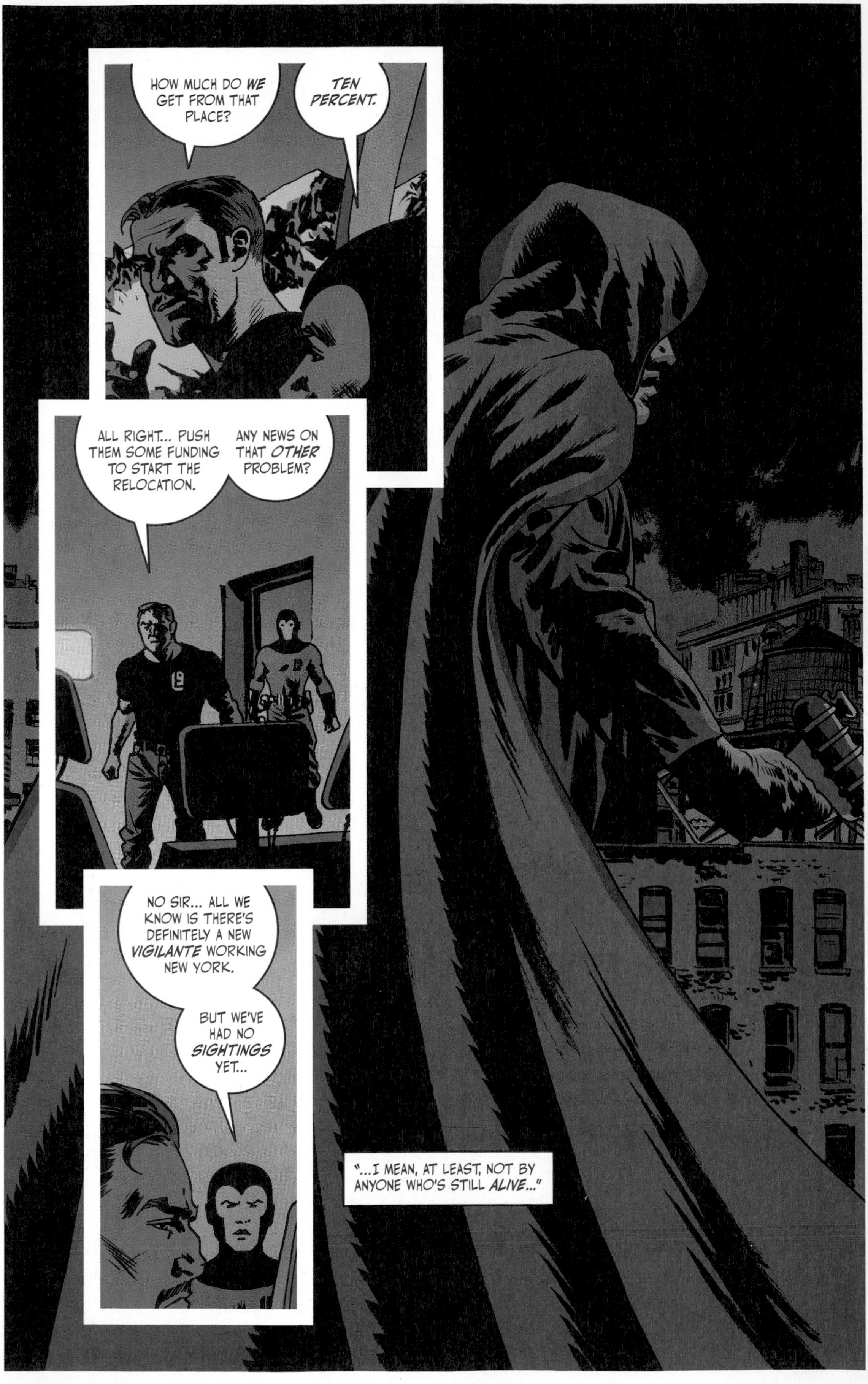
HOW MUCH DO WE GET FROM THAT PLACE?
TEN PERCENT.
ALL RIGHT... PUSH THEM SOME FUNDING TO START THE RELOCATION.
ANY NEWS ON THAT OTHER PROBLEM?
NO SIR... ALL WE KNOW IS THERE'S DEFINITELY A NEW VIGILANTE WORKING NEW YORK.
BUT WE'VE HAD NO SIGHTINGS YET...
"...I MEAN, AT LEAST, NOT BY ANYONE WHO'S STILL ALIVE..."

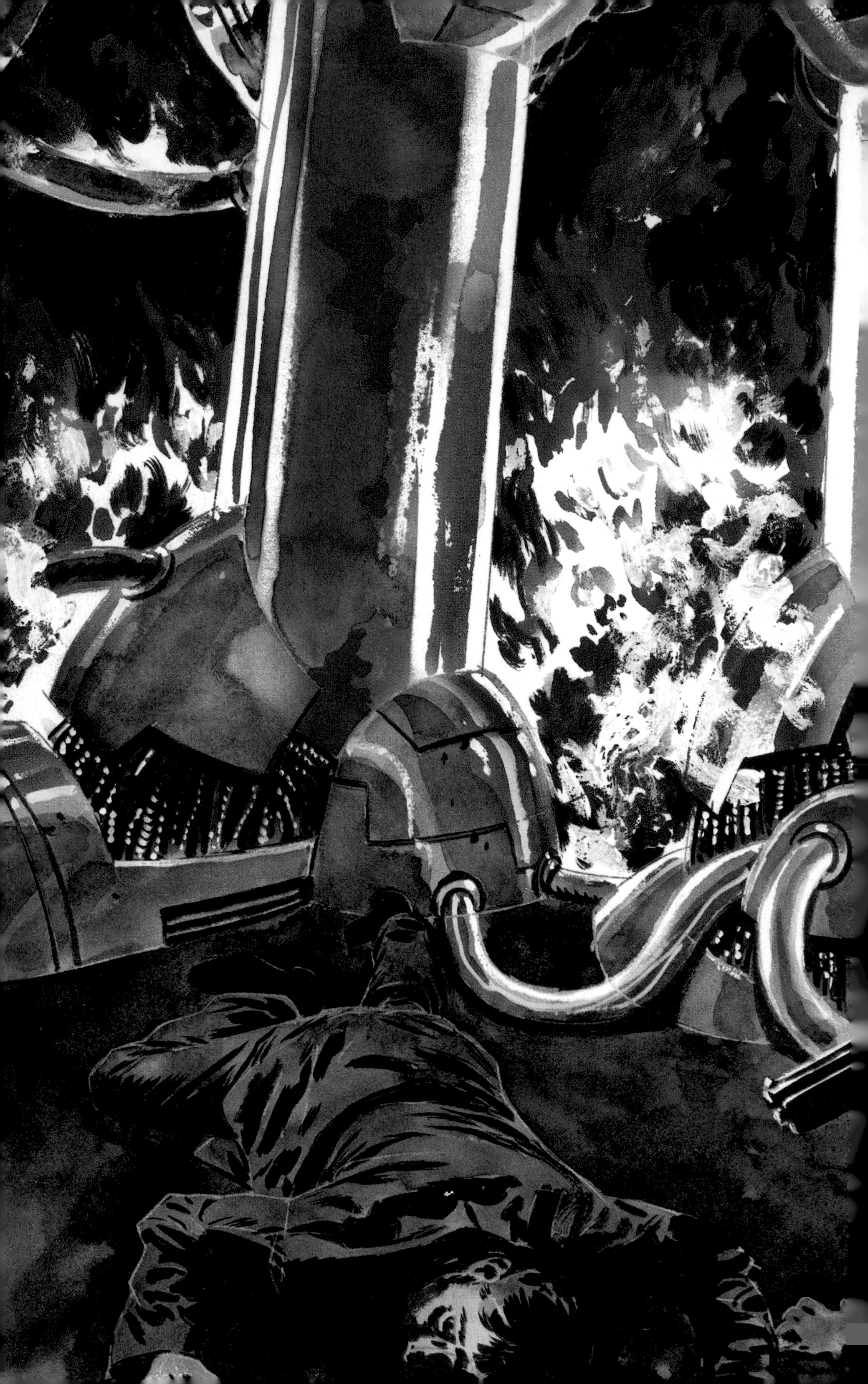

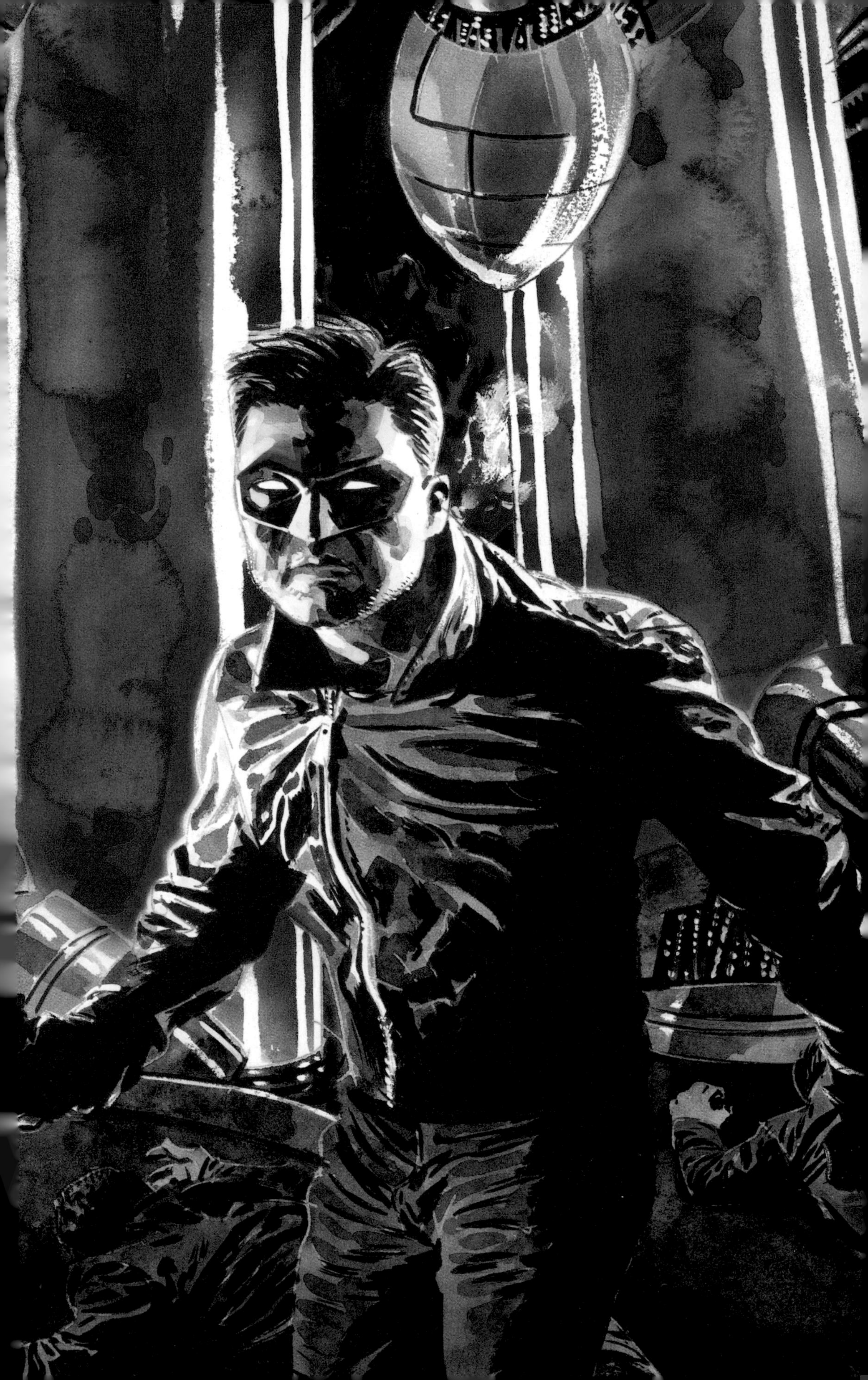

Chapter Three

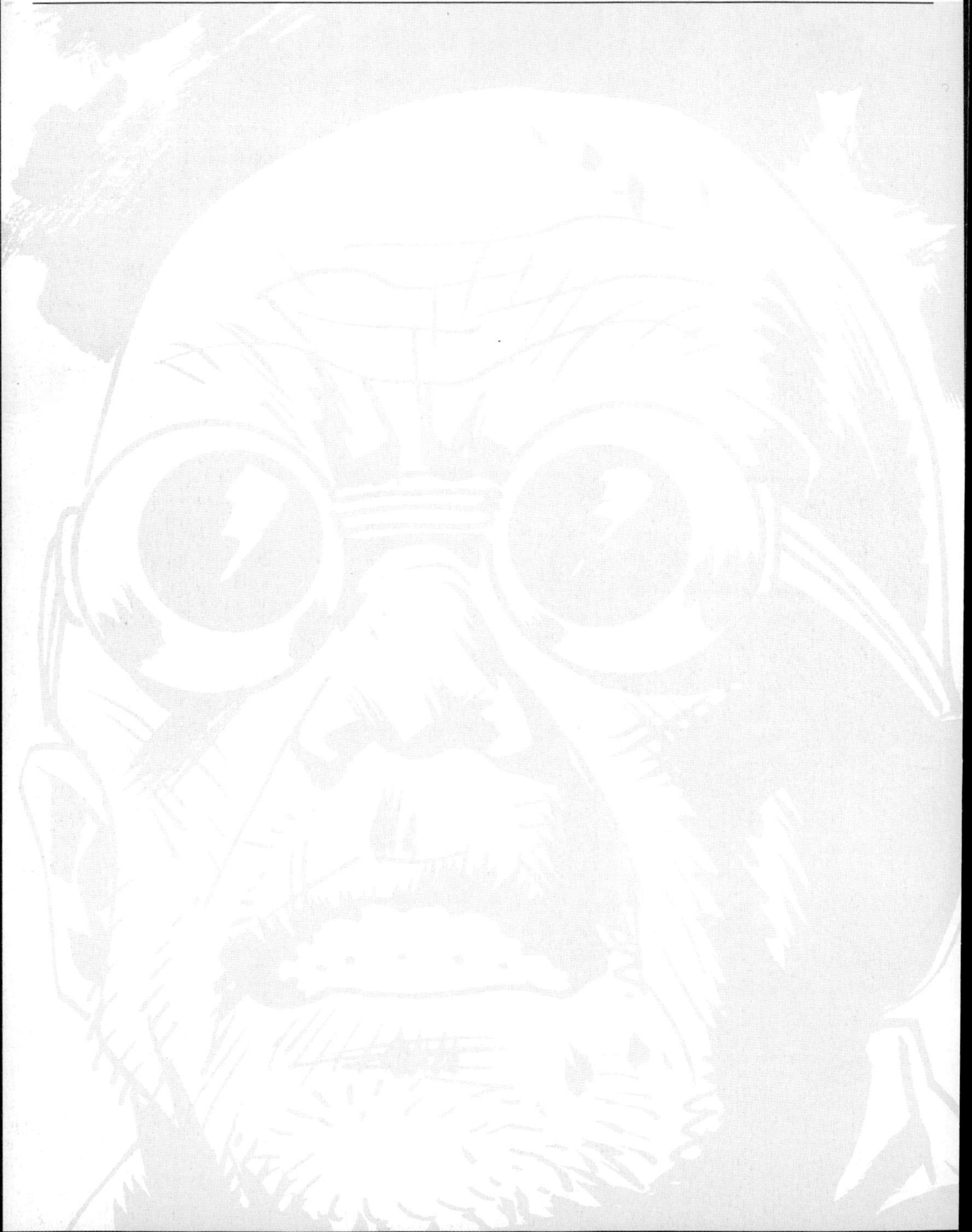

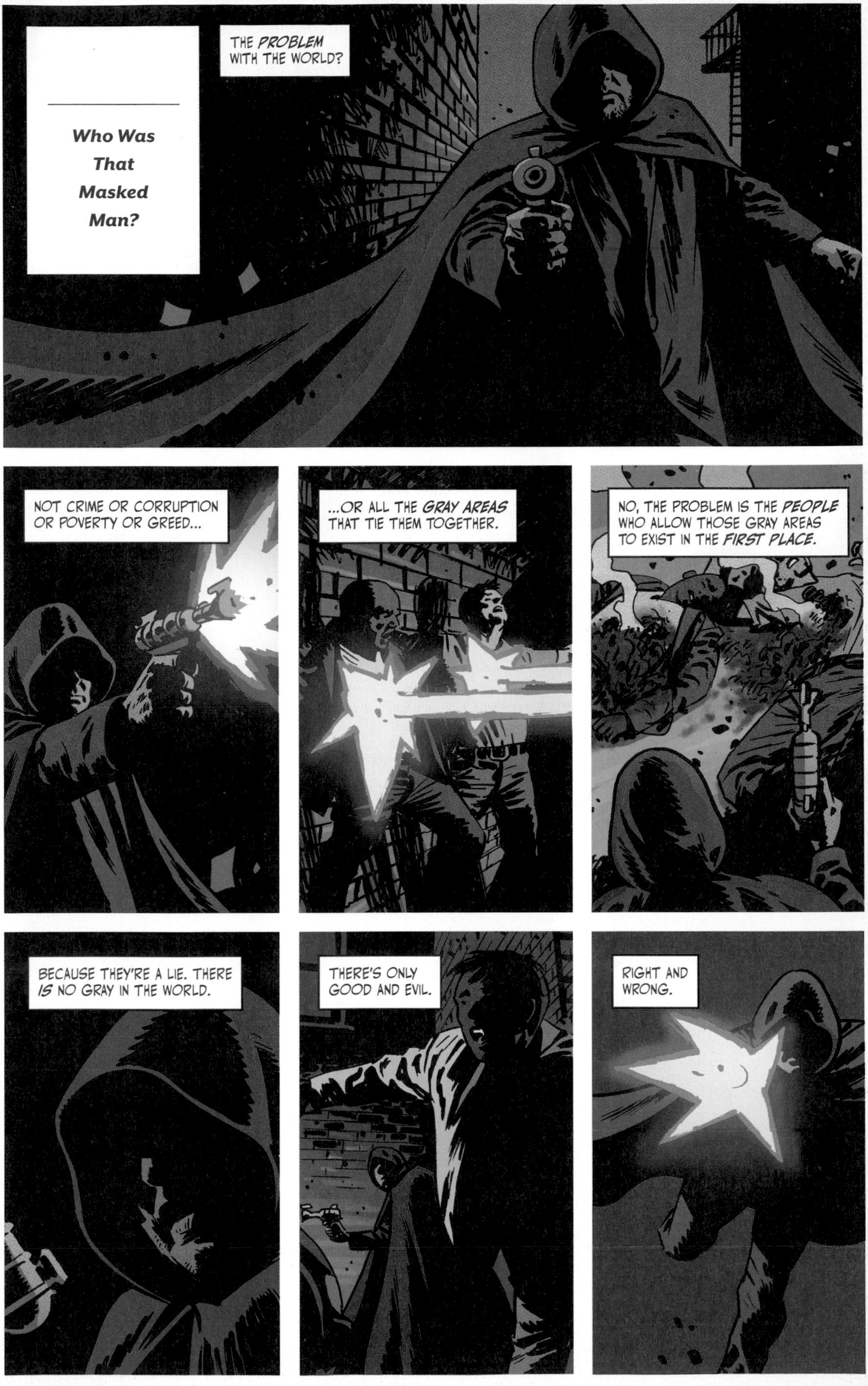
Who Was That Masked Man?
THE PROBLEM WITH THE WORLD?
NOT CRIME OR CORRUPTION OR POVERTY OR GREED...
...OR ALL THE GRAY AREAS THAT TIE THEM TOGETHER.
NO, THE PROBLEM IS THE PEOPLE WHO ALLOW THOSE GRAY AREAS TO EXIST IN THE FIRST PLACE.
BECAUSE THEY'RE A LIE. THERE IS NO GRAY IN THE WORLD.
THERE'S ONLY GOOD AND EVIL.
RIGHT AND WRONG.

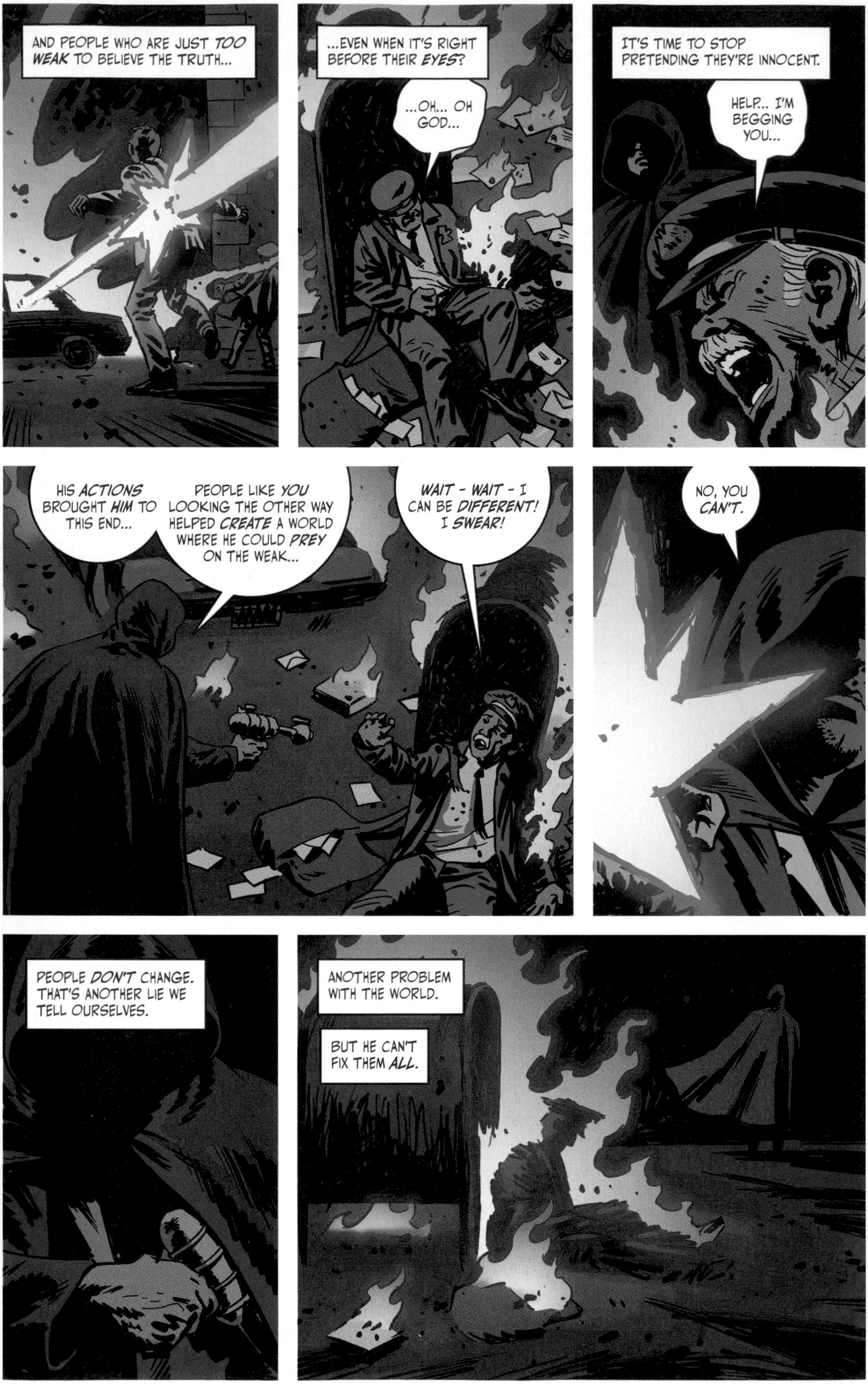
AND PEOPLE WHO ARE JUST *TOO WEAK* TO BELIEVE THE TRUTH...
...EVEN WHEN IT'S RIGHT BEFORE THEIR *EYES*?
...OH... OH GOD...
IT'S TIME TO STOP PRETENDING THEY'RE INNOCENT.
HELP... I'M BEGGING YOU...
HIS *ACTIONS* BROUGHT *HIM* TO THIS END...
PEOPLE LIKE *YOU* LOOKING THE OTHER WAY HELPED *CREATE* A WORLD WHERE HE COULD *PREY* ON THE WEAK...
WAIT - WAIT - I CAN BE *DIFFERENT*! I *SWEAR*!
NO, YOU *CAN'T*.
PEOPLE *DON'T* CHANGE. THAT'S ANOTHER LIE WE TELL OURSELVES.
ANOTHER PROBLEM WITH THE WORLD.
BUT HE CAN'T FIX THEM *ALL*.

THREE ATTACKS IN *TWO* DAYS?

THAT WE *KNOW* OF.

SO... WHAT'VE WE COME UP WITH SO FAR?

THE *GRANDSON* OF THE OLD MAN WHO TRIED TO BLOW ZACK UP.

ONE *RANDALL BEEKMAN*... AGE FIFTY-ONE.

APPARENTLY, RANDY AND GRAND-DAD HAD SOME *TIME* TOGETHER AFTER HE WOKE UP.

PRESUMPTION IS HE HELPED HIM RAID LAZARUS'S *HIDEOUT.*

AND WE'RE ZEROING IN ON THIS RANDALL *BECAUSE...?*

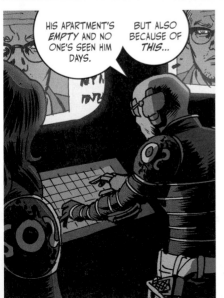

HIS APARTMENT'S *EMPTY* AND NO ONE'S SEEN HIM DAYS.

BUT ALSO BECAUSE OF *THIS...*

SECURITY FOOTAGE SCANS FROM ZACK'S ATTACK...

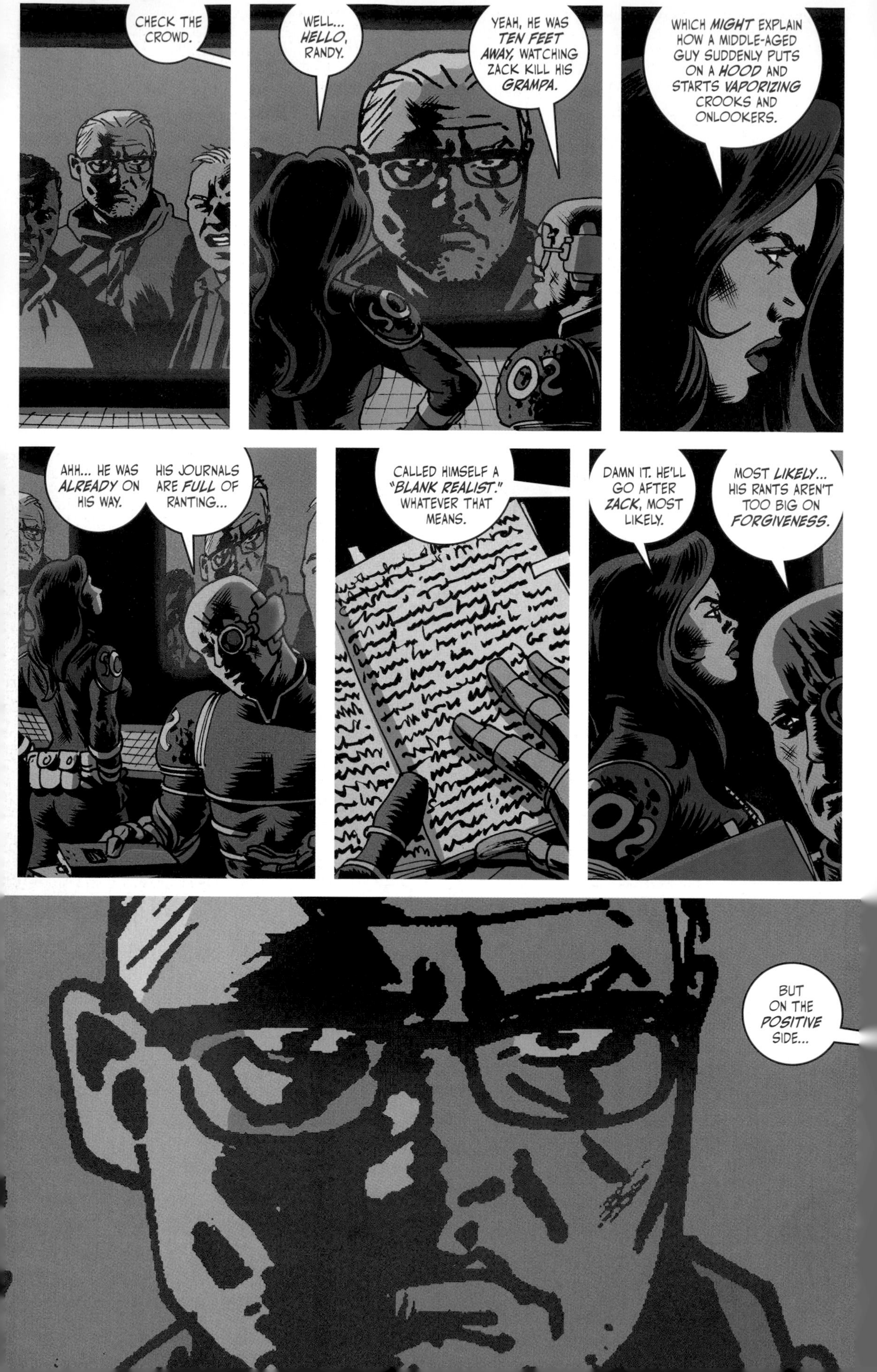

CHECK THE CROWD.
WELL... HELLO, RANDY.
YEAH, HE WAS TEN FEET AWAY, WATCHING ZACK KILL HIS GRAMPA.
WHICH MIGHT EXPLAIN HOW A MIDDLE-AGED GUY SUDDENLY PUTS ON A HOOD AND STARTS VAPORIZING CROOKS AND ONLOOKERS.
AHH... HE WAS ALREADY ON HIS WAY.
HIS JOURNALS ARE FULL OF RANTING...
CALLED HIMSELF A "BLANK REALIST." WHATEVER THAT MEANS.
DAMN IT. HE'LL GO AFTER ZACK, MOST LIKELY.
MOST LIKELY... HIS RANTS AREN'T TOO BIG ON FORGIVENESS.
BUT ON THE POSITIVE SIDE...

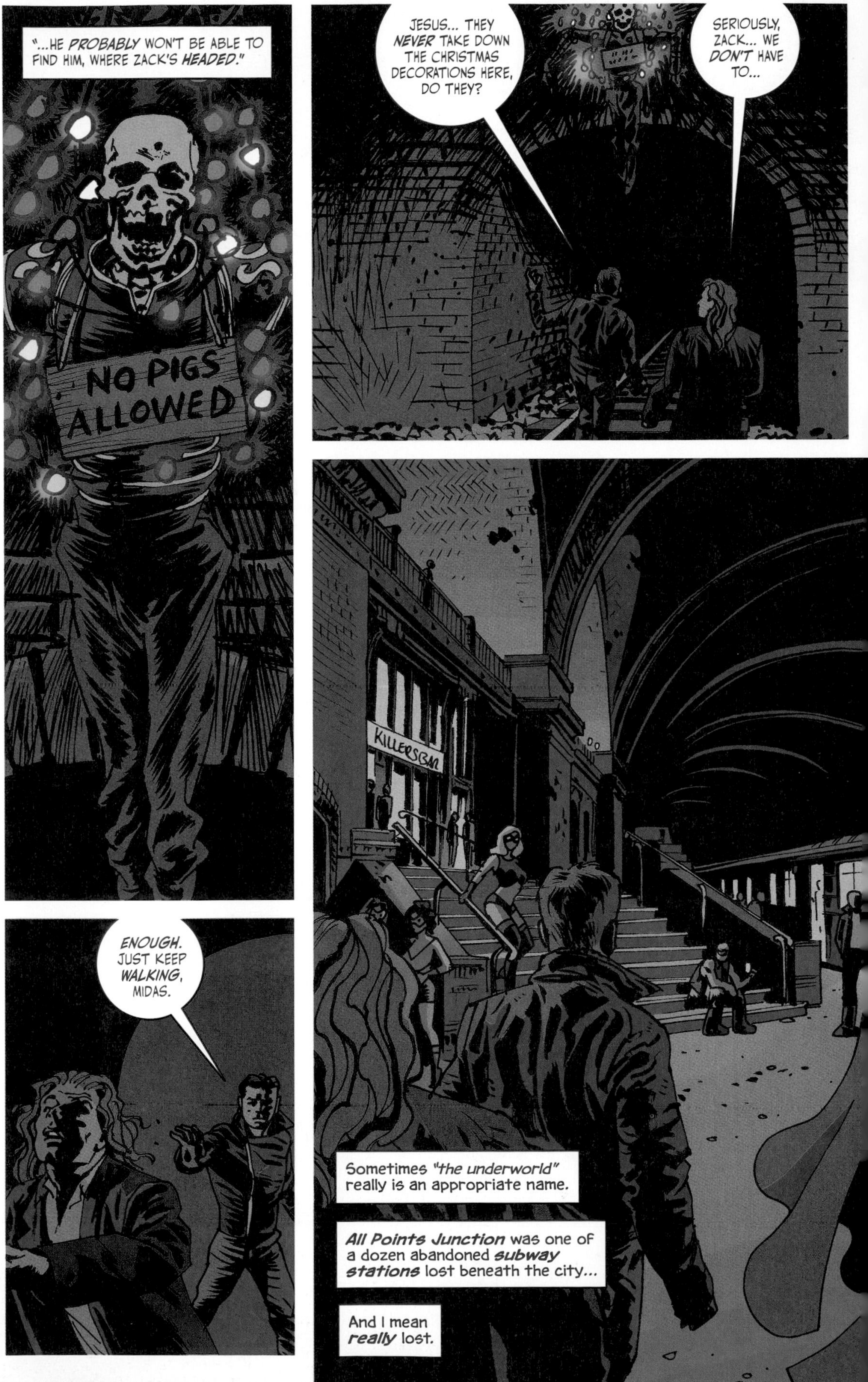
"...HE PROBABLY WON'T BE ABLE TO FIND HIM, WHERE ZACK'S HEADED."
NO PIGS ALLOWED
JESUS... THEY NEVER TAKE DOWN THE CHRISTMAS DECORATIONS HERE, DO THEY?
SERIOUSLY, ZACK... WE DON'T HAVE TO...
ENOUGH. JUST KEEP WALKING, MIDAS.
KILLERS BAR
Sometimes "the underworld" really is an appropriate name.
All Points Junction was one of a dozen abandoned subway stations lost beneath the city...
And I mean really lost.

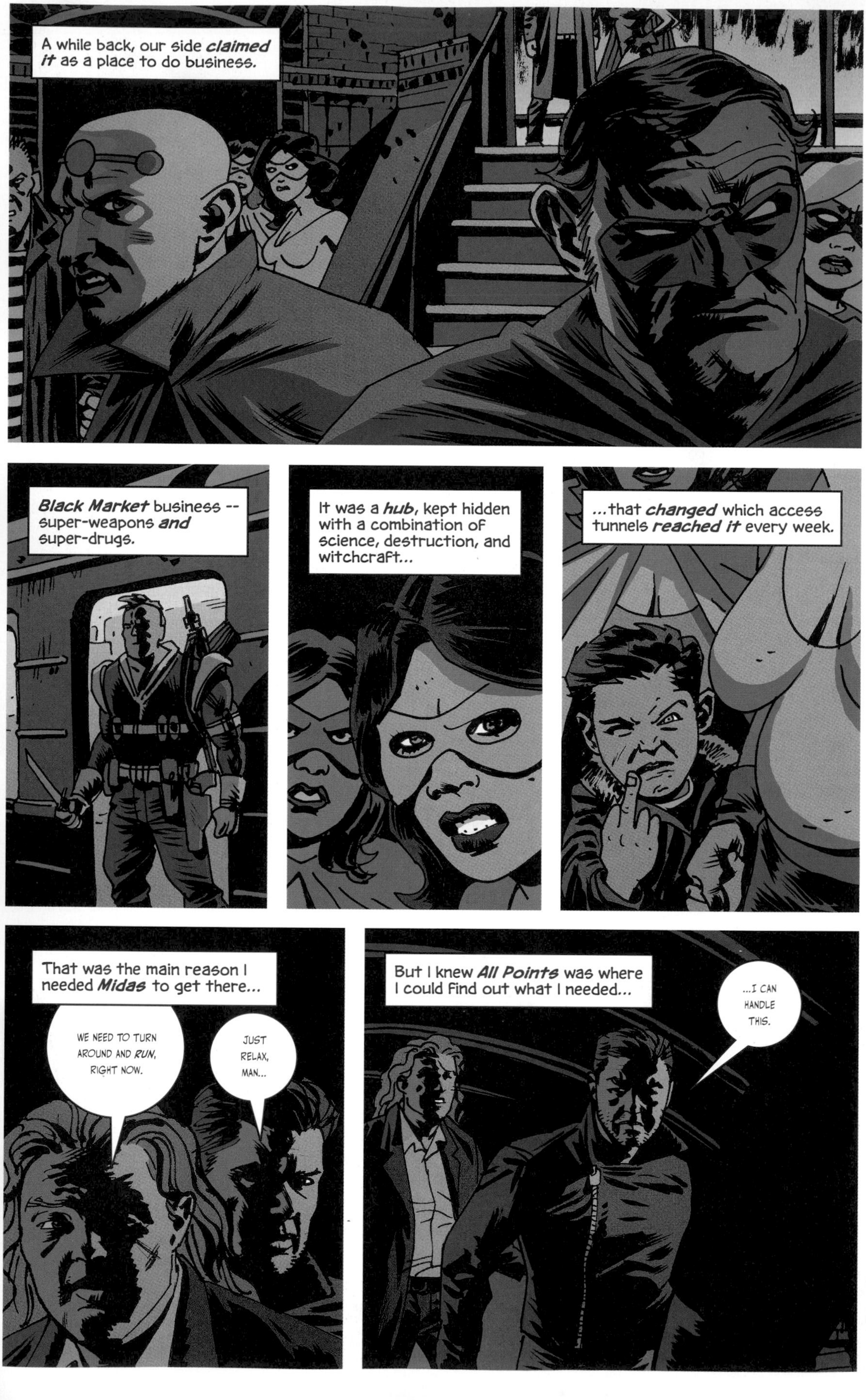
A while back, our side claimed it as a place to do business.
Black Market business -- super-weapons and super-drugs.
It was a hub, kept hidden with a combination of science, destruction, and witchcraft...
...that changed which access tunnels reached it every week.
That was the main reason I needed Midas to get there...
WE NEED TO TURN AROUND AND RUN, RIGHT NOW.
JUST RELAX, MAN...
But I knew All Points was where I could find out what I needed...
...I CAN HANDLE THIS.

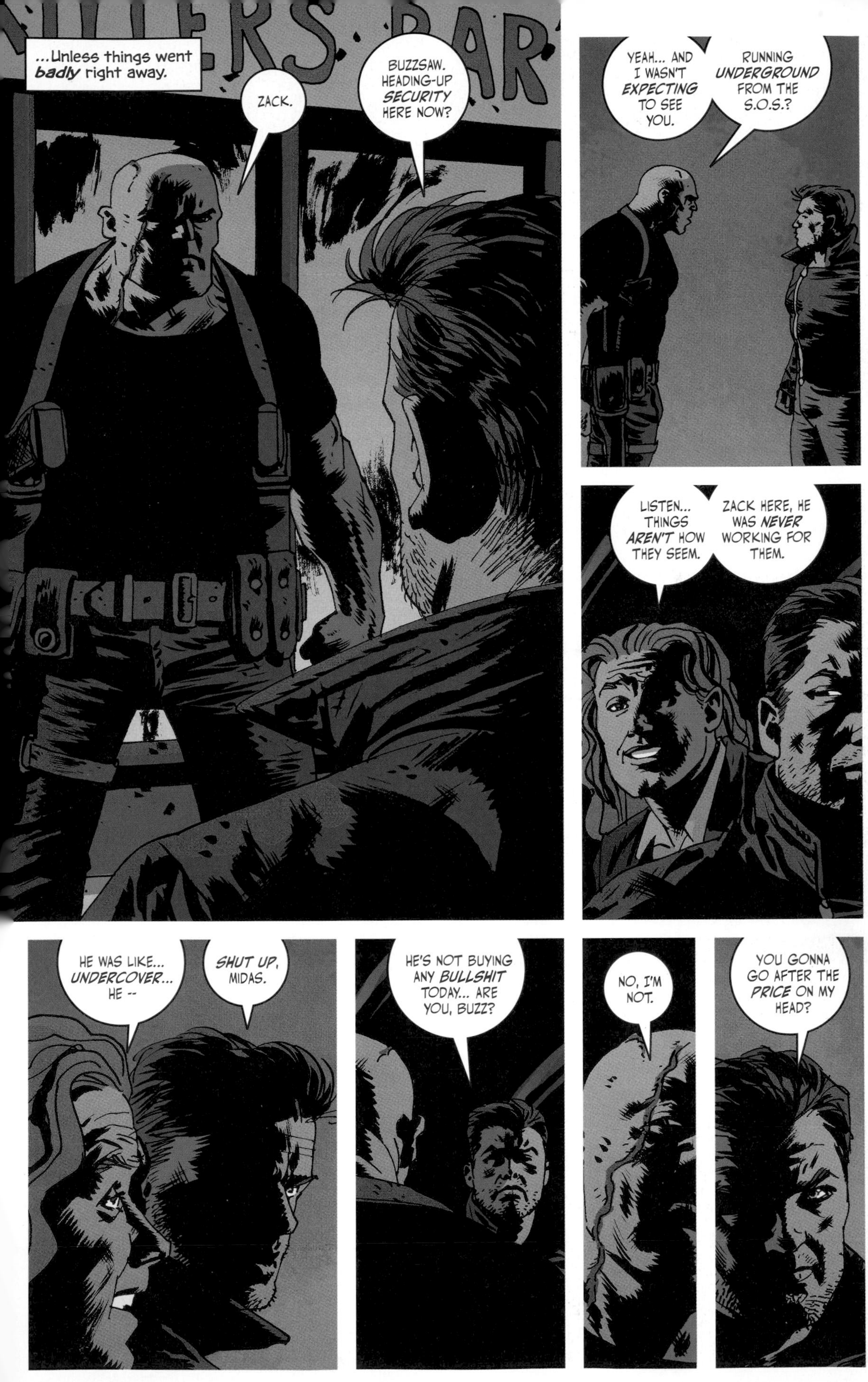
...Unless things went *badly* right away.
ZACK.
BUZZSAW. HEADING-UP *SECURITY* HERE NOW?
YEAH... AND I WASN'T *EXPECTING* TO SEE YOU.
RUNNING *UNDERGROUND* FROM THE S.O.S.?
LISTEN... THINGS *AREN'T* HOW THEY SEEM.
ZACK HERE, HE WAS *NEVER* WORKING FOR THEM.
HE WAS LIKE... *UNDERCOVER*... HE --
SHUT UP, MIDAS.
HE'S NOT BUYING ANY *BULLSHIT* TODAY... ARE YOU, BUZZ?
NO, I'M NOT.
YOU GONNA GO AFTER THE *PRICE* ON MY HEAD?

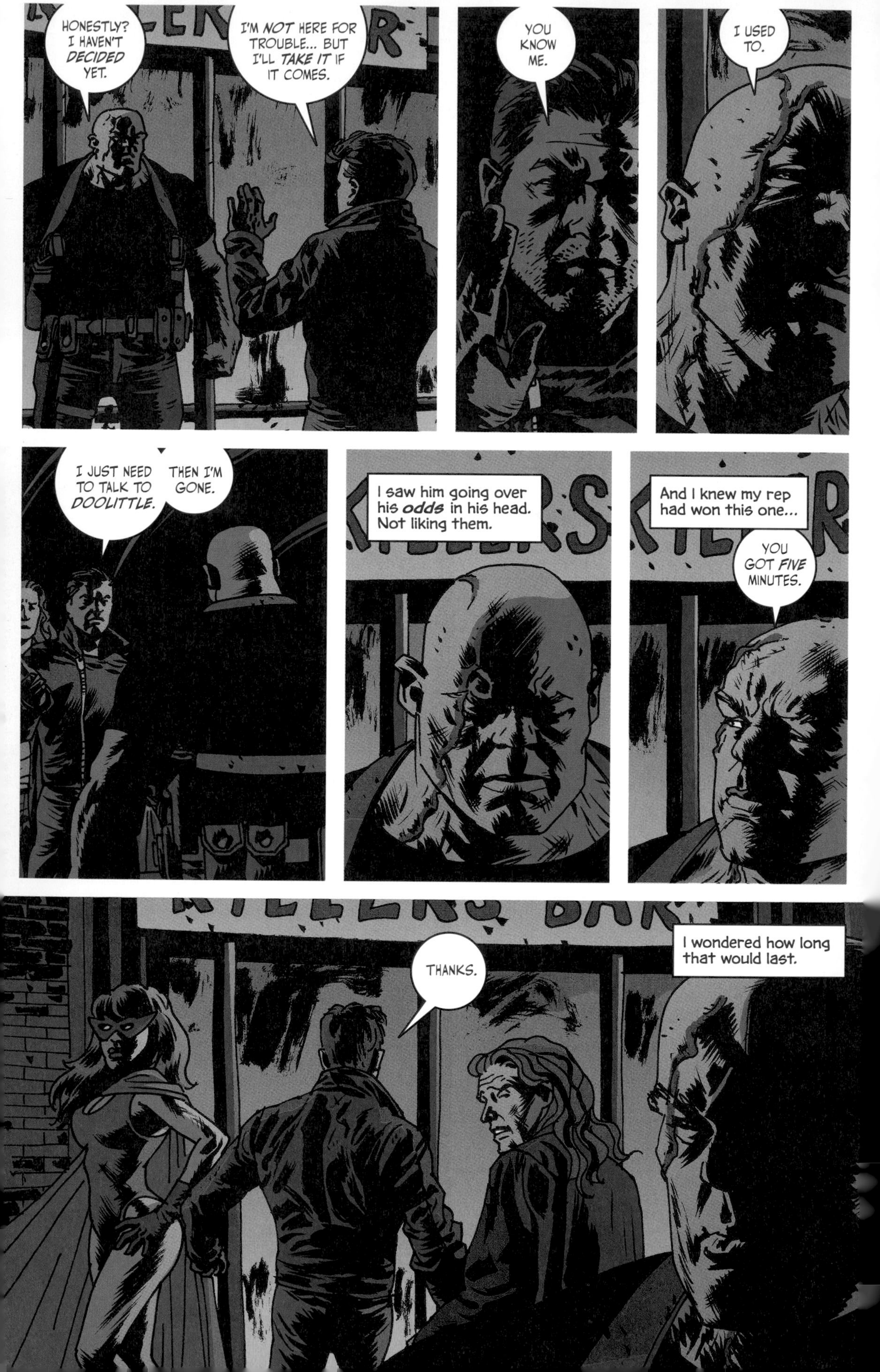
HONESTLY? I HAVEN'T DECIDED YET.
I'M NOT HERE FOR TROUBLE... BUT I'LL TAKE IT IF IT COMES.
YOU KNOW ME.
I USED TO.
I JUST NEED TO TALK TO DOOLITTLE.
THEN I'M GONE.
I saw him going over his odds in his head. Not liking them.
And I knew my rep had won this one...
YOU GOT FIVE MINUTES.
THANKS.
I wondered how long that would last.

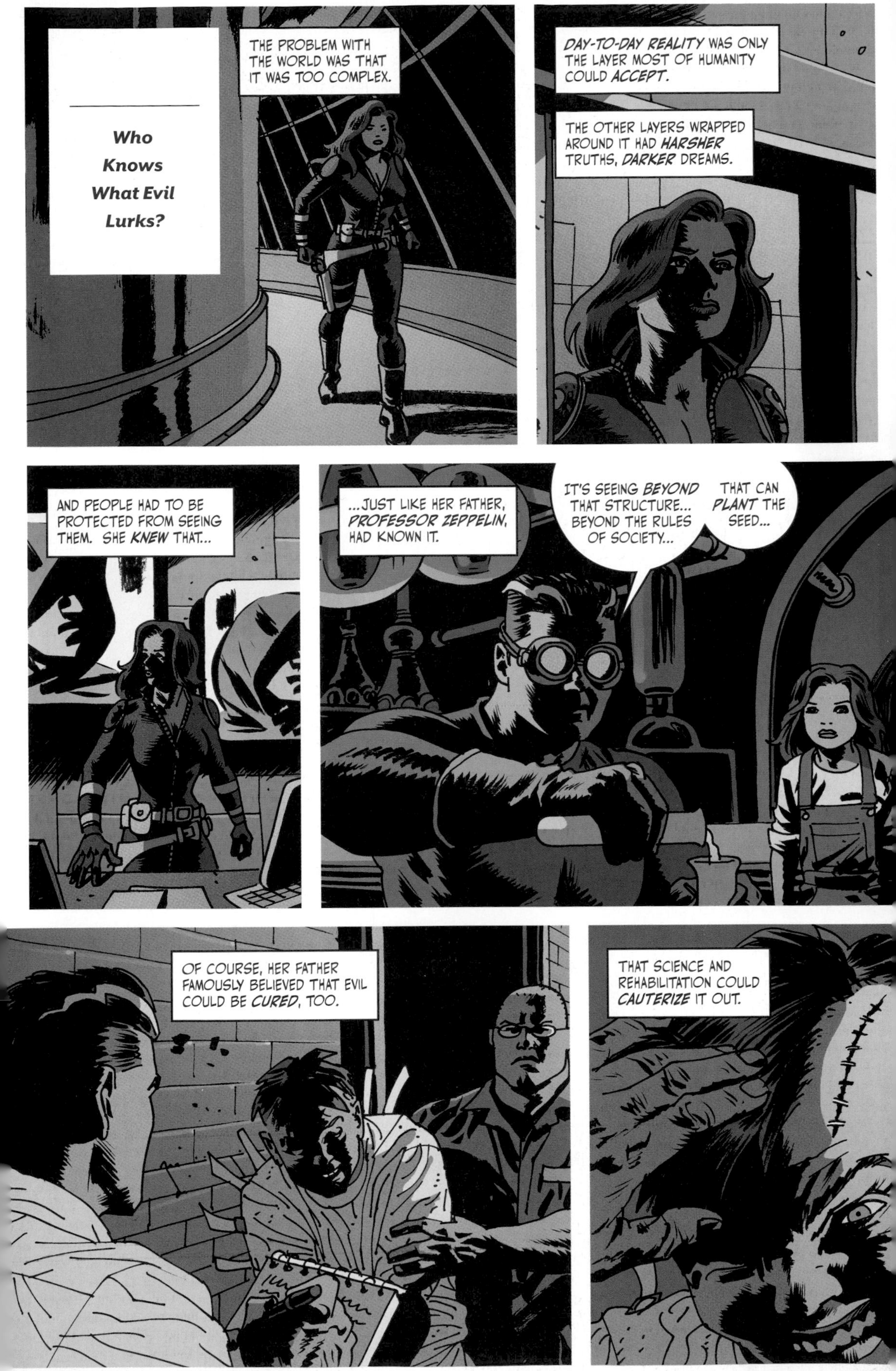
Who Knows What Evil Lurks?
THE PROBLEM WITH THE WORLD WAS THAT IT WAS TOO COMPLEX.
DAY-TO-DAY REALITY WAS ONLY THE LAYER MOST OF HUMANITY COULD ACCEPT.
THE OTHER LAYERS WRAPPED AROUND IT HAD HARSHER TRUTHS, DARKER DREAMS.
AND PEOPLE HAD TO BE PROTECTED FROM SEEING THEM. SHE KNEW THAT...
...JUST LIKE HER FATHER, PROFESSOR ZEPPELIN, HAD KNOWN IT.
IT'S SEEING BEYOND THAT STRUCTURE... BEYOND THE RULES OF SOCIETY...
THAT CAN PLANT THE SEED...
OF COURSE, HER FATHER FAMOUSLY BELIEVED THAT EVIL COULD BE CURED, TOO.
THAT SCIENCE AND REHABILITATION COULD CAUTERIZE IT OUT.

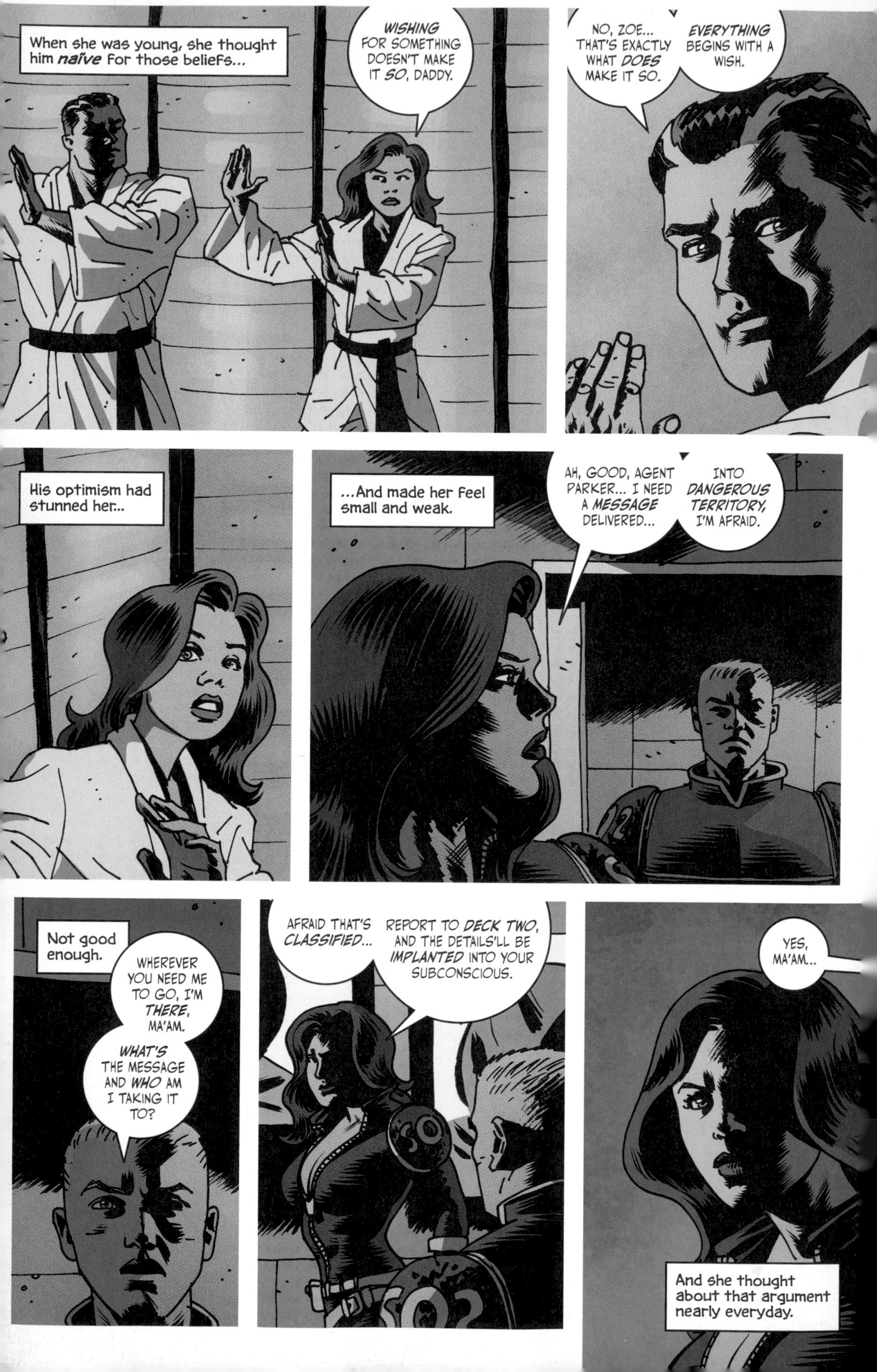
When she was young, she thought him naïve for those beliefs...
WISHING FOR SOMETHING DOESN'T MAKE IT SO, DADDY.
NO, ZOE... THAT'S EXACTLY WHAT DOES MAKE IT SO.
EVERYTHING BEGINS WITH A WISH.
His optimism had stunned her...
...And made her feel small and weak.
AH, GOOD, AGENT PARKER... I NEED A MESSAGE DELIVERED...
INTO DANGEROUS TERRITORY, I'M AFRAID.
Not good enough.
WHEREVER YOU NEED ME TO GO, I'M THERE, MA'AM.
WHAT'S THE MESSAGE AND WHO AM I TAKING IT TO?
AFRAID THAT'S CLASSIFIED...
REPORT TO DECK TWO, AND THE DETAILS'LL BE IMPLANTED INTO YOUR SUBCONSCIOUS.
YES, MA'AM...
And she thought about that argument nearly everyday.

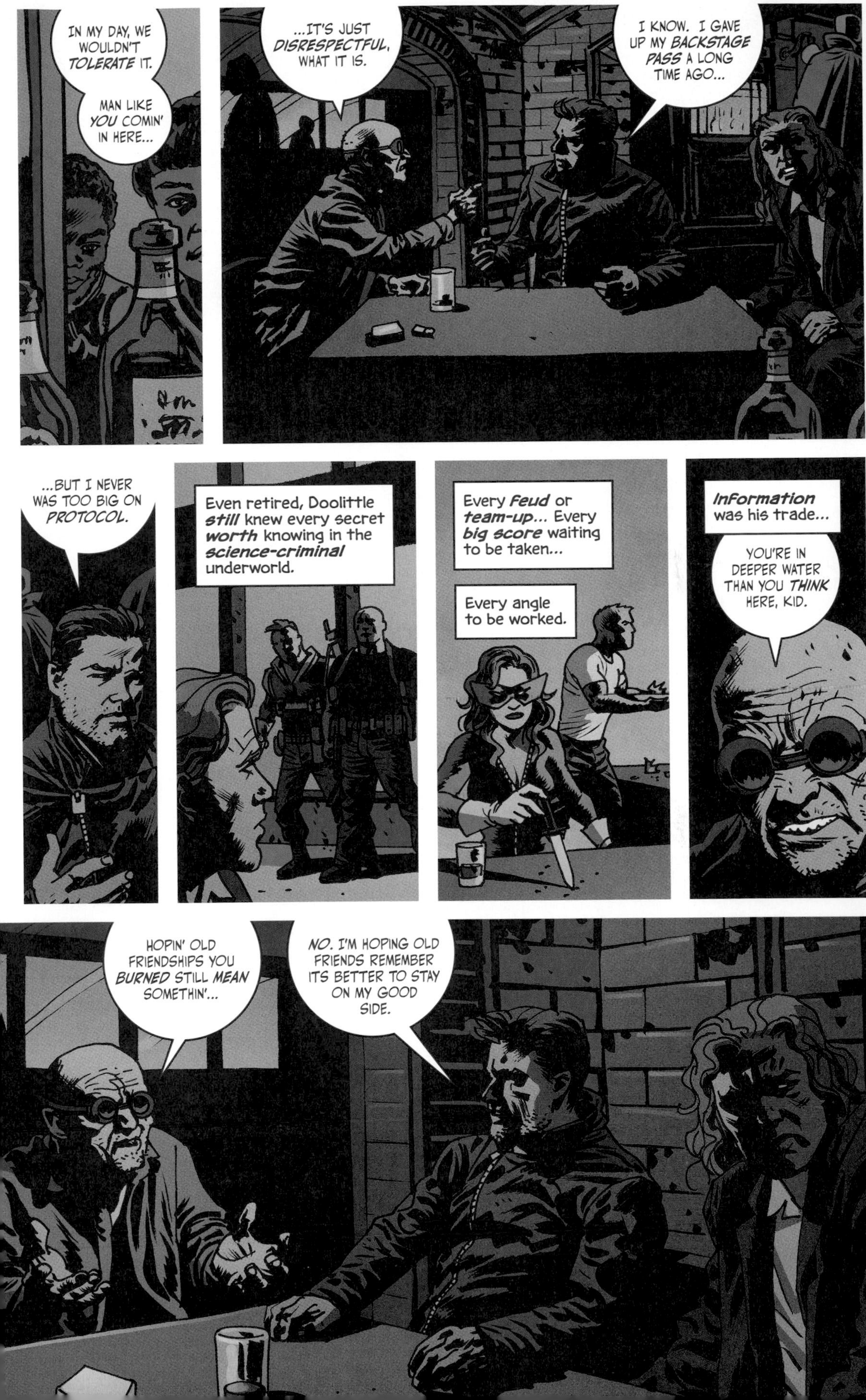

IN MY DAY, WE WOULDN'T TOLERATE IT.
MAN LIKE YOU COMIN' IN HERE...
...IT'S JUST DISRESPECTFUL, WHAT IT IS.
I KNOW. I GAVE UP MY BACKSTAGE PASS A LONG TIME AGO...
...BUT I NEVER WAS TOO BIG ON PROTOCOL.
Even retired, Doolittle still knew every secret worth knowing in the science-criminal underworld.
Every feud or team-up... Every big score waiting to be taken...
Every angle to be worked.
Information was his trade...
YOU'RE IN DEEPER WATER THAN YOU THINK HERE, KID.
HOPIN' OLD FRIENDSHIPS YOU BURNED STILL MEAN SOMETHIN'...
NO. I'M HOPING OLD FRIENDS REMEMBER ITS BETTER TO STAY ON MY GOOD SIDE.

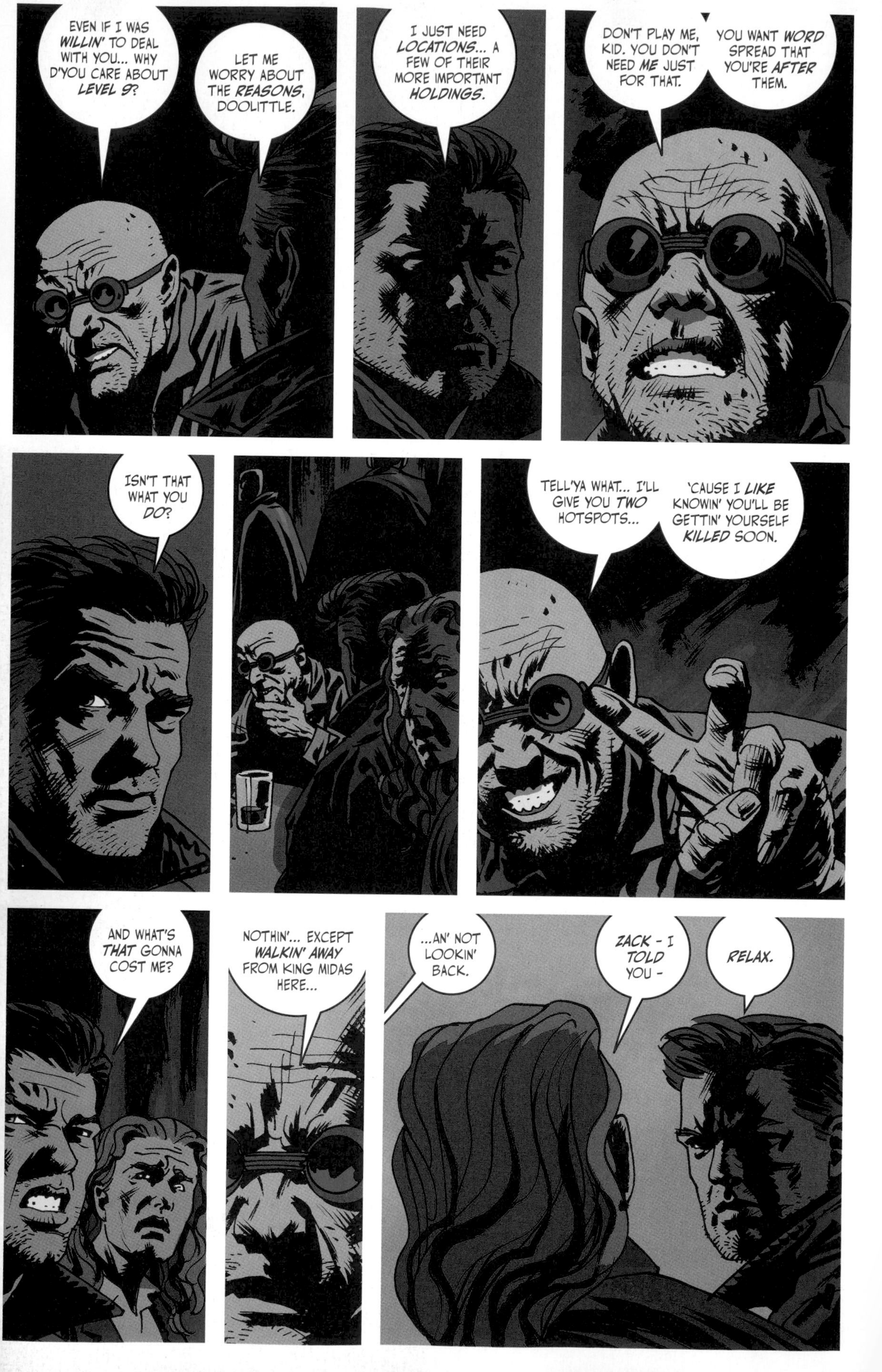
EVEN IF I WAS WILLIN' TO DEAL WITH YOU... WHY D'YOU CARE ABOUT LEVEL 9?
LET ME WORRY ABOUT THE REASONS, DOOLITTLE.
I JUST NEED LOCATIONS... A FEW OF THEIR MORE IMPORTANT HOLDINGS.
DON'T PLAY ME, KID. YOU DON'T NEED ME JUST FOR THAT.
YOU WANT WORD SPREAD THAT YOU'RE AFTER THEM.
ISN'T THAT WHAT YOU DO?
TELL'YA WHAT... I'LL GIVE YOU TWO HOTSPOTS...
'CAUSE I LIKE KNOWIN' YOU'LL BE GETTIN' YOURSELF KILLED SOON.
AND WHAT'S THAT GONNA COST ME?
NOTHIN'... EXCEPT WALKIN' AWAY FROM KING MIDAS HERE...
...AN' NOT LOOKIN' BACK.
ZACK - I TOLD YOU -
RELAX.

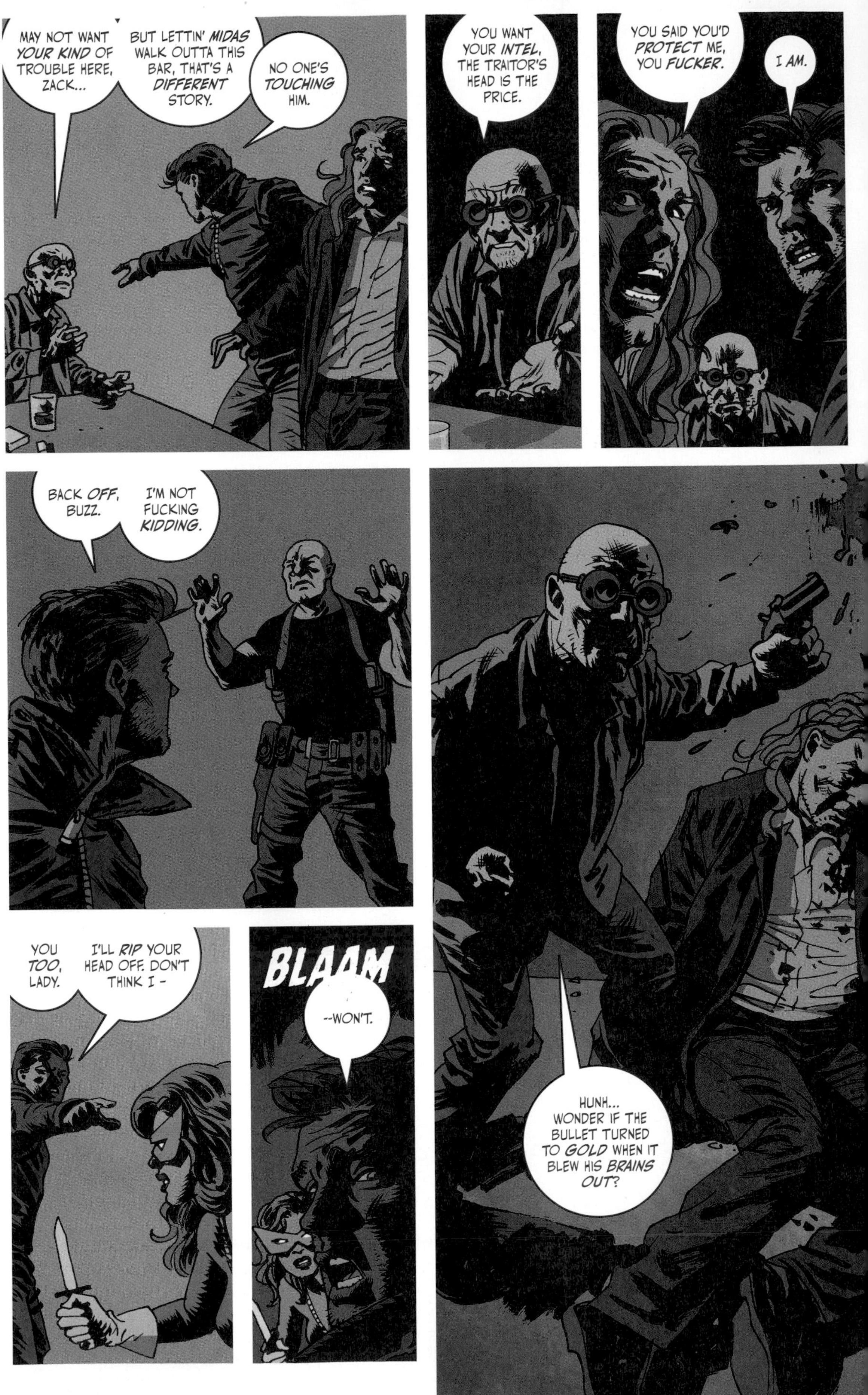
MAY NOT WANT YOUR KIND OF TROUBLE HERE, ZACK...
BUT LETTIN' MIDAS WALK OUTTA THIS BAR, THAT'S A DIFFERENT STORY.
NO ONE'S TOUCHING HIM.
YOU WANT YOUR INTEL, THE TRAITOR'S HEAD IS THE PRICE.
YOU SAID YOU'D PROTECT ME, YOU FUCKER.
I AM.
BACK OFF, BUZZ.
I'M NOT FUCKING KIDDING.
YOU TOO, LADY.
I'LL RIP YOUR HEAD OFF. DON'T THINK I -
BLAAM
--WON'T.
HUNH... WONDER IF THE BULLET TURNED TO GOLD WHEN IT BLEW HIS BRAINS OUT?

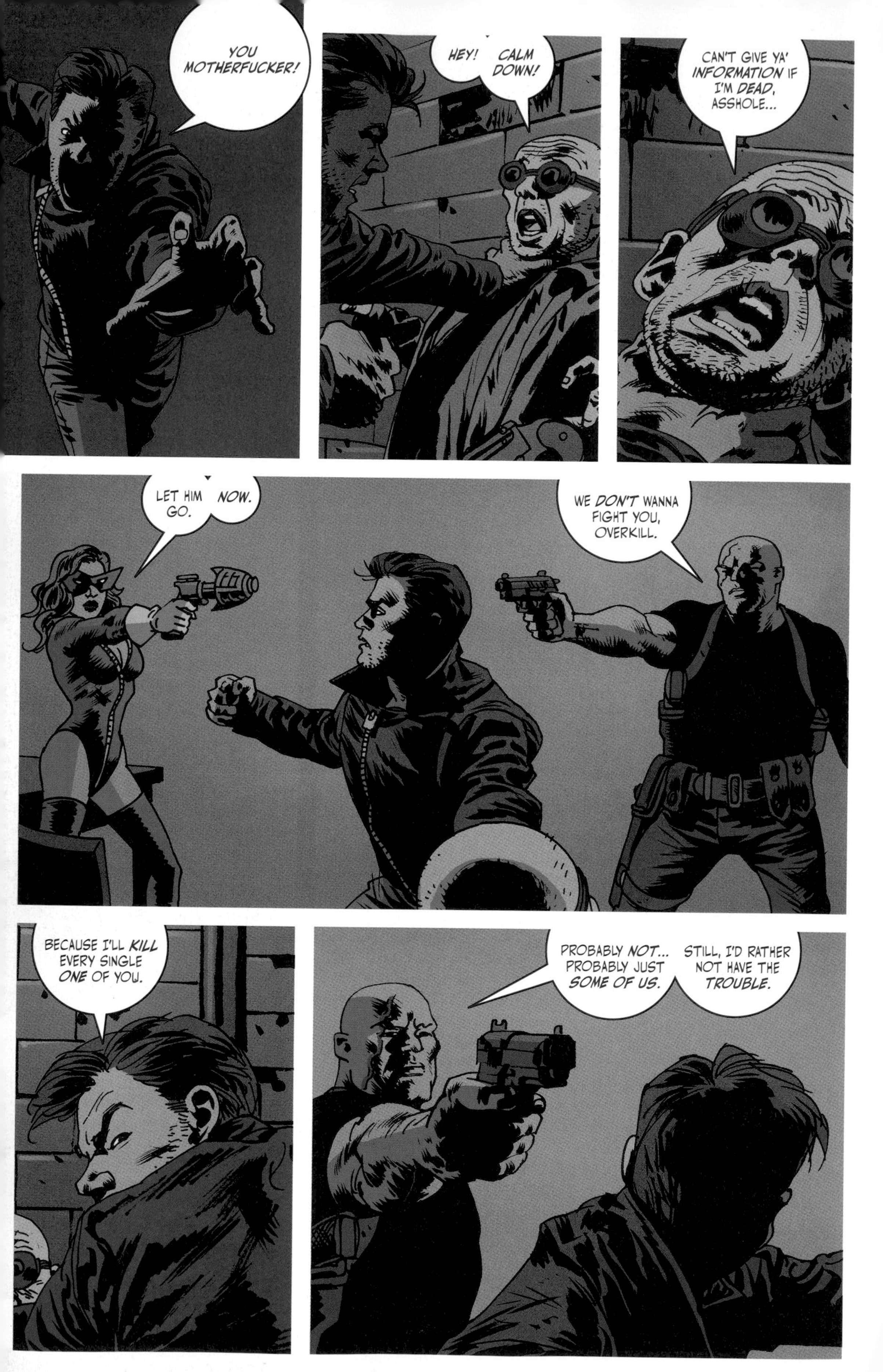
YOU MOTHERFUCKER!
HEY!
CALM DOWN!
CAN'T GIVE YA' INFORMATION IF I'M DEAD, ASSHOLE...
LET HIM GO.
NOW.
WE DON'T WANNA FIGHT YOU, OVERKILL.
BECAUSE I'LL KILL EVERY SINGLE ONE OF YOU.
PROBABLY NOT... PROBABLY JUST SOME OF US.
STILL, I'D RATHER NOT HAVE THE TROUBLE.

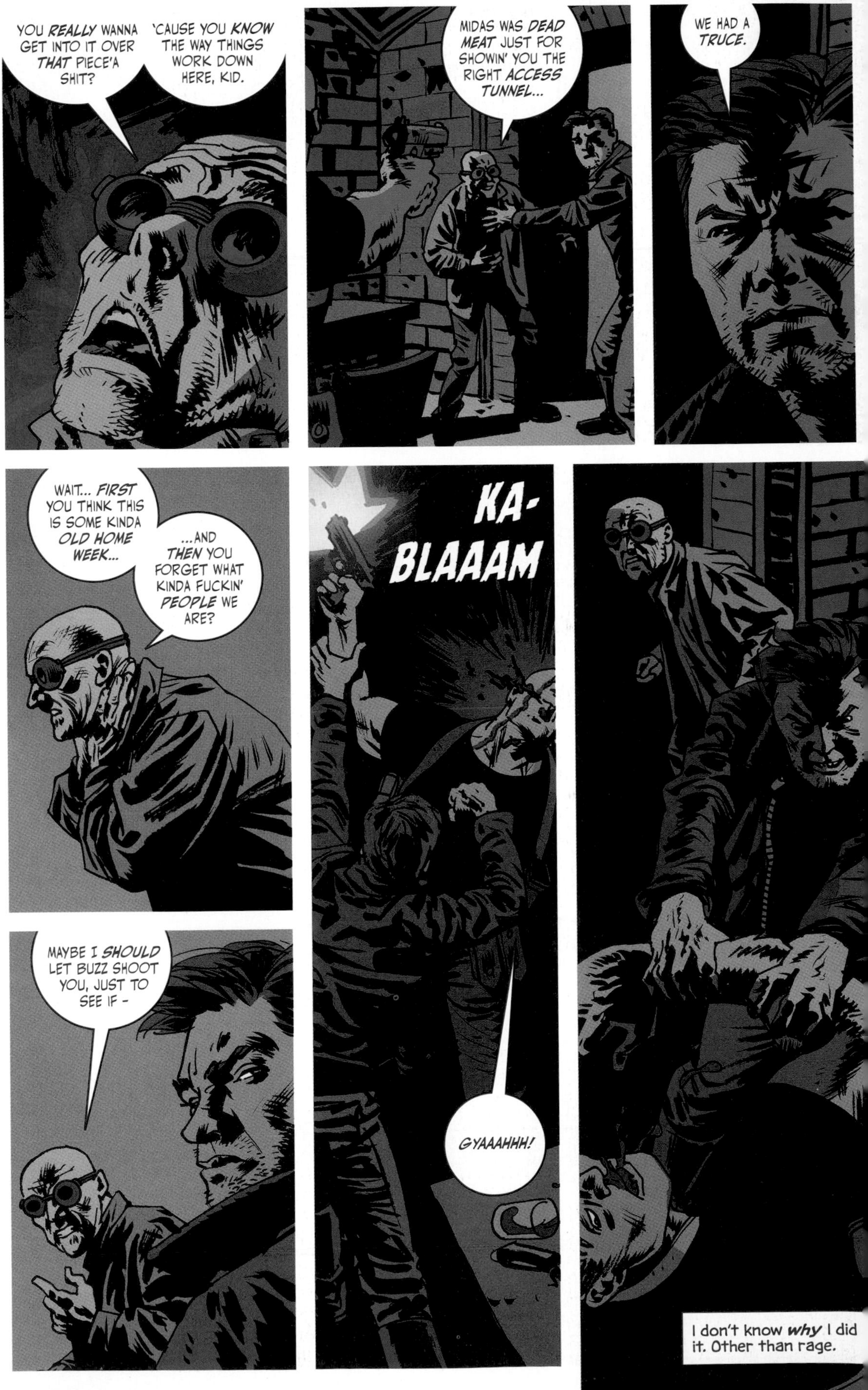
YOU REALLY WANNA GET INTO IT OVER THAT PIECE'A SHIT?
'CAUSE YOU KNOW THE WAY THINGS WORK DOWN HERE, KID.
MIDAS WAS DEAD MEAT JUST FOR SHOWIN' YOU THE RIGHT ACCESS TUNNEL...
WE HAD A TRUCE.
WAIT... FIRST YOU THINK THIS IS SOME KINDA OLD HOME WEEK...
...AND THEN YOU FORGET WHAT KINDA FUCKIN' PEOPLE WE ARE?
MAYBE I SHOULD LET BUZZ SHOOT YOU, JUST TO SEE IF -
KA-BLAAAM
GYAAAHHH!
I don't know why I did it. Other than rage.

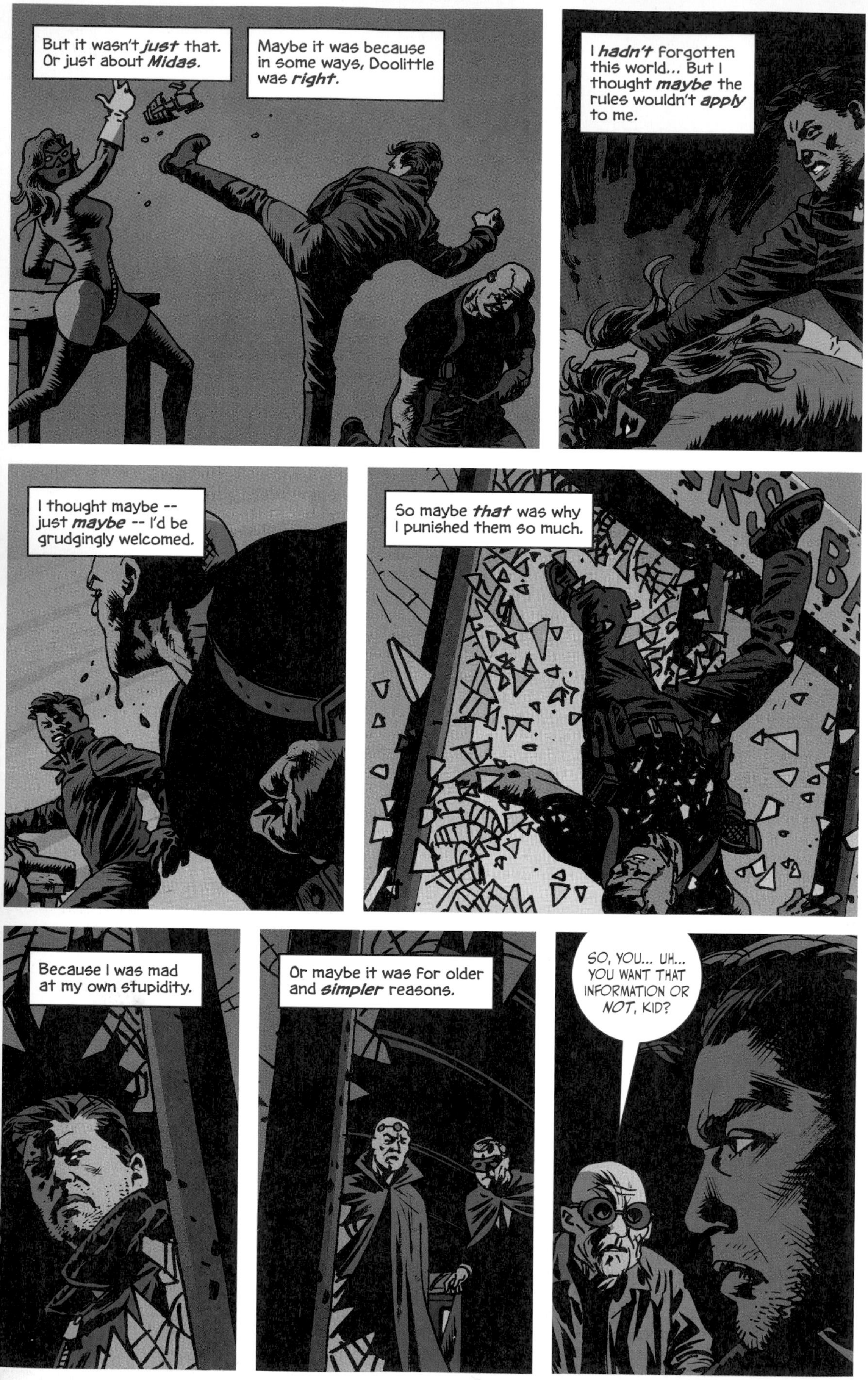

But it wasn't just that. Or just about Midas.
Maybe it was because in some ways, Doolittle was right.
I hadn't forgotten this world... But I thought maybe the rules wouldn't apply to me.
I thought maybe -- just maybe -- I'd be grudgingly welcomed.
So maybe that was why I punished them so much.
Because I was mad at my own stupidity.
Or maybe it was for older and simpler reasons.
SO, YOU... UH... YOU WANT THAT INFORMATION OR NOT, KID?

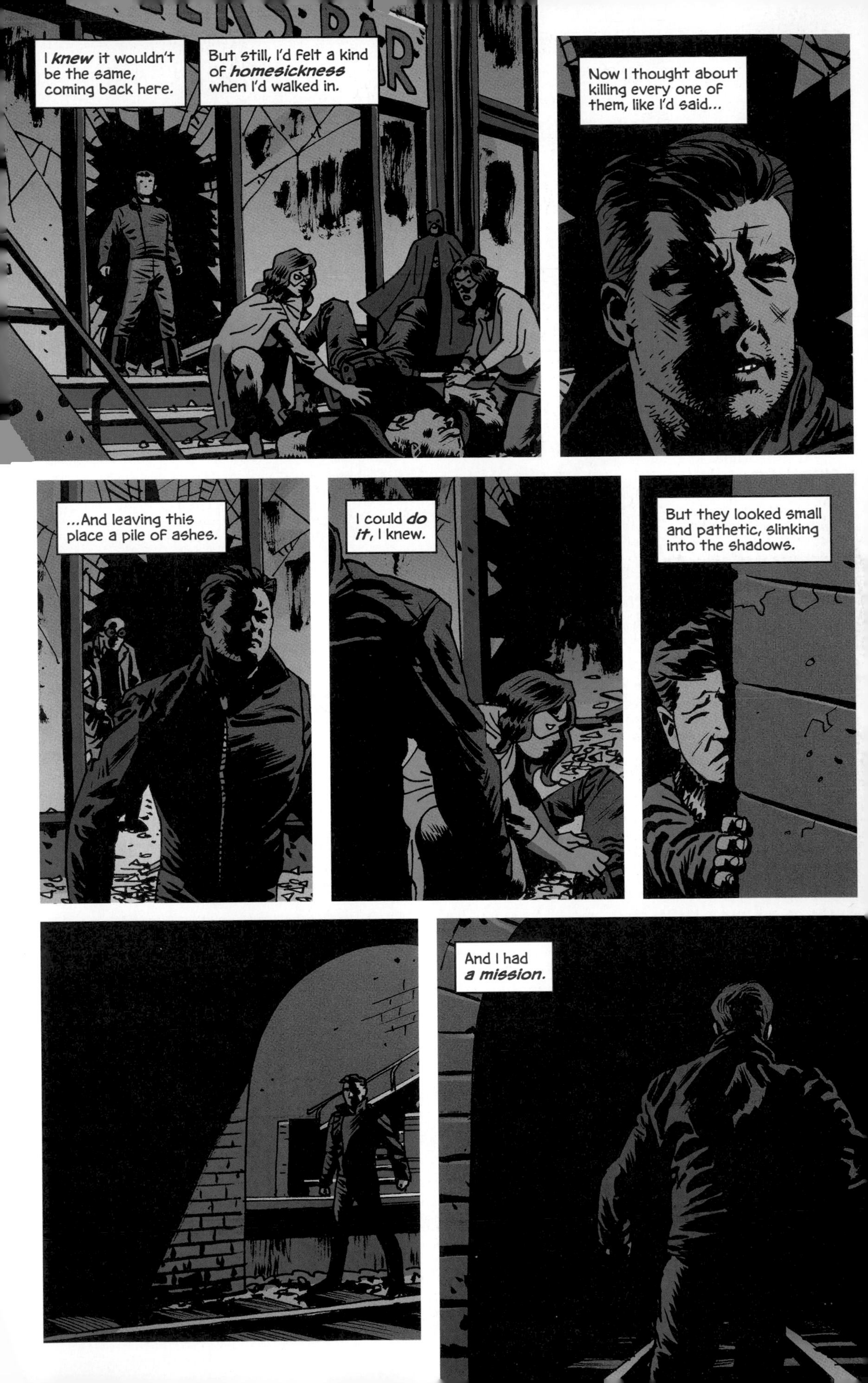
I knew it wouldn't be the same, coming back here.
But still, I'd felt a kind of homesickness when I'd walked in.
Now I thought about killing every one of them, like I'd said...
...And leaving this place a pile of ashes.
I could do it, I knew.
But they looked small and pathetic, slinking into the shadows.
And I had a mission.

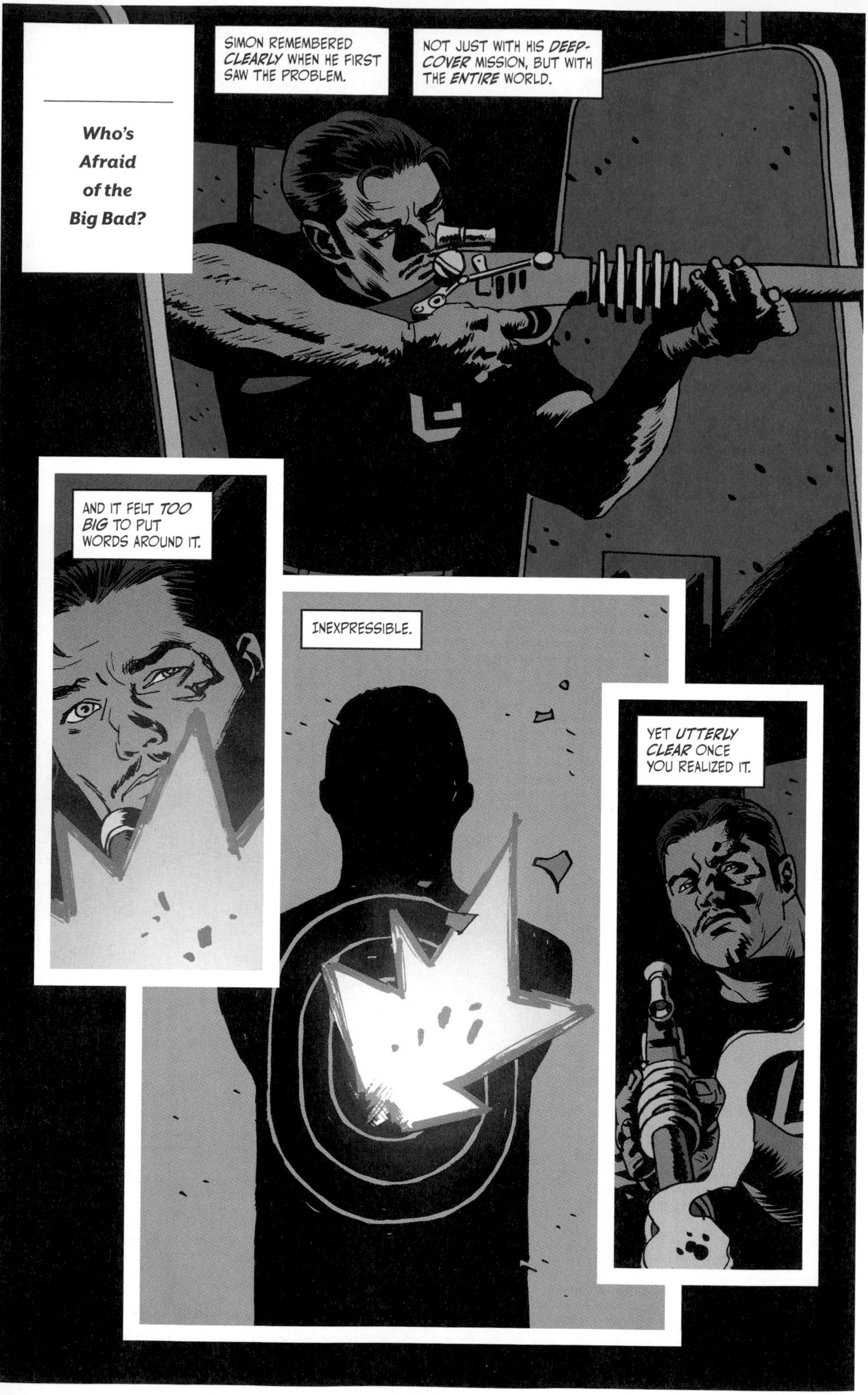
Who's Afraid of the Big Bad?
SIMON REMEMBERED CLEARLY WHEN HE FIRST SAW THE PROBLEM.
NOT JUST WITH HIS DEEP-COVER MISSION, BUT WITH THE ENTIRE WORLD.
AND IT FELT TOO BIG TO PUT WORDS AROUND IT.
INEXPRESSIBLE.
YET UTTERLY CLEAR ONCE YOU REALIZED IT.

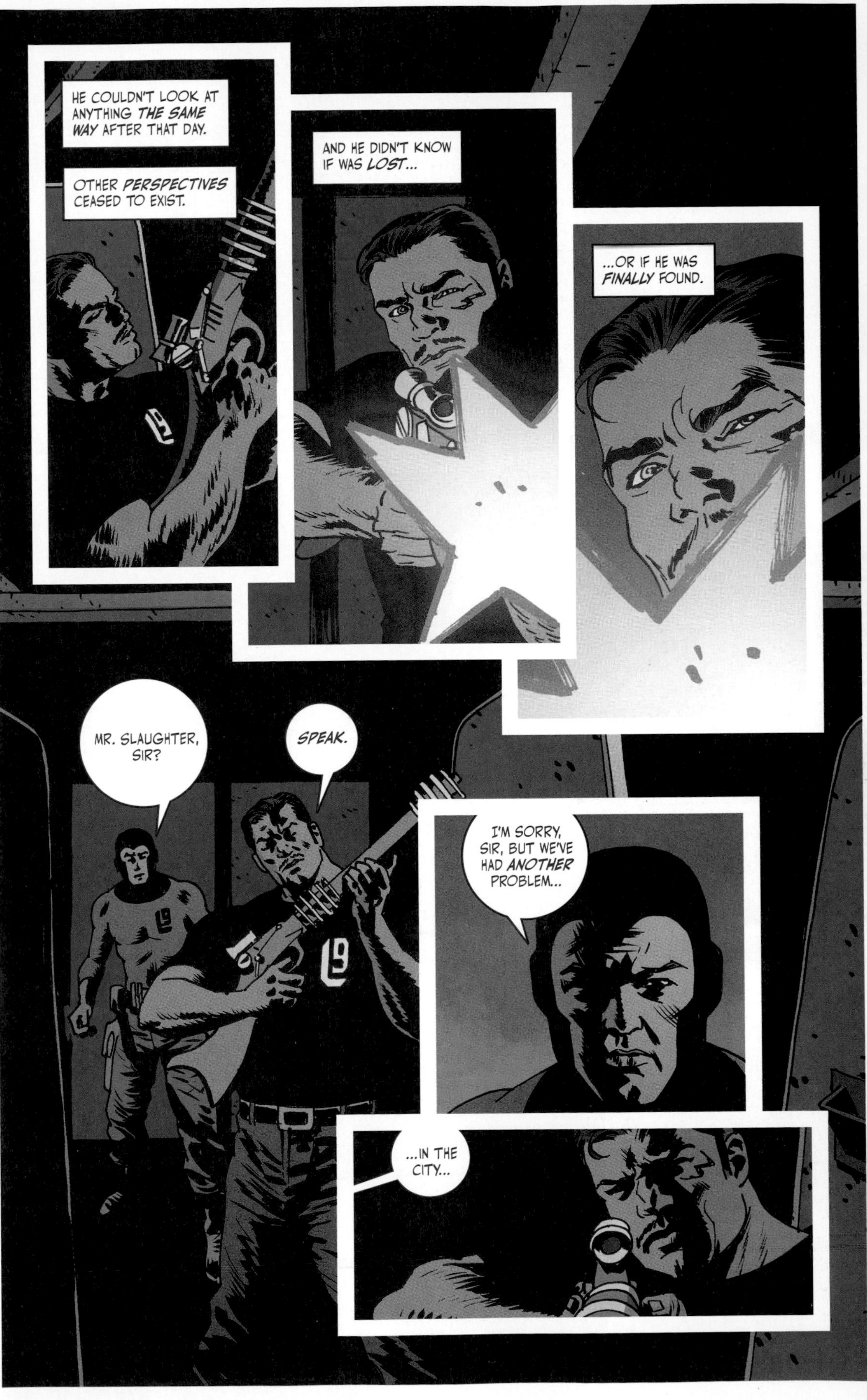
HE COULDN'T LOOK AT ANYTHING *THE SAME WAY* AFTER THAT DAY.
OTHER *PERSPECTIVES* CEASED TO EXIST.
AND HE DIDN'T KNOW IF WAS *LOST*...
...OR IF HE WAS *FINALLY* FOUND.
MR. SLAUGHTER, SIR?
SPEAK.
I'M SORRY, SIR, BUT WE'VE HAD *ANOTHER* PROBLEM...
...IN THE CITY...

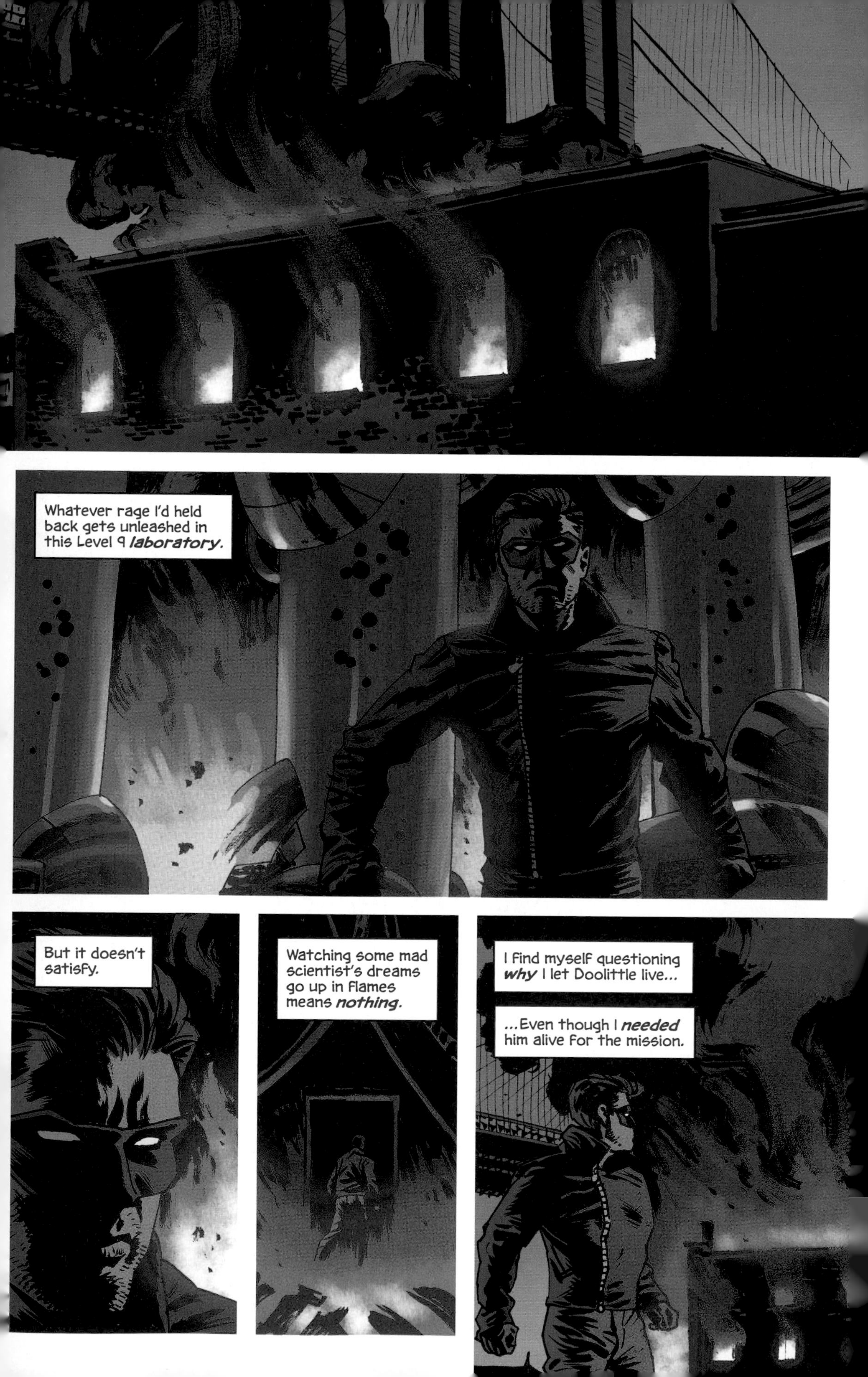
Whatever rage I'd held back gets unleashed in this Level 9 *laboratory.*
But it doesn't satisfy.
Watching some mad scientist's dreams go up in flames means *nothing.*
I find myself questioning *why* I let Doolittle live...
...Even though I *needed* him alive for the mission.

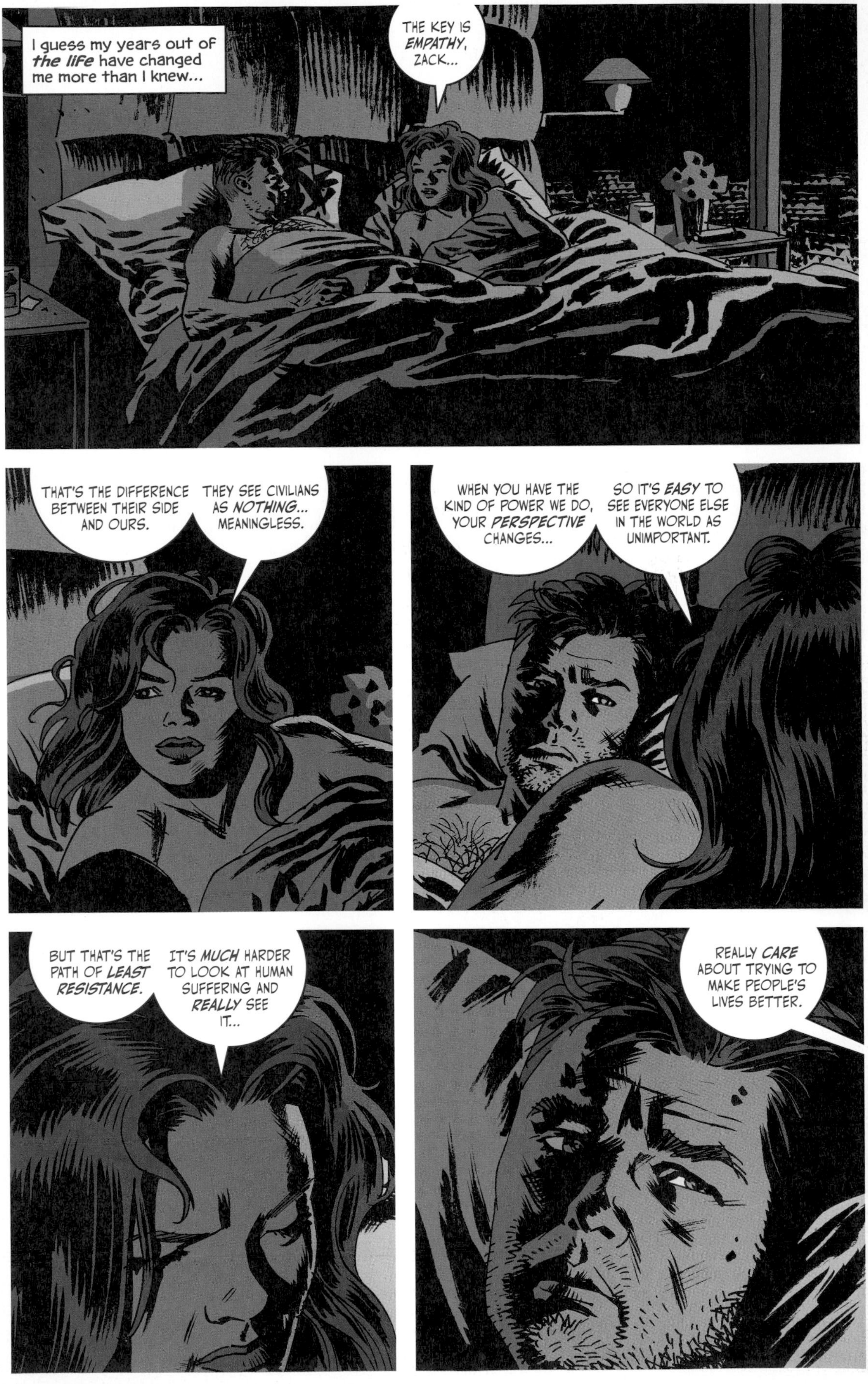
I guess my years out of *the life* have changed me more than I knew...
THE KEY IS *EMPATHY*, ZACK...
THAT'S THE DIFFERENCE BETWEEN THEIR SIDE AND OURS.
THEY SEE CIVILIANS AS *NOTHING*... MEANINGLESS.
WHEN YOU HAVE THE KIND OF POWER WE DO, YOUR *PERSPECTIVE* CHANGES...
SO IT'S *EASY* TO SEE EVERYONE ELSE IN THE WORLD AS UNIMPORTANT.
BUT THAT'S THE PATH OF *LEAST RESISTANCE*.
IT'S *MUCH* HARDER TO LOOK AT HUMAN SUFFERING AND *REALLY* SEE IT...
REALLY *CARE* ABOUT TRYING TO MAKE PEOPLE'S LIVES BETTER.

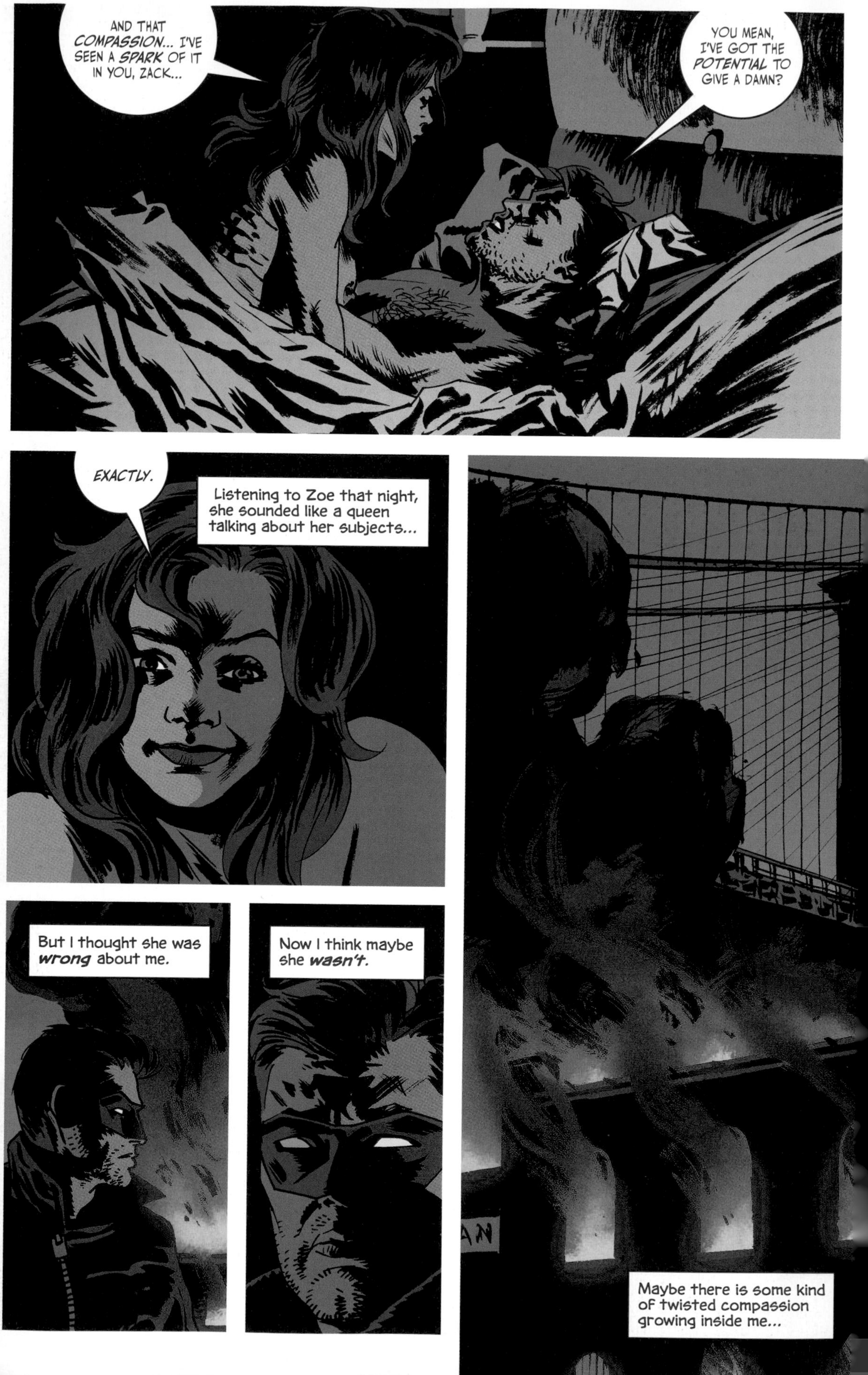
AND THAT COMPASSION... I'VE SEEN A SPARK OF IT IN YOU, ZACK...
YOU MEAN, I'VE GOT THE POTENTIAL TO GIVE A DAMN?
EXACTLY.
Listening to Zoe that night, she sounded like a queen talking about her subjects...
But I thought she was wrong about me.
Now I think maybe she wasn't.
Maybe there is some kind of twisted compassion growing inside me...

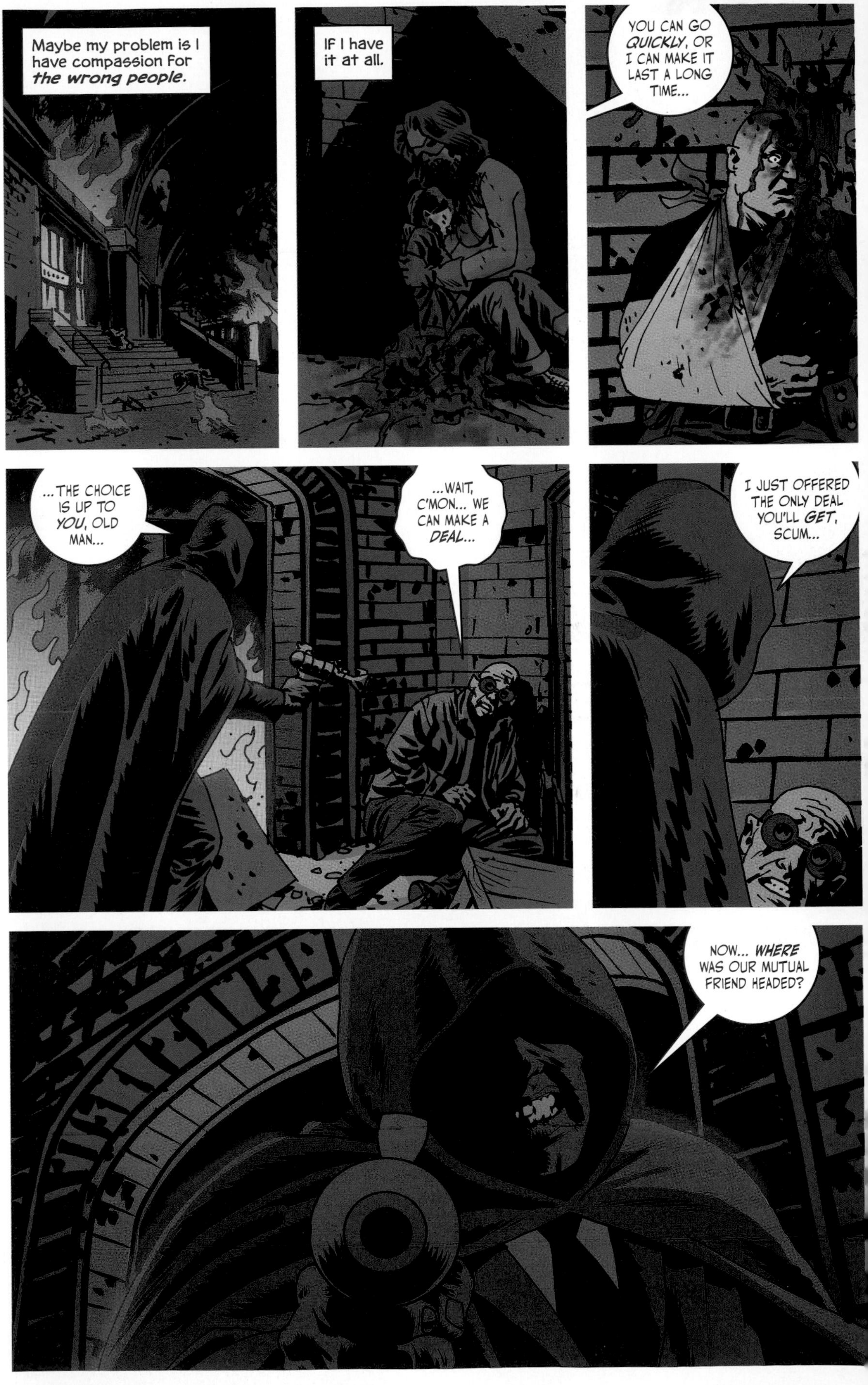
Maybe my problem is I have compassion for *the wrong people*.
If I have it at all.
YOU CAN GO *QUICKLY*, OR I CAN MAKE IT LAST A LONG TIME...
...THE CHOICE IS UP TO *YOU*, OLD MAN...
...WAIT, C'MON... WE CAN MAKE A *DEAL*...
I JUST OFFERED THE ONLY DEAL YOU'LL *GET*, SCUM...
NOW... *WHERE* WAS OUR MUTUAL FRIEND HEADED?

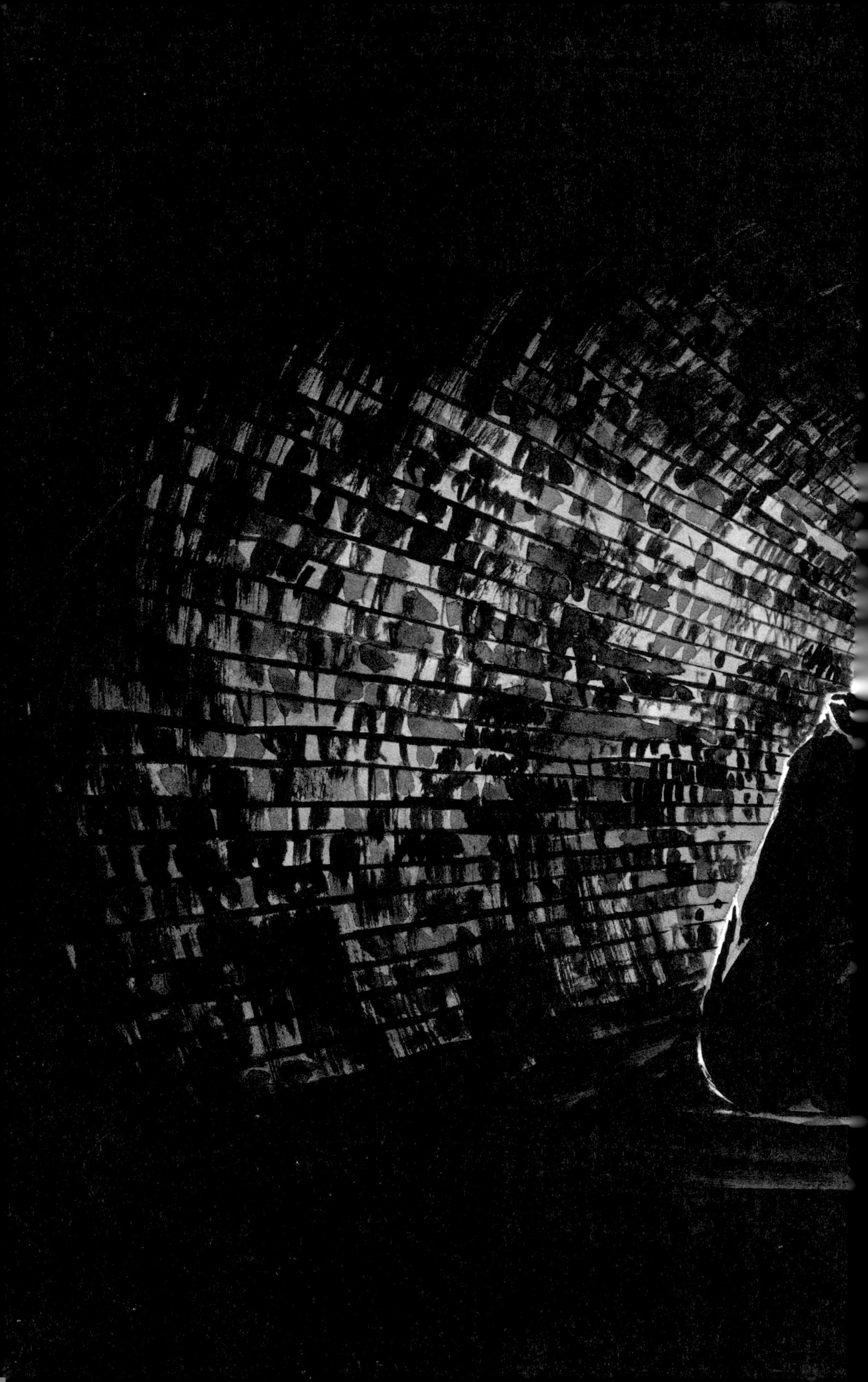

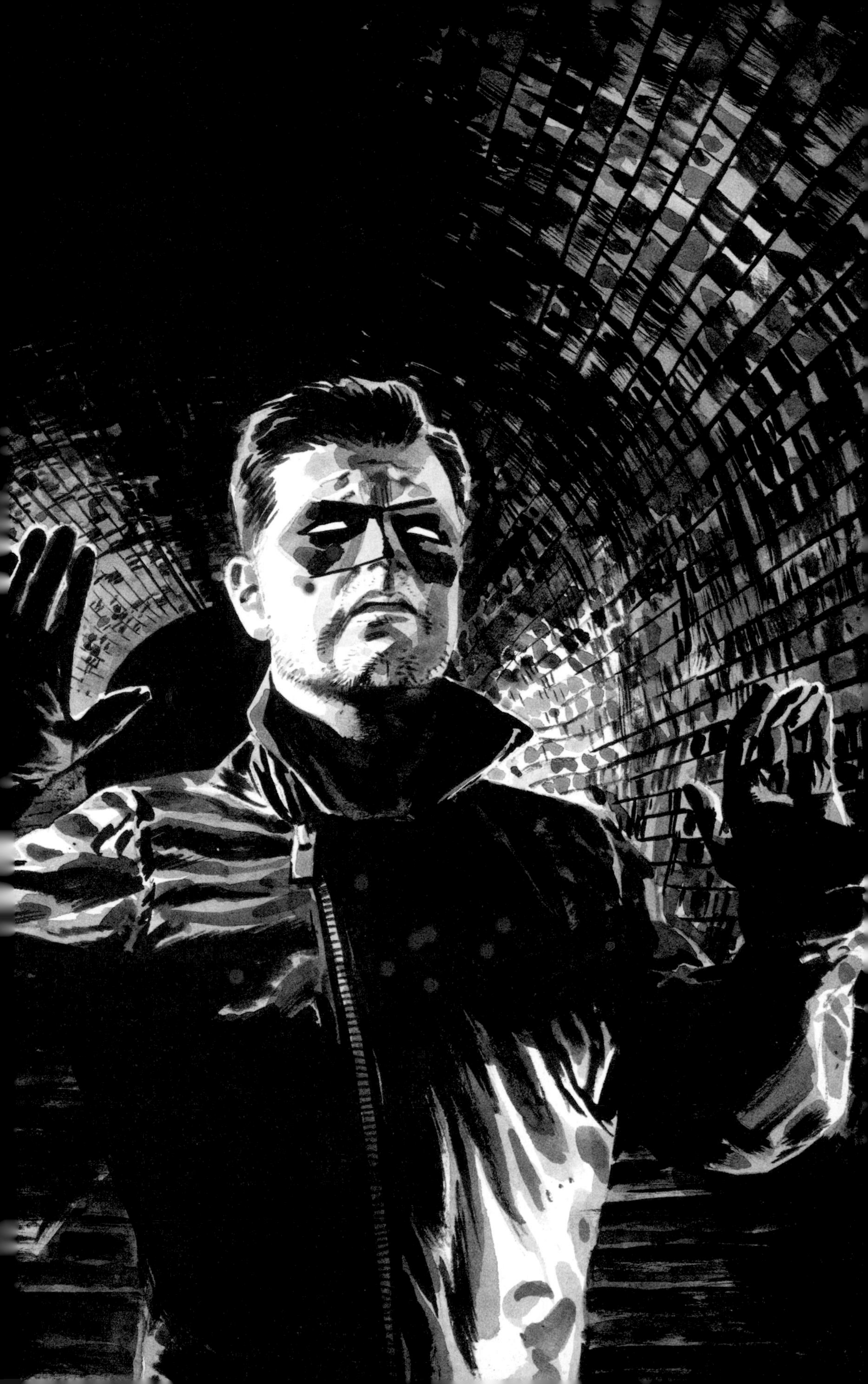

Chapter Four

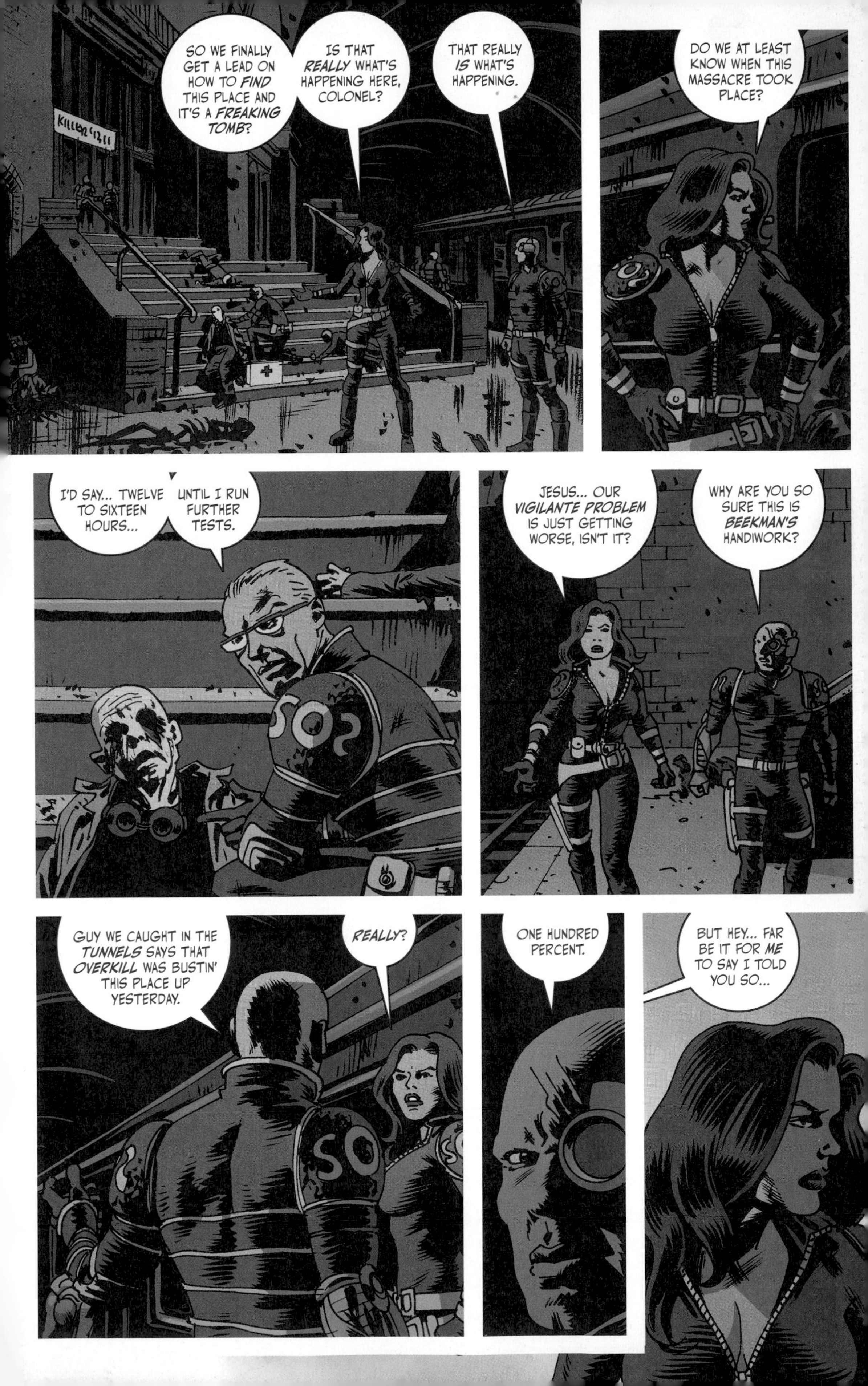

KILLER'S 1211
SO WE FINALLY GET A LEAD ON HOW TO *FIND* THIS PLACE AND IT'S A *FREAKING TOMB*?
IS THAT *REALLY* WHAT'S HAPPENING HERE, COLONEL?
THAT REALLY *IS* WHAT'S HAPPENING.
DO WE AT LEAST KNOW WHEN THIS MASSACRE TOOK PLACE?
I'D SAY... TWELVE TO SIXTEEN HOURS...
UNTIL I RUN FURTHER TESTS.
JESUS... OUR *VIGILANTE PROBLEM* IS JUST GETTING WORSE, ISN'T IT?
WHY ARE YOU SO SURE THIS IS *BEEKMAN'S* HANDIWORK?
GUY WE CAUGHT IN THE *TUNNELS* SAYS THAT *OVERKILL* WAS BUSTIN' THIS PLACE UP YESTERDAY.
REALLY?
ONE HUNDRED PERCENT.
BUT HEY... FAR BE IT FOR *ME* TO SAY I TOLD YOU SO...

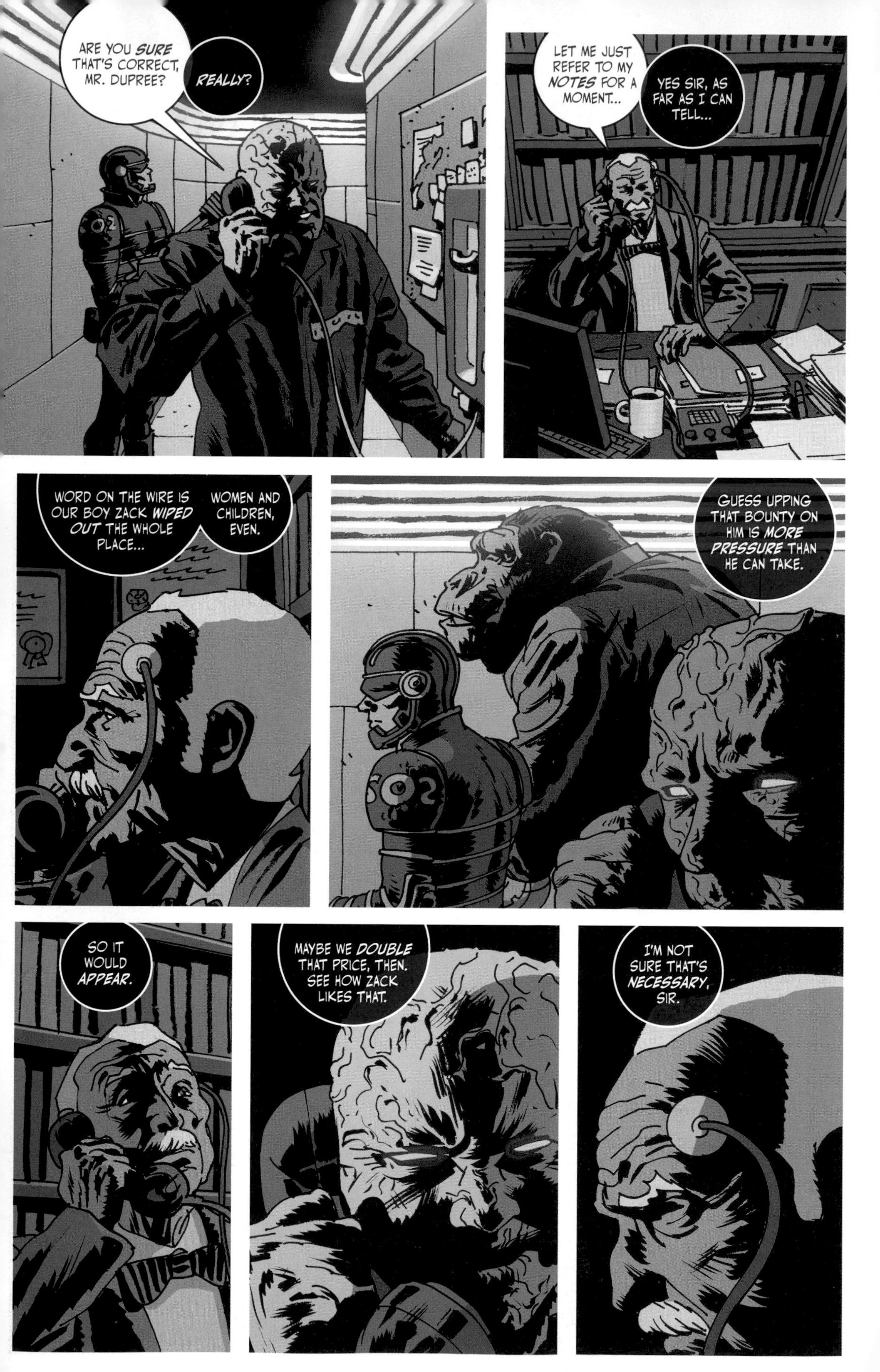
ARE YOU SURE THAT'S CORRECT, MR. DUPREE?
REALLY?
LET ME JUST REFER TO MY NOTES FOR A MOMENT...
YES SIR, AS FAR AS I CAN TELL...
WORD ON THE WIRE IS OUR BOY ZACK WIPED OUT THE WHOLE PLACE...
WOMEN AND CHILDREN, EVEN.
GUESS UPPING THAT BOUNTY ON HIM IS MORE PRESSURE THAN HE CAN TAKE.
SO IT WOULD APPEAR.
MAYBE WE DOUBLE THAT PRICE, THEN. SEE HOW ZACK LIKES THAT.
I'M NOT SURE THAT'S NECESSARY, SIR.

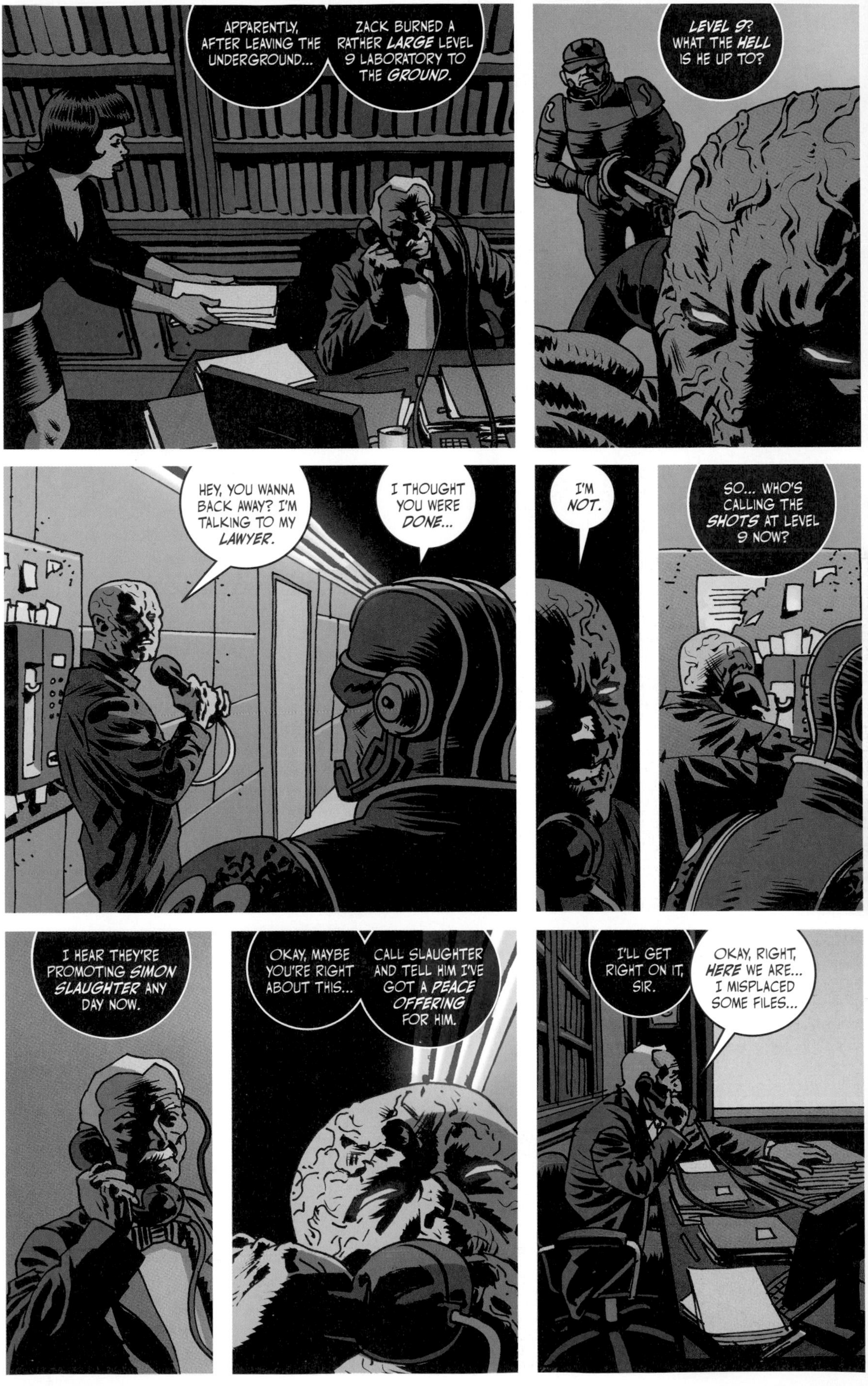
APPARENTLY, AFTER LEAVING THE UNDERGROUND...
ZACK BURNED A RATHER LARGE LEVEL 9 LABORATORY TO THE GROUND.
LEVEL 9? WHAT THE HELL IS HE UP TO?
HEY, YOU WANNA BACK AWAY? I'M TALKING TO MY LAWYER.
I THOUGHT YOU WERE DONE...
I'M NOT.
SO... WHO'S CALLING THE SHOTS AT LEVEL 9 NOW?
I HEAR THEY'RE PROMOTING SIMON SLAUGHTER ANY DAY NOW.
OKAY, MAYBE YOU'RE RIGHT ABOUT THIS...
CALL SLAUGHTER AND TELL HIM I'VE GOT A PEACE OFFERING FOR HIM.
I'LL GET RIGHT ON IT, SIR.
OKAY, RIGHT, HERE WE ARE... I MISPLACED SOME FILES...

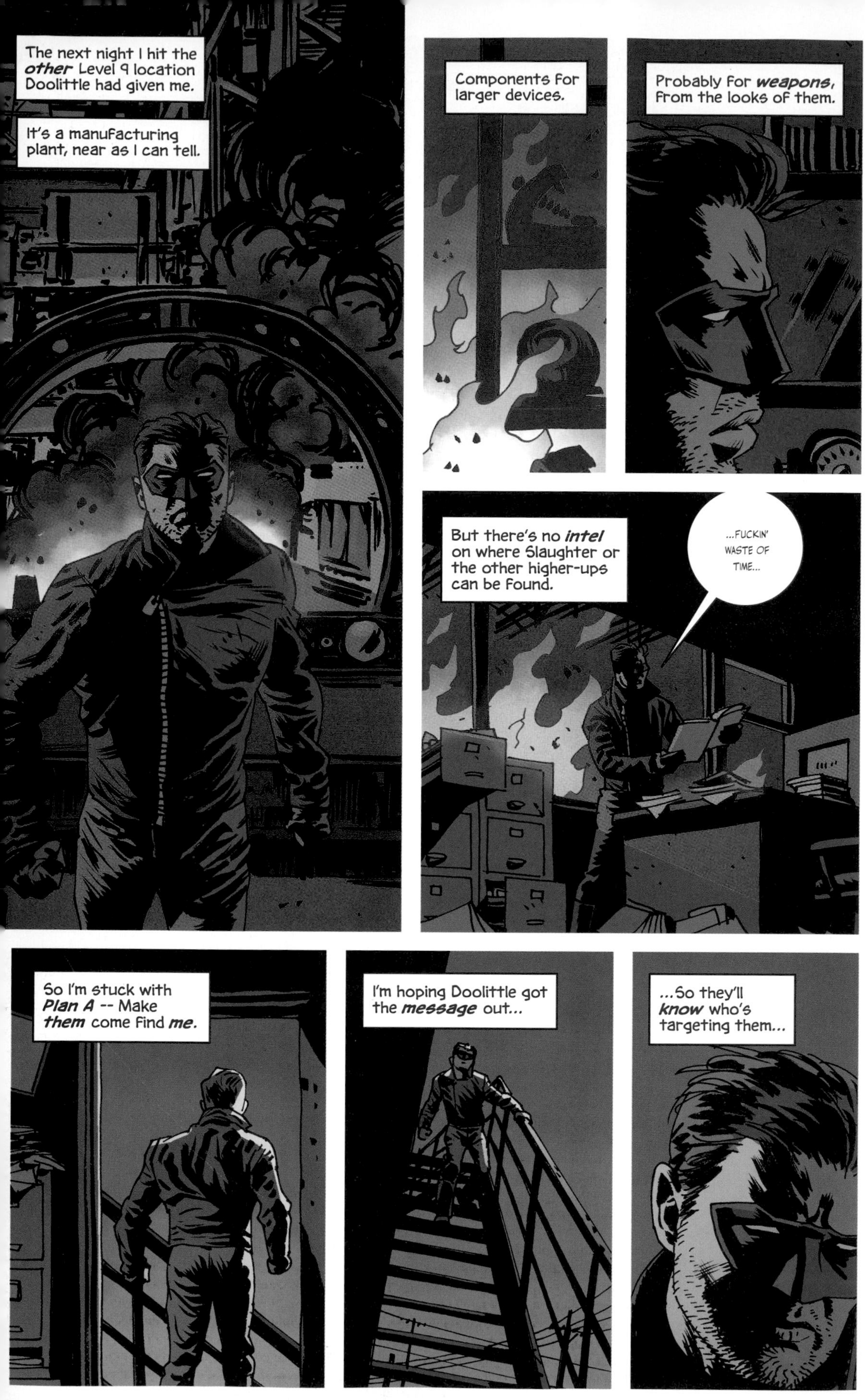
The next night I hit the *other* Level 9 location Doolittle had given me.
It's a manufacturing plant, near as I can tell.
Components for larger devices.
Probably for *weapons*, from the looks of them.
But there's no *intel* on where Slaughter or the other higher-ups can be found.
...FUCKIN' WASTE OF TIME...
So I'm stuck with *Plan A* -- Make *them* come find *me.*
I'm hoping Doolittle got the *message* out...
...So they'll *know* who's targeting them...

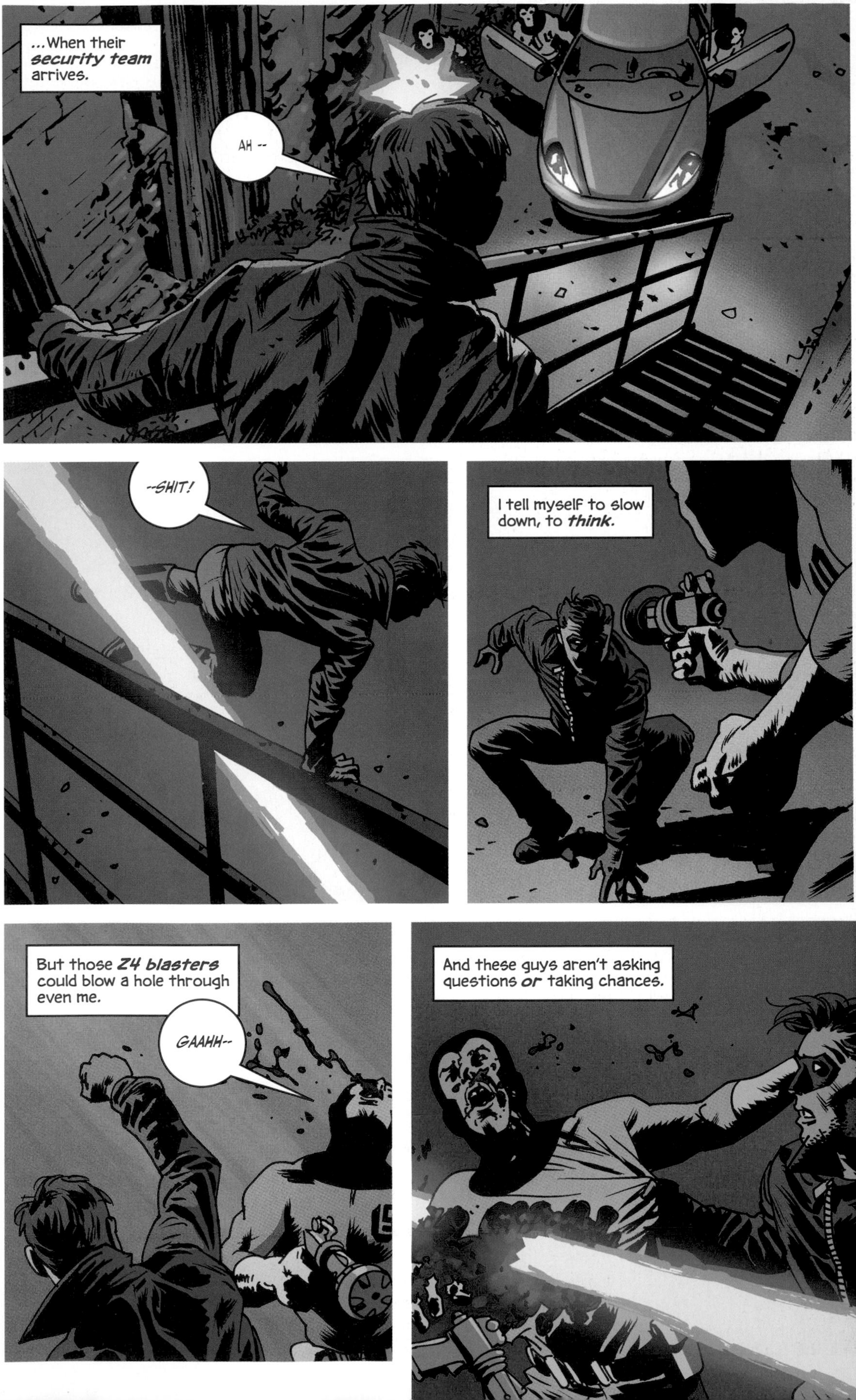
...When their *security team* arrives.
AH --
--SHIT!
I tell myself to slow down, to *think.*
But those *24 blasters* could blow a hole through even me.
GAAHH--
And these guys aren't asking questions *or* taking chances.

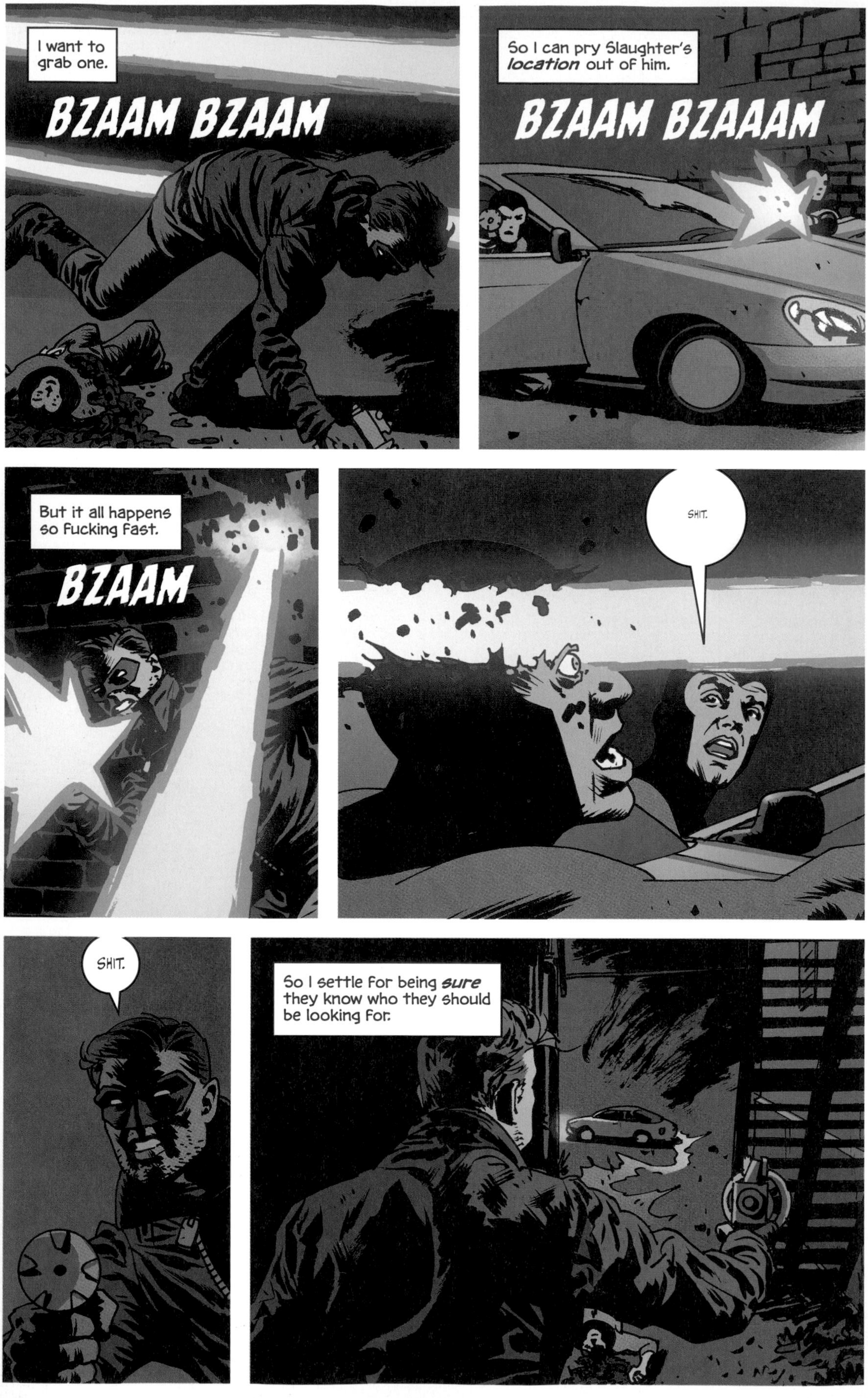
I want to grab one.
BZAAM BZAAM
So I can pry Slaughter's *location* out of him.
BZAAM BZAAAM
But it all happens so fucking fast.
BZAAM
SHIT.
SHIT.
So I settle for being *sure* they know who they should be looking for.

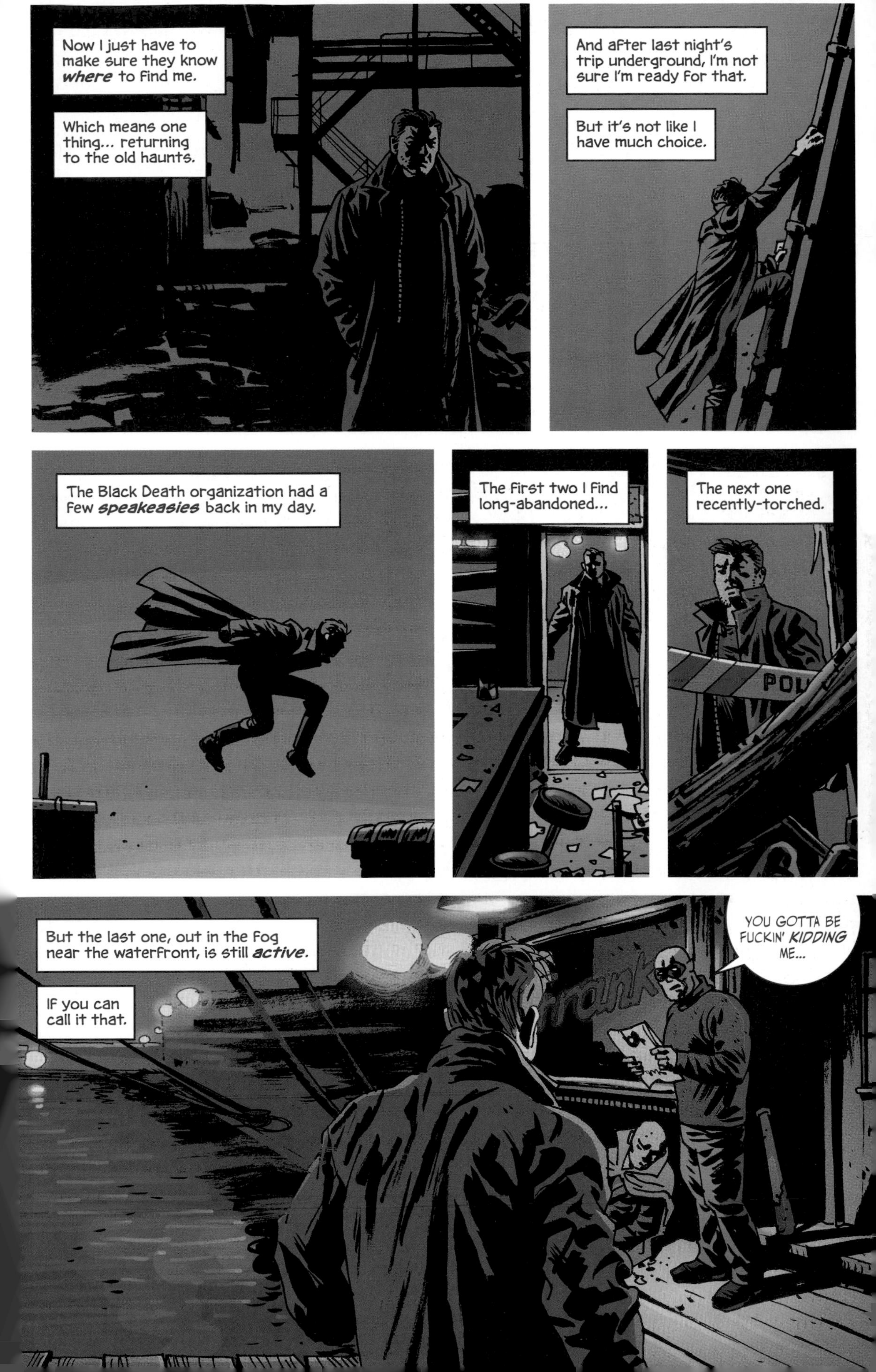
Now I just have to make sure they know *where* to find me.
Which means one thing... returning to the old haunts.
And after last night's trip underground, I'm not sure I'm ready for that.
But it's not like I have much choice.
The Black Death organization had a few *speakeasies* back in my day.
The first two I find long-abandoned...
The next one recently-torched.
POL
But the last one, out in the fog near the waterfront, is still *active*.
If you can call it that.
YOU GOTTA BE FUCKIN' *KIDDING* ME...

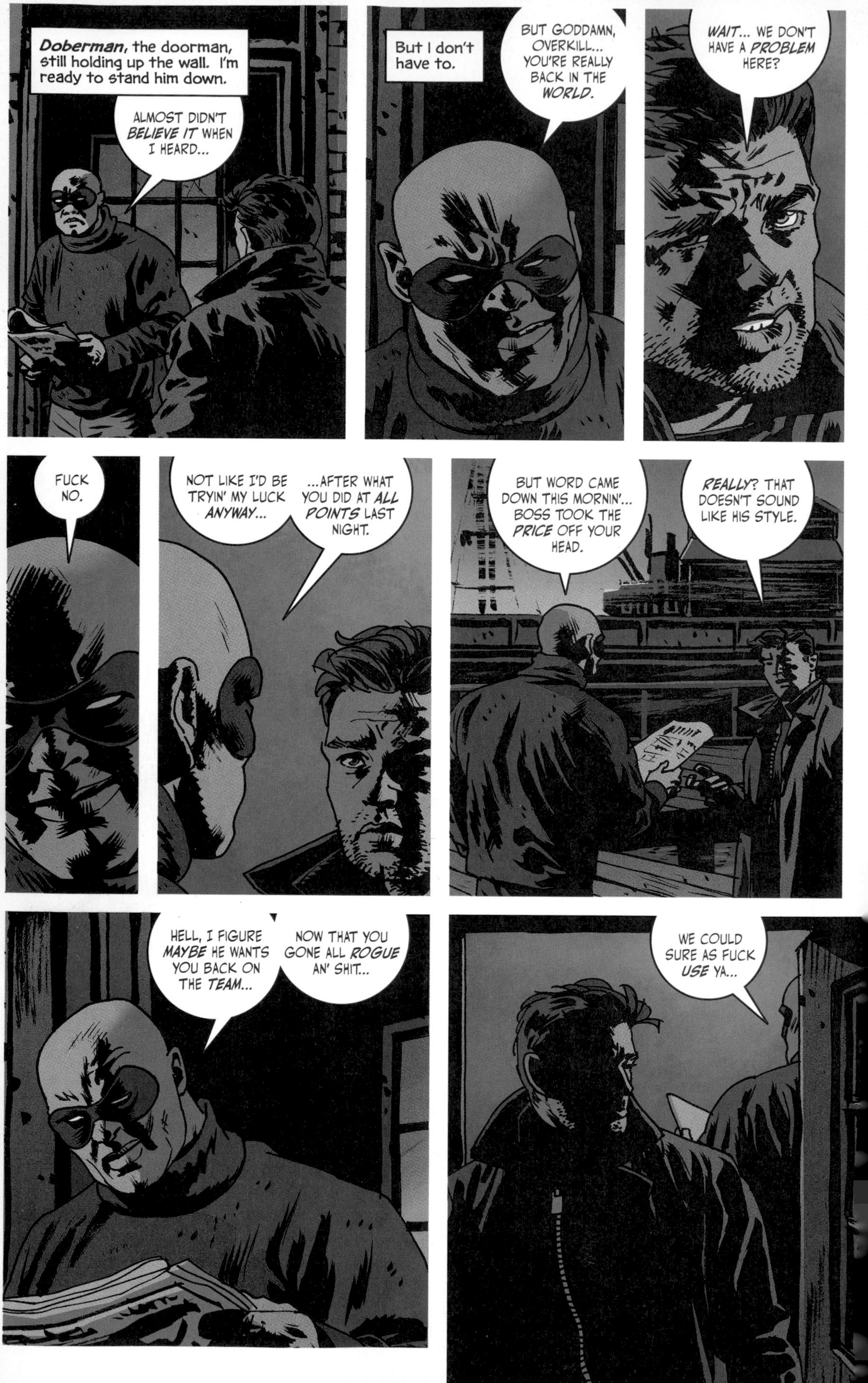

Doberman, the doorman, still holding up the wall. I'm ready to stand him down.
ALMOST DIDN'T BELIEVE IT WHEN I HEARD...
But I don't have to.
BUT GODDAMN, OVERKILL... YOU'RE REALLY BACK IN THE WORLD.
WAIT... WE DON'T HAVE A PROBLEM HERE?
FUCK NO.
NOT LIKE I'D BE TRYIN' MY LUCK ANYWAY...
...AFTER WHAT YOU DID AT ALL POINTS LAST NIGHT.
BUT WORD CAME DOWN THIS MORNIN'... BOSS TOOK THE PRICE OFF YOUR HEAD.
REALLY? THAT DOESN'T SOUND LIKE HIS STYLE.
HELL, I FIGURE MAYBE HE WANTS YOU BACK ON THE TEAM...
NOW THAT YOU GONE ALL ROGUE AN' SHIT...
WE COULD SURE AS FUCK USE YA...

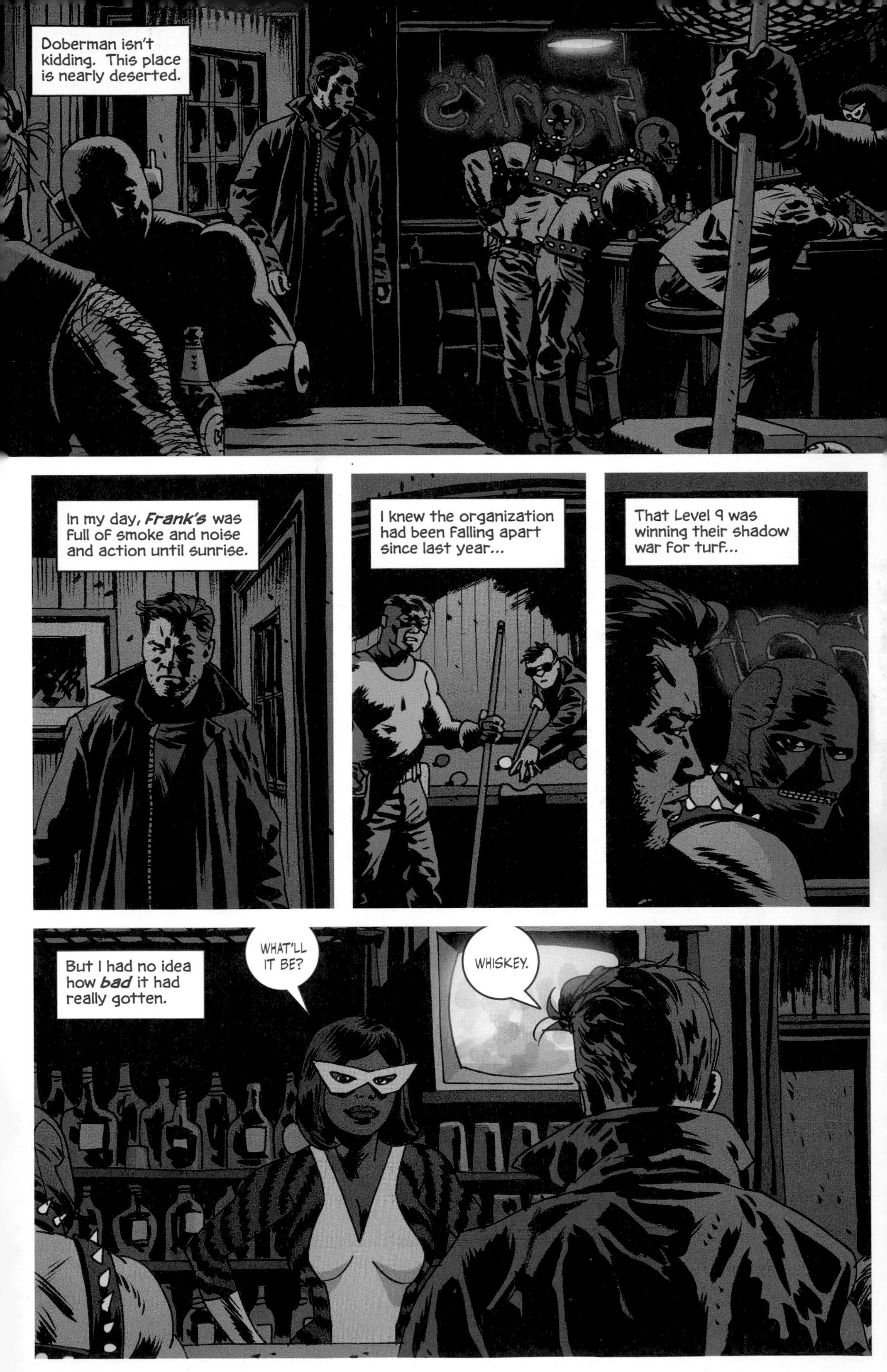
Doberman isn't kidding. This place is nearly deserted.
FRANK'S
In my day, Frank's was full of smoke and noise and action until sunrise.
I knew the organization had been falling apart since last year...
That Level 9 was winning their shadow war for turf...
But I had no idea how bad it had really gotten.
WHAT'LL IT BE?
WHISKEY.

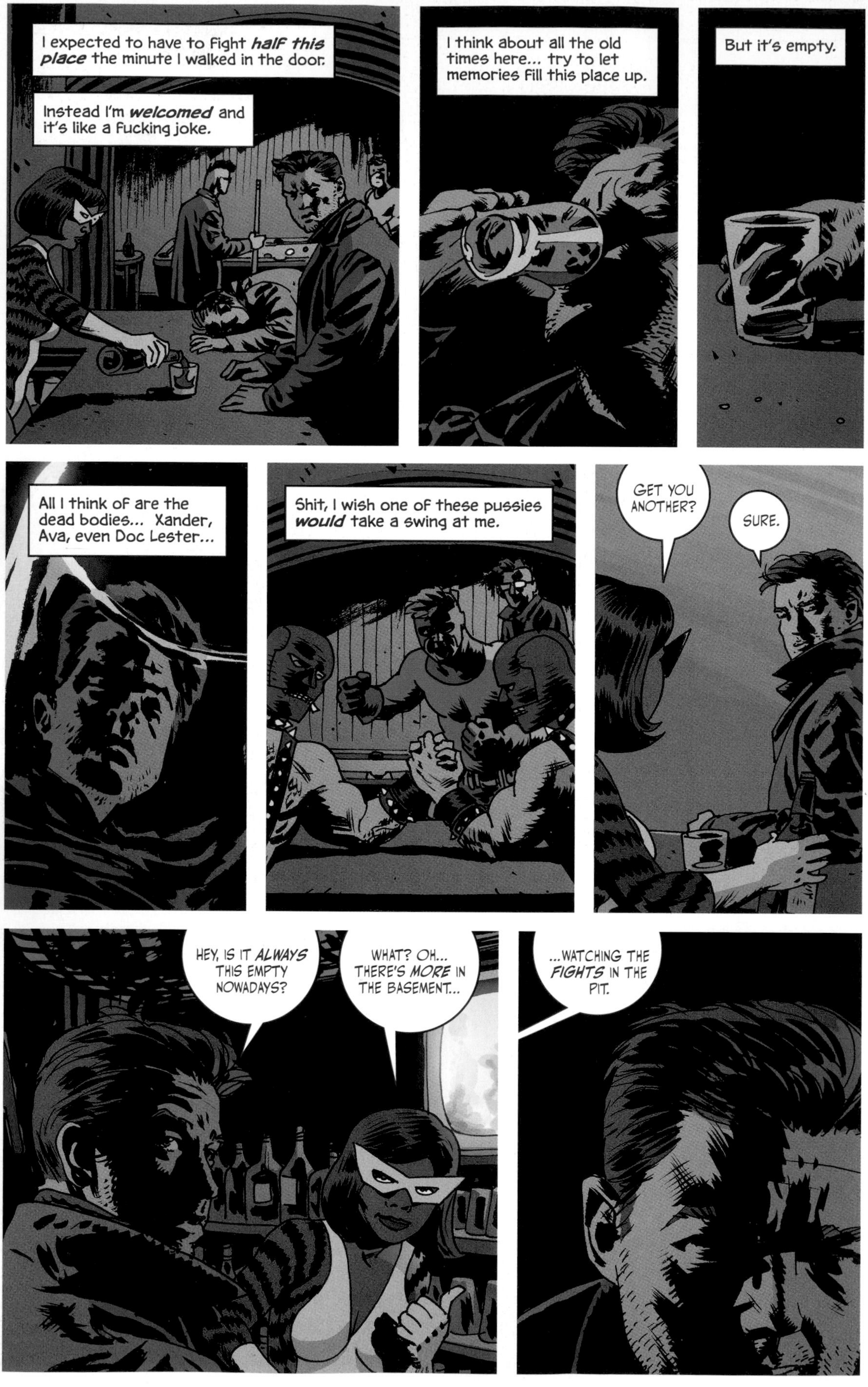

I expected to have to fight *half this place* the minute I walked in the door.
Instead I'm *welcomed* and it's like a fucking joke.
I think about all the old times here... try to let memories fill this place up.
But it's empty.
All I think of are the dead bodies... Xander, Ava, even Doc Lester...
Shit, I wish one of these pussies *would* take a swing at me.
GET YOU ANOTHER?
SURE.
HEY, IS IT *ALWAYS* THIS EMPTY NOWADAYS?
WHAT? OH... THERE'S *MORE* IN THE BASEMENT...
...WATCHING THE *FIGHTS* IN THE PIT.

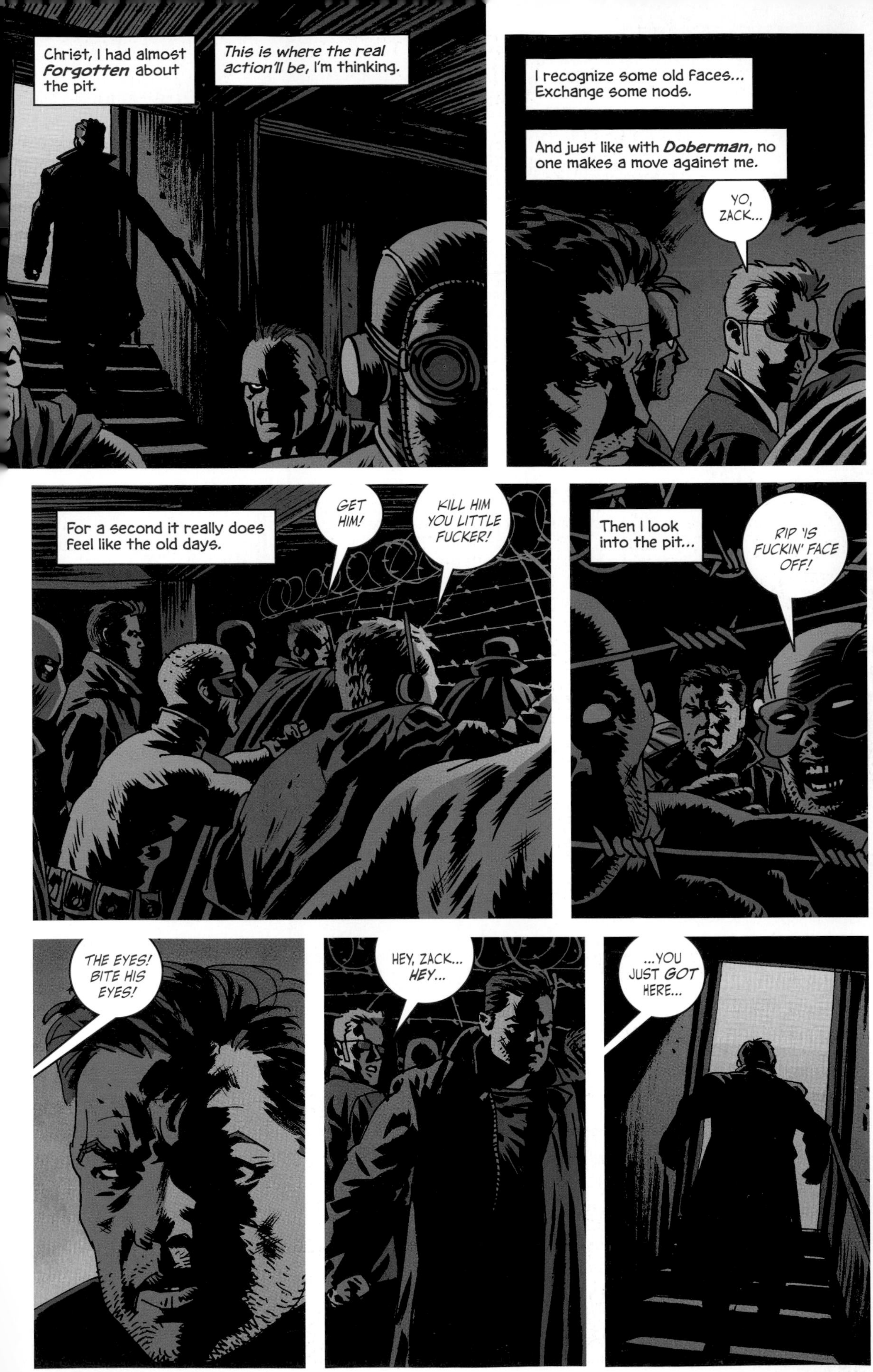
Christ, I had almost *Forgotten* about the pit.
This is where the real action'll be, I'm thinking.
I recognize some old faces... Exchange some nods.
And just like with *Doberman*, no one makes a move against me.
YO, ZACK...
For a second it really does feel like the old days.
GET HIM!
KILL HIM YOU LITTLE FUCKER!
Then I look into the pit...
RIP 'IS FUCKIN' FACE OFF!
THE EYES! BITE HIS EYES!
HEY, ZACK... *HEY*...
...YOU JUST *GOT* HERE...

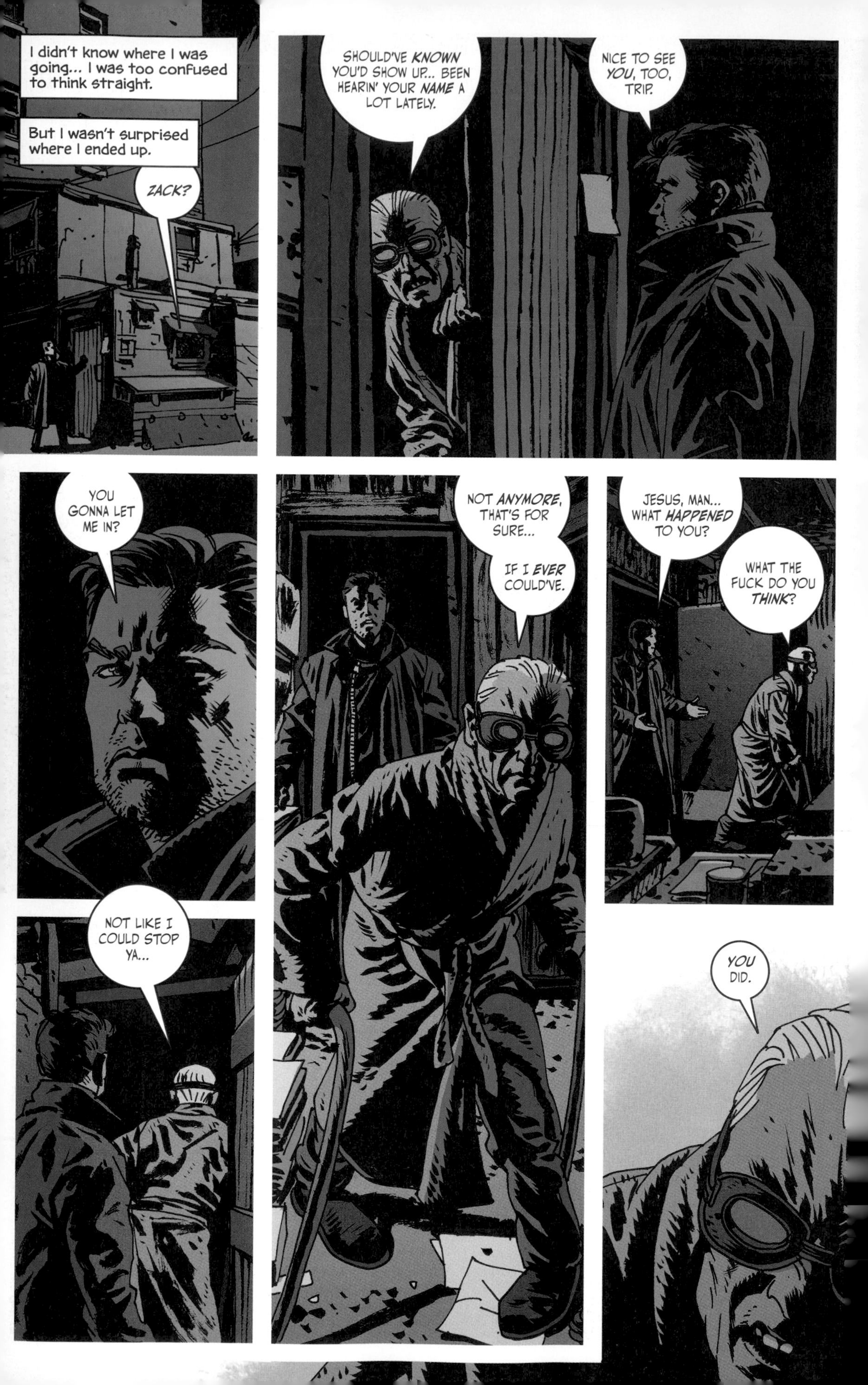
I didn't know where I was going... I was too confused to think straight.
But I wasn't surprised where I ended up.
ZACK?
SHOULD'VE KNOWN YOU'D SHOW UP... BEEN HEARIN' YOUR NAME A LOT LATELY.
NICE TO SEE YOU, TOO, TRIP.
YOU GONNA LET ME IN?
NOT LIKE I COULD STOP YA...
NOT ANYMORE, THAT'S FOR SURE...
IF I EVER COULD'VE.
JESUS, MAN... WHAT HAPPENED TO YOU?
WHAT THE FUCK DO YOU THINK?
YOU DID.

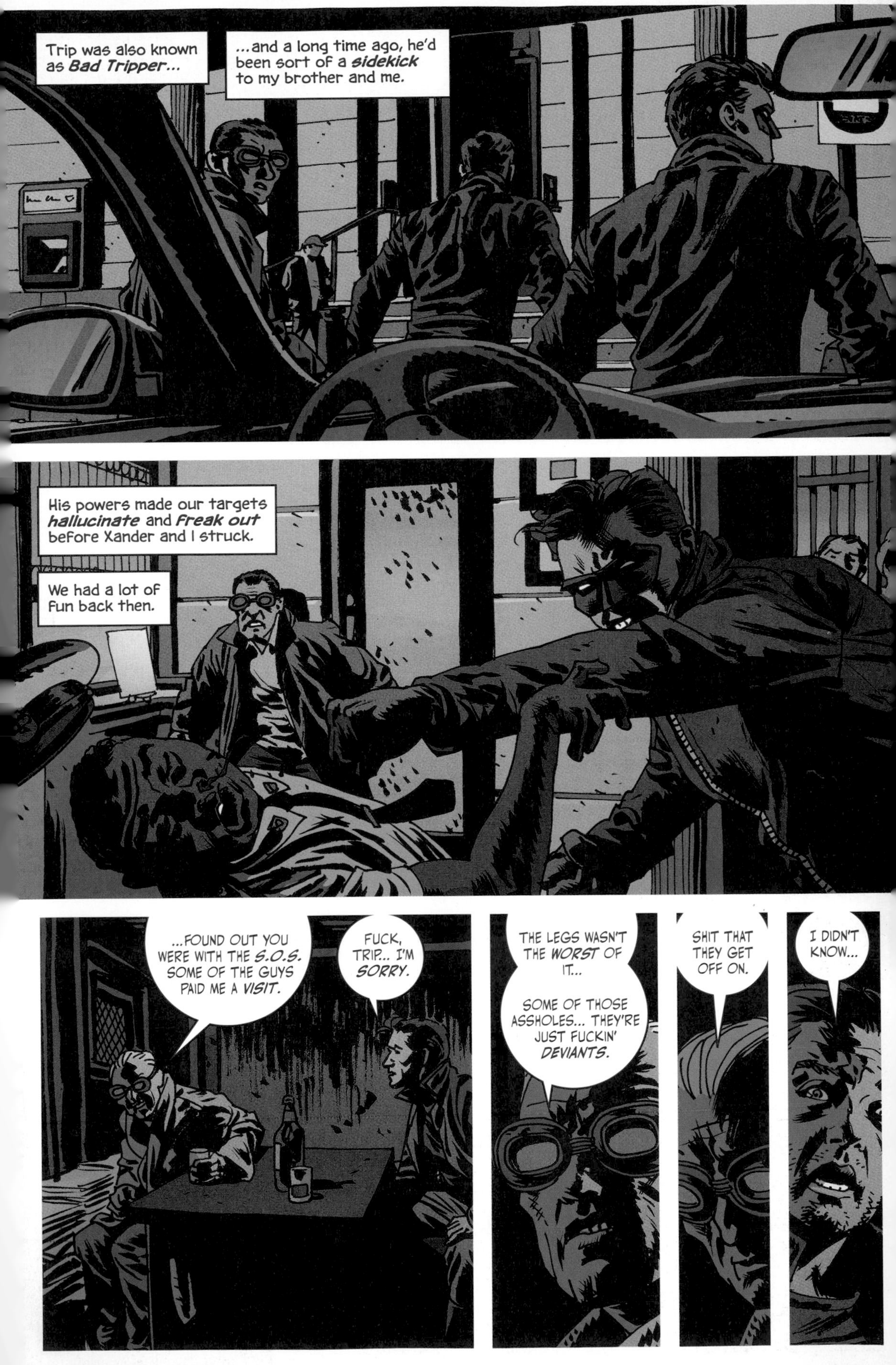
Trip was also known as *Bad Tripper*...
...and a long time ago, he'd been sort of a *sidekick* to my brother and me.
His powers made our targets ***hallucinate*** and ***freak out*** before Xander and I struck.
We had a lot of fun back then.
...FOUND OUT YOU WERE WITH THE *S.O.S.* SOME OF THE GUYS PAID ME A *VISIT*.
FUCK, TRIP... I'M *SORRY*.
THE LEGS WASN'T THE *WORST* OF IT...
SOME OF THOSE ASSHOLES... THEY'RE JUST FUCKIN' *DEVIANTS*.
SHIT THAT THEY GET OFF ON.
I DIDN'T KNOW...

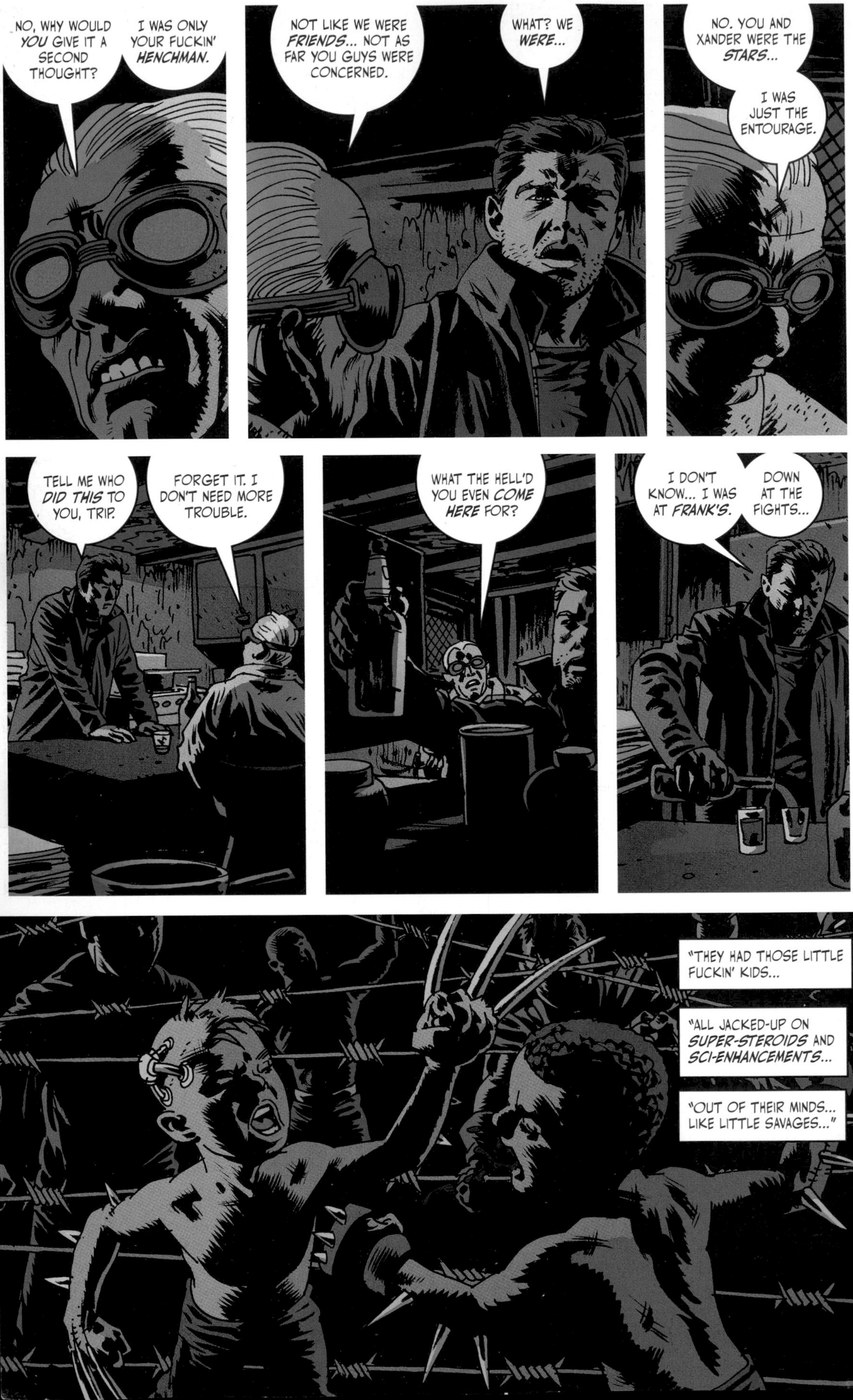
NO, WHY WOULD *YOU* GIVE IT A SECOND THOUGHT?
I WAS ONLY YOUR FUCKIN' *HENCHMAN.*
NOT LIKE WE WERE *FRIENDS*... NOT AS FAR YOU GUYS WERE CONCERNED.
WHAT? WE *WERE*...
NO. YOU AND XANDER WERE THE *STARS*...
I WAS JUST THE ENTOURAGE.
TELL ME WHO *DID THIS* TO YOU, TRIP.
FORGET IT. I DON'T NEED MORE TROUBLE.
WHAT THE HELL'D YOU EVEN *COME HERE* FOR?
I DON'T KNOW... I WAS AT *FRANK'S.*
DOWN AT THE FIGHTS...
"THEY HAD THOSE LITTLE FUCKIN' KIDS...
"ALL JACKED-UP ON *SUPER-STEROIDS* AND *SCI-ENHANCEMENTS*...
"OUT OF THEIR MINDS... LIKE LITTLE SAVAGES..."

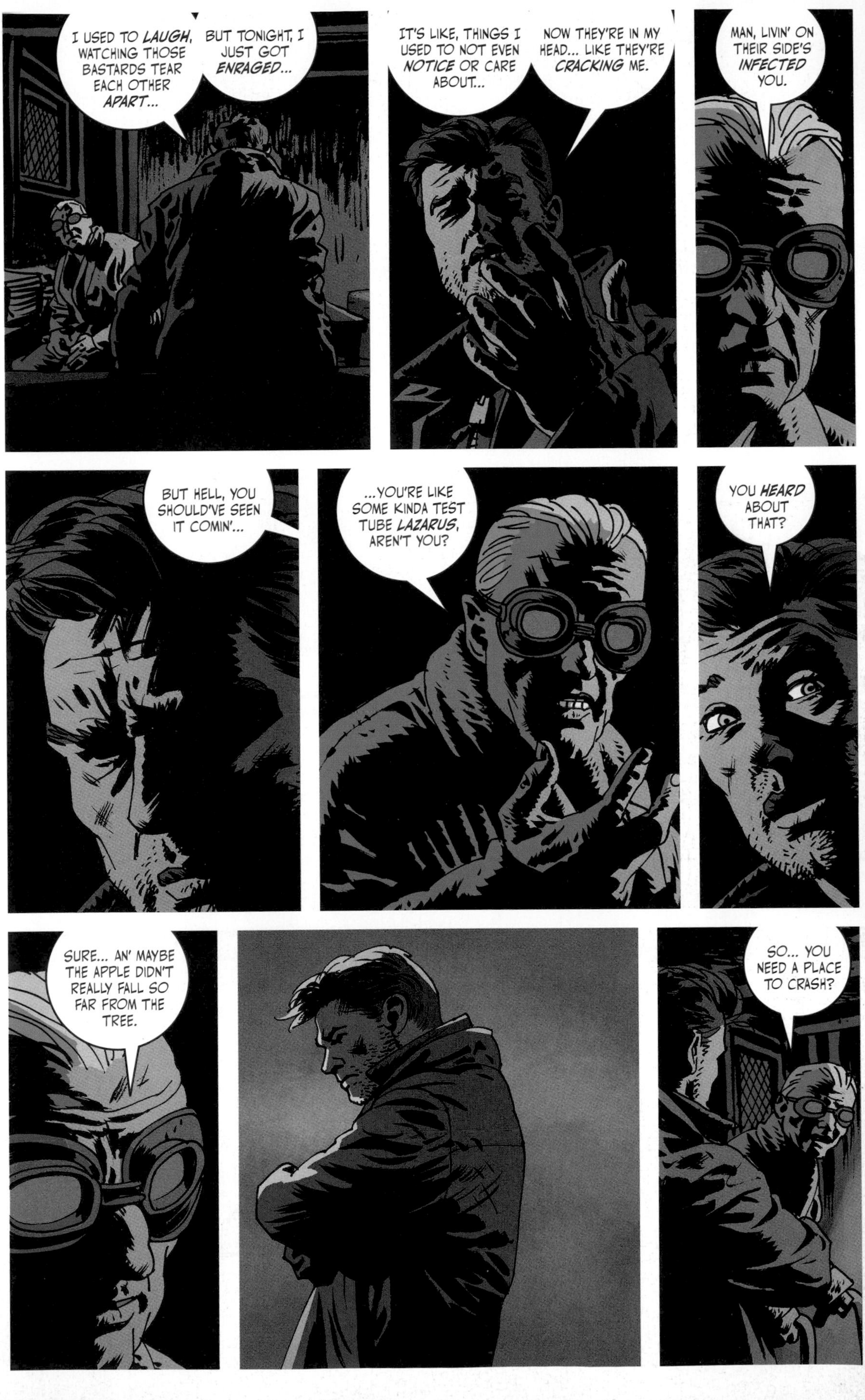
I USED TO LAUGH, WATCHING THOSE BASTARDS TEAR EACH OTHER APART...
BUT TONIGHT, I JUST GOT ENRAGED...
IT'S LIKE, THINGS I USED TO NOT EVEN NOTICE OR CARE ABOUT...
NOW THEY'RE IN MY HEAD... LIKE THEY'RE CRACKING ME.
MAN, LIVIN' ON THEIR SIDE'S INFECTED YOU.
BUT HELL, YOU SHOULD'VE SEEN IT COMIN'...
...YOU'RE LIKE SOME KINDA TEST TUBE LAZARUS, AREN'T YOU?
YOU HEARD ABOUT THAT?
SURE... AN' MAYBE THE APPLE DIDN'T REALLY FALL SO FAR FROM THE TREE.
SO... YOU NEED A PLACE TO CRASH?

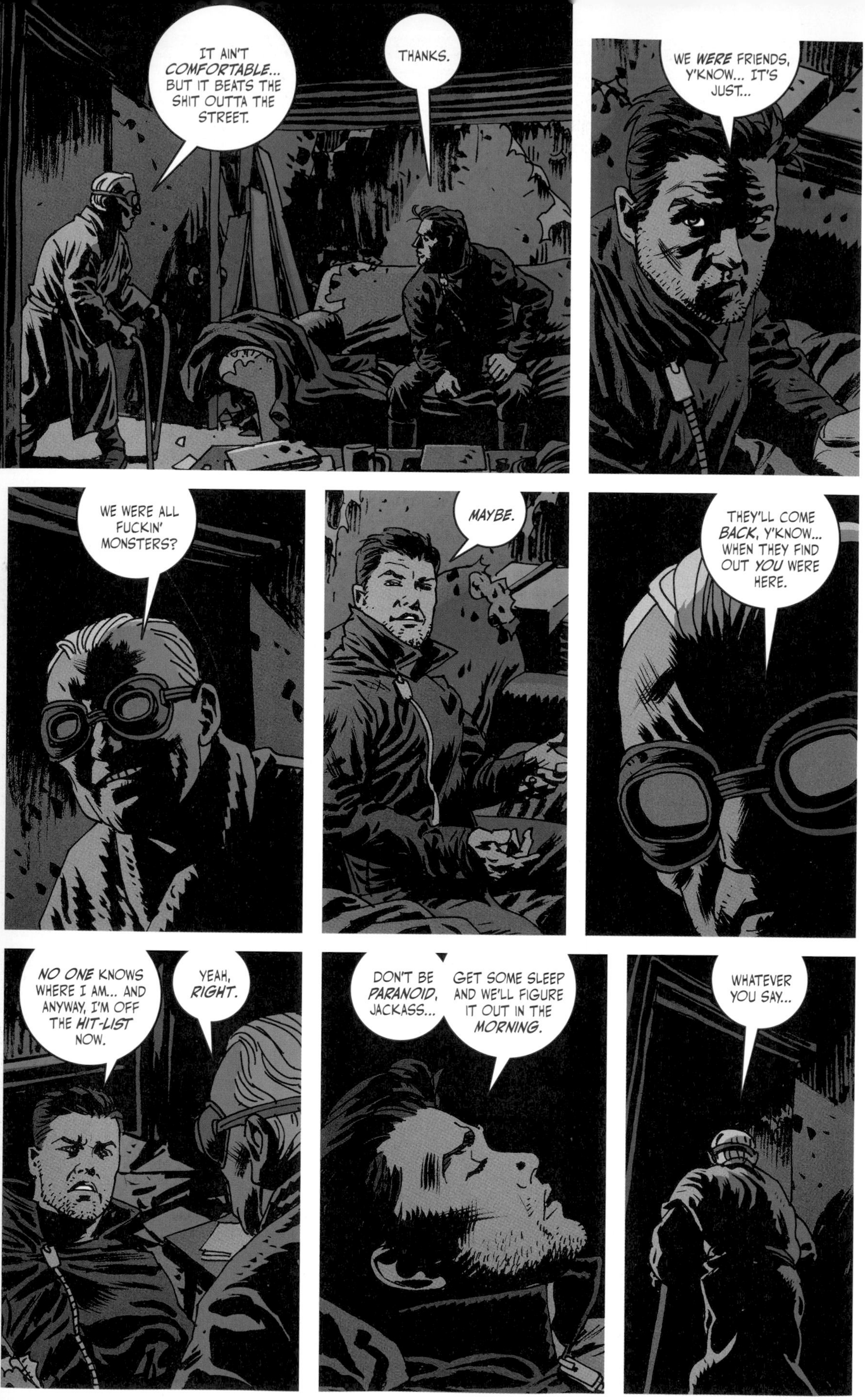
IT AIN'T COMFORTABLE... BUT IT BEATS THE SHIT OUTTA THE STREET.
THANKS.
WE WERE FRIENDS, Y'KNOW... IT'S JUST...
WE WERE ALL FUCKIN' MONSTERS?
MAYBE.
THEY'LL COME BACK, Y'KNOW... WHEN THEY FIND OUT YOU WERE HERE.
NO ONE KNOWS WHERE I AM... AND ANYWAY, I'M OFF THE HIT-LIST NOW.
YEAH, RIGHT.
DON'T BE PARANOID, JACKASS...
GET SOME SLEEP AND WE'LL FIGURE IT OUT IN THE MORNING.
WHATEVER YOU SAY...

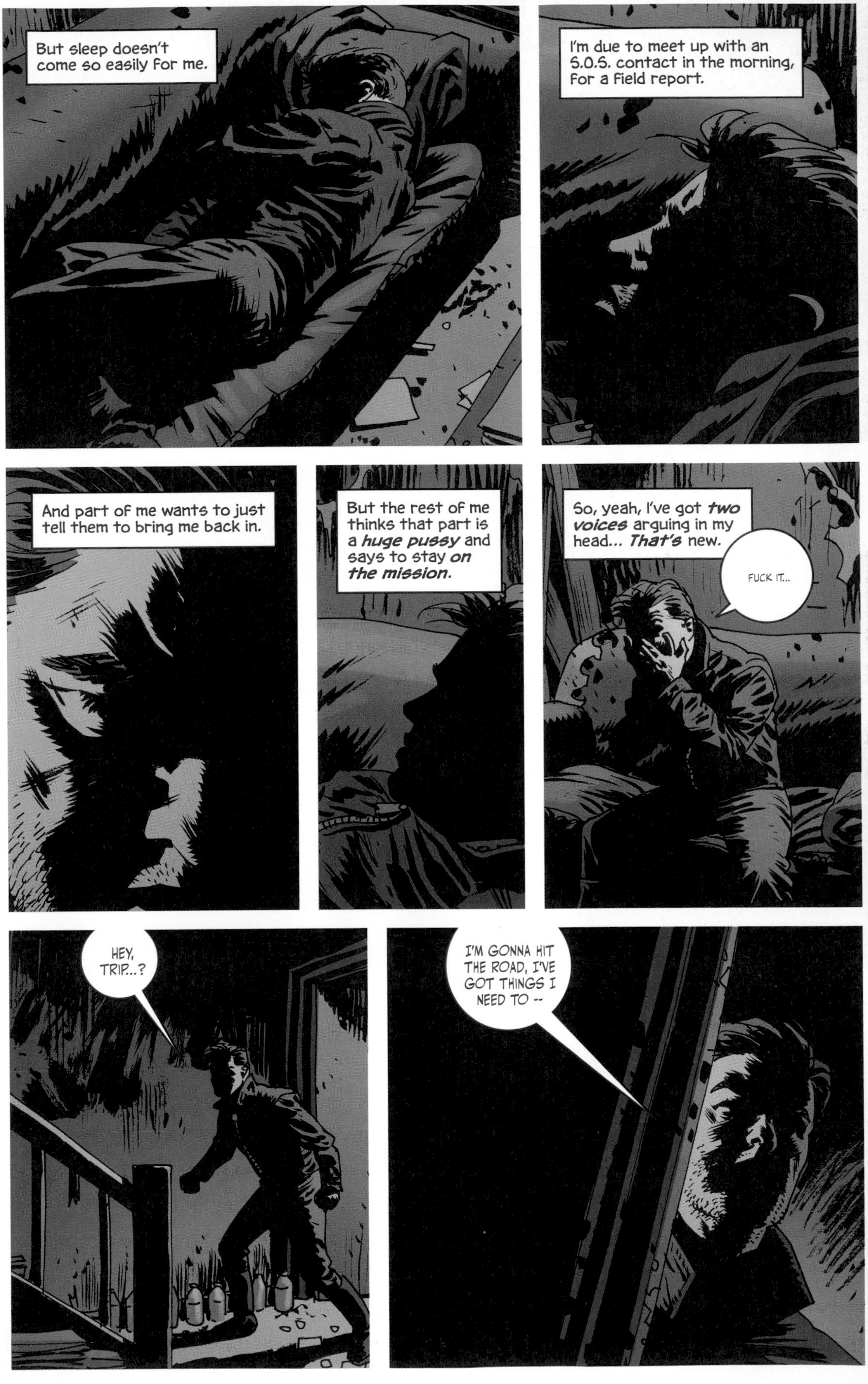
But sleep doesn't come so easily for me.
I'm due to meet up with an S.O.S. contact in the morning, for a field report.
And part of me wants to just tell them to bring me back in.
But the rest of me thinks that part is a *huge pussy* and says to stay *on the mission*.
So, yeah, I've got *two voices* arguing in my head... *That's* new.
FUCK IT...
HEY, TRIP...?
I'M GONNA HIT THE ROAD, I'VE GOT THINGS I NEED TO --

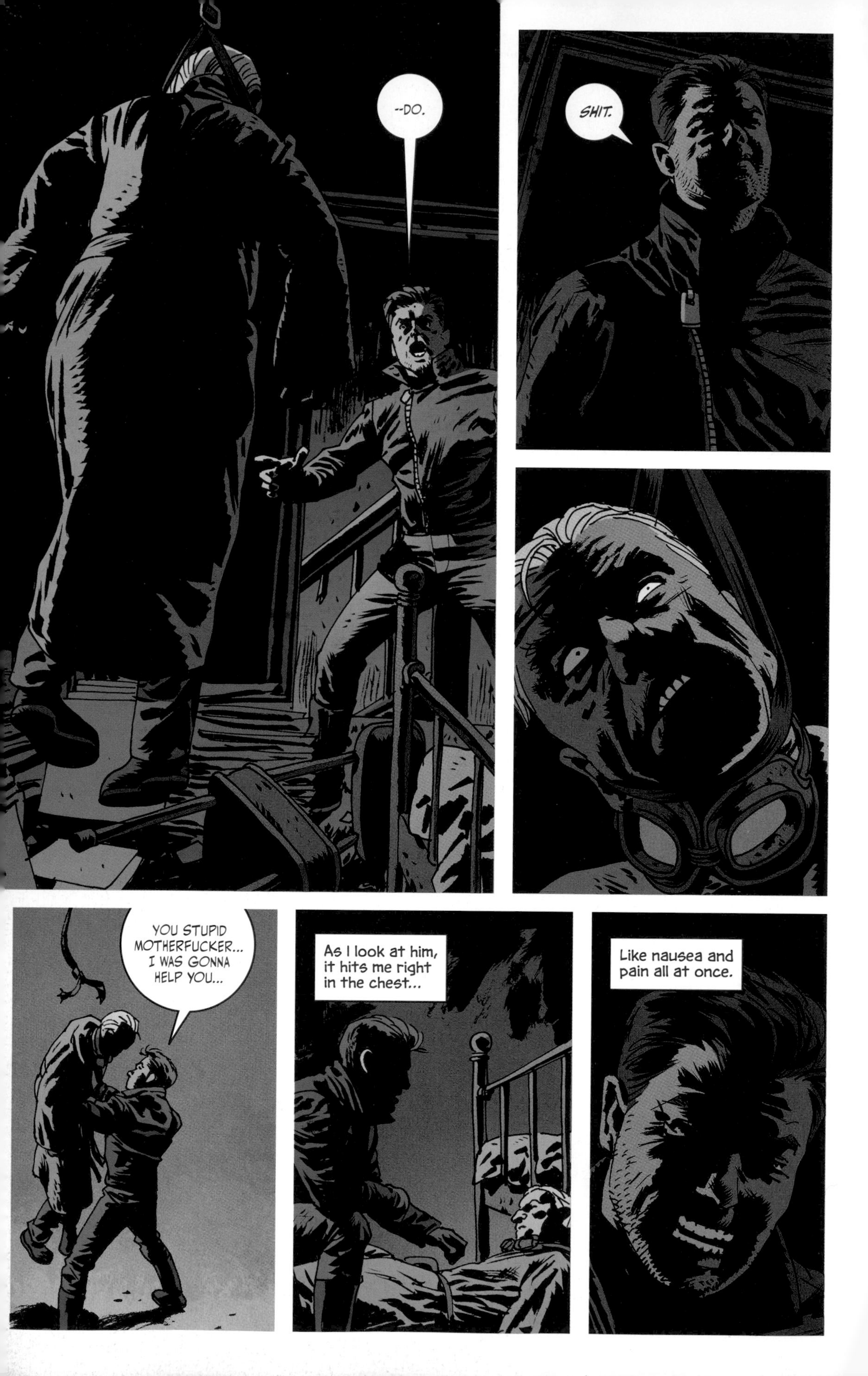
--DO.
SHIT.
YOU STUPID MOTHERFUCKER... I WAS GONNA HELP YOU...
As I look at him, it hits me right in the chest...
Like nausea and pain all at once.

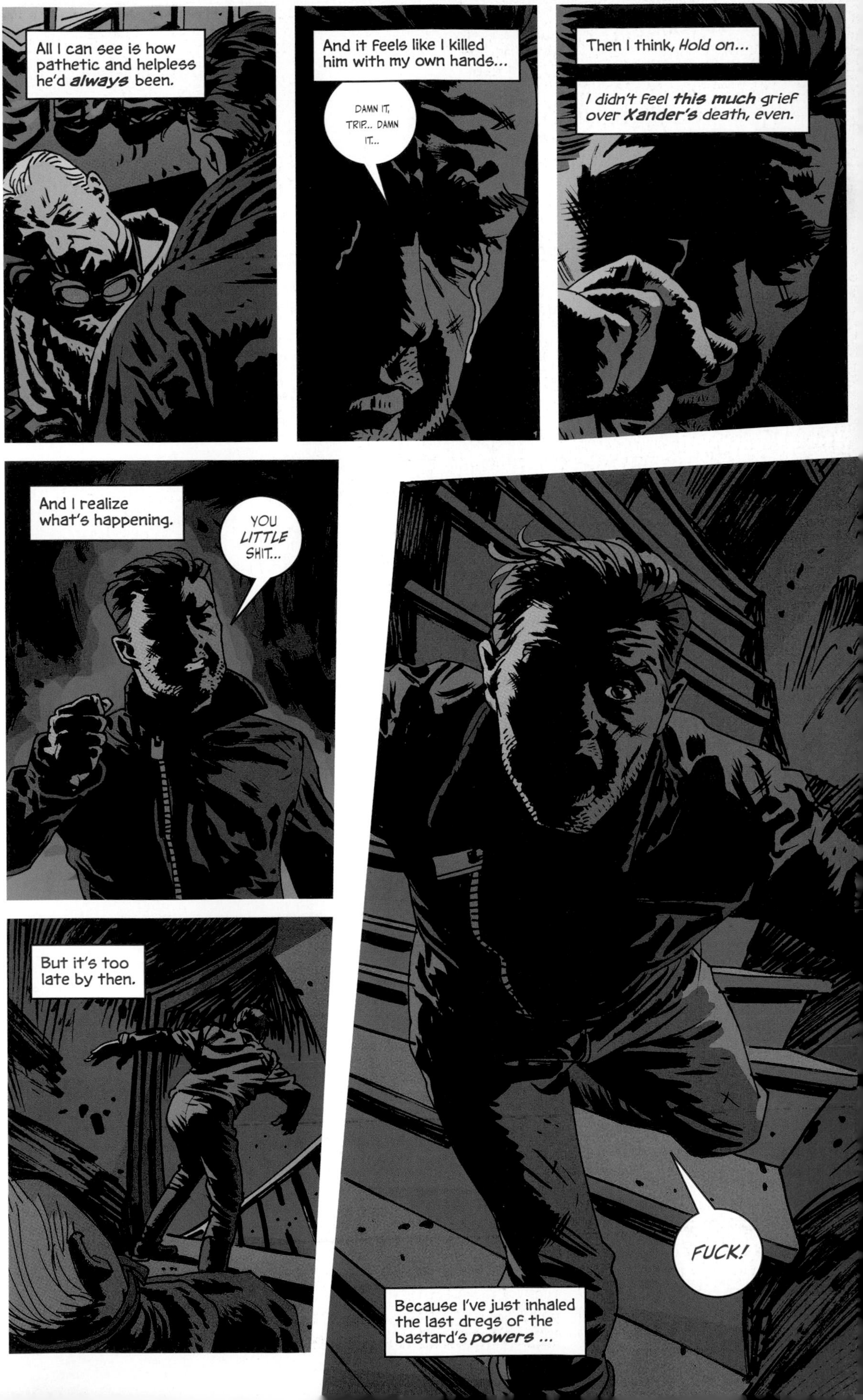
All I can see is how pathetic and helpless he'd ***always*** been.
And it feels like I killed him with my own hands...
DAMN IT, TRIP... DAMN IT...
Then I think, *Hold on...*
I didn't feel ***this much*** *grief over* ***Xander's*** *death, even.*
And I realize what's happening.
YOU *LITTLE* SHIT...
But it's too late by then.
FUCK!
Because I've just inhaled the last dregs of the bastard's ***powers*** ...

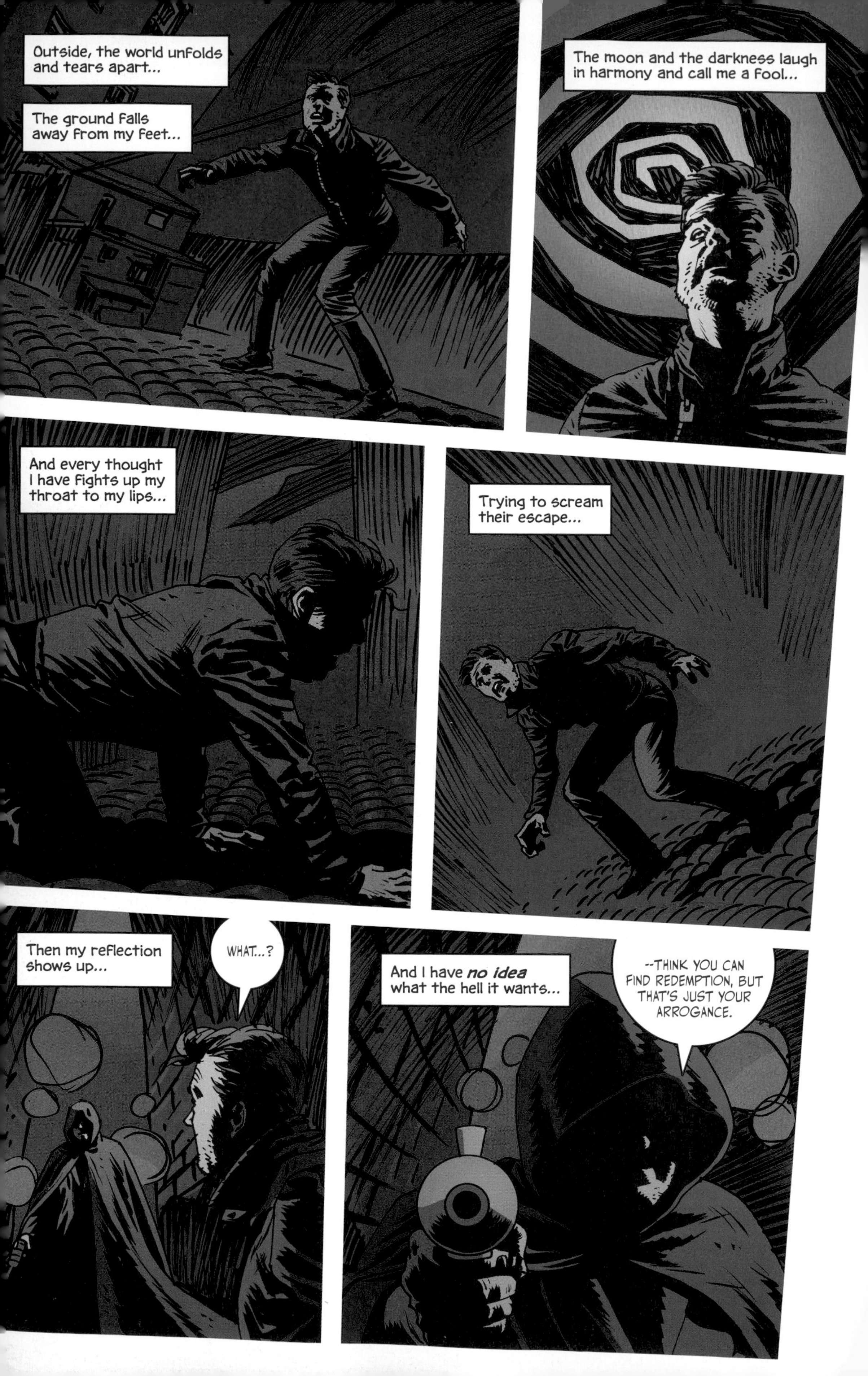
Outside, the world unfolds and tears apart...
The ground falls away from my feet...
The moon and the darkness laugh in harmony and call me a fool...
And every thought I have fights up my throat to my lips...
Trying to scream their escape...
Then my reflection shows up...
WHAT...?
And I have **no idea** what the hell it wants...
--THINK YOU CAN FIND REDEMPTION, BUT THAT'S JUST YOUR ARROGANCE.

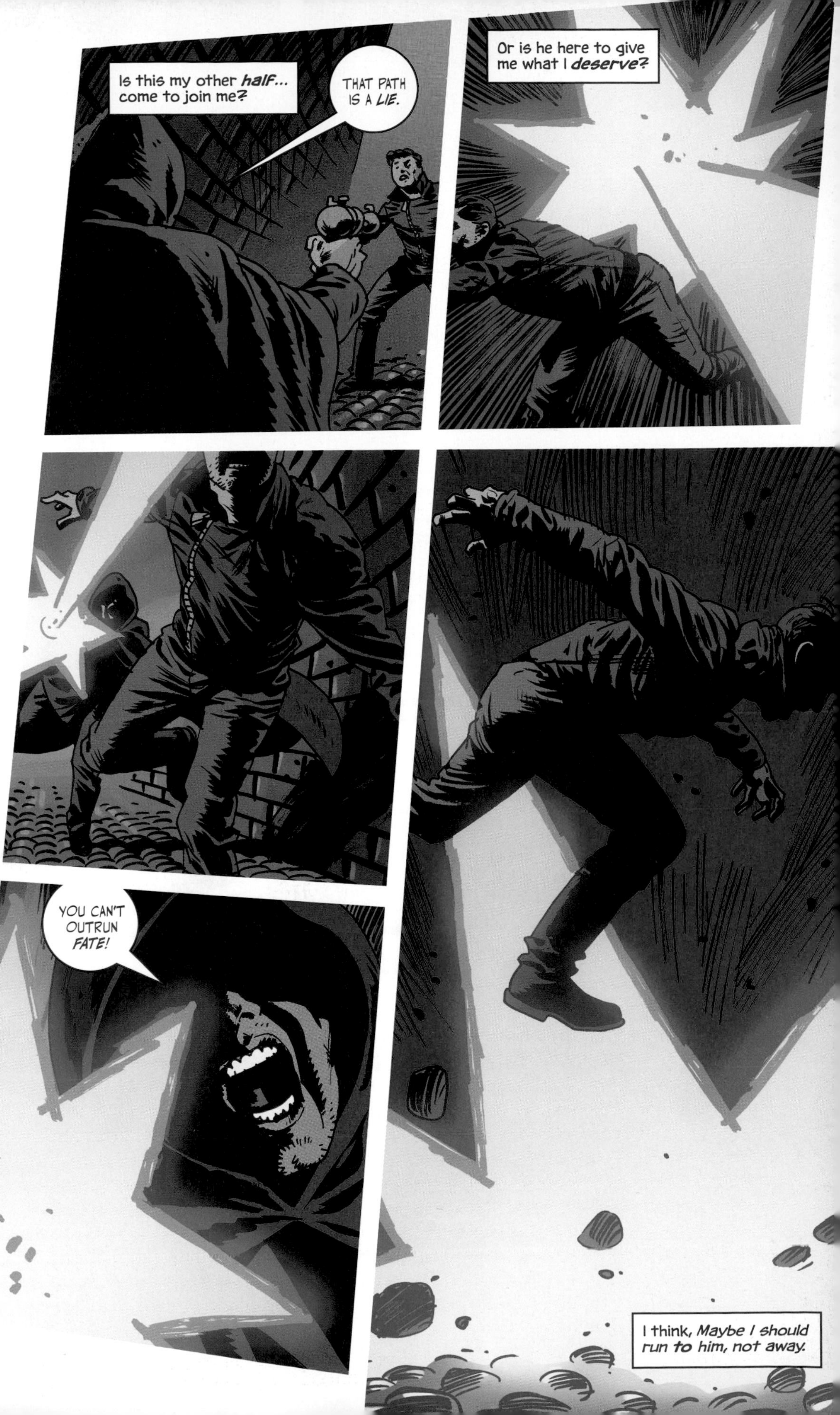
Is this my other *half*... come to join me?
THAT PATH IS A *LIE*.
Or is he here to give me what I *deserve*?
YOU CAN'T OUTRUN *FATE*!
I think, *Maybe I should run **to** him, not away.*

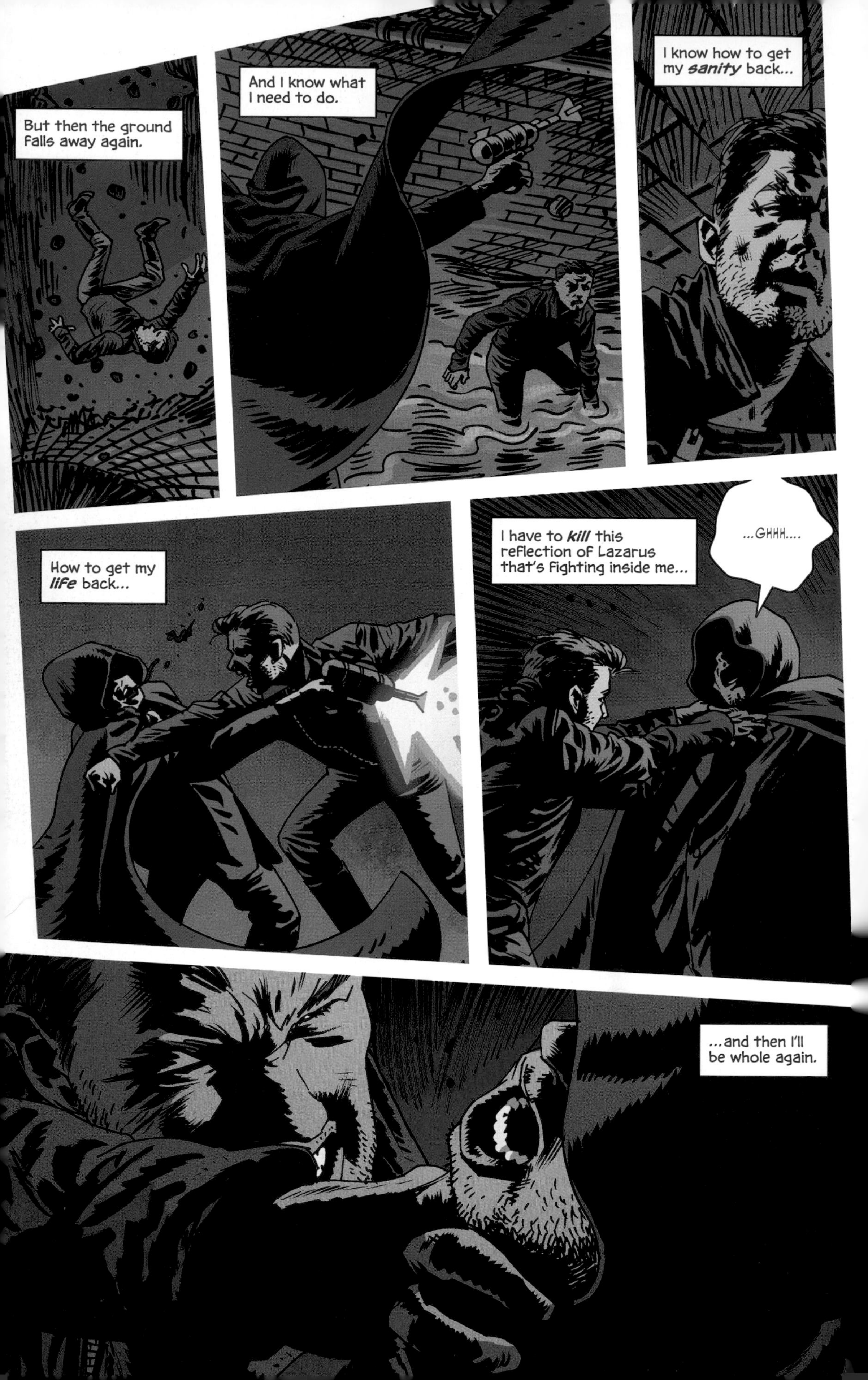
But then the ground falls away again.
And I know what I need to do.
I know how to get my *sanity* back...
How to get my *life* back...
I have to *kill* this reflection of Lazarus that's fighting inside me...
...GHHH....
...and then I'll be whole again.

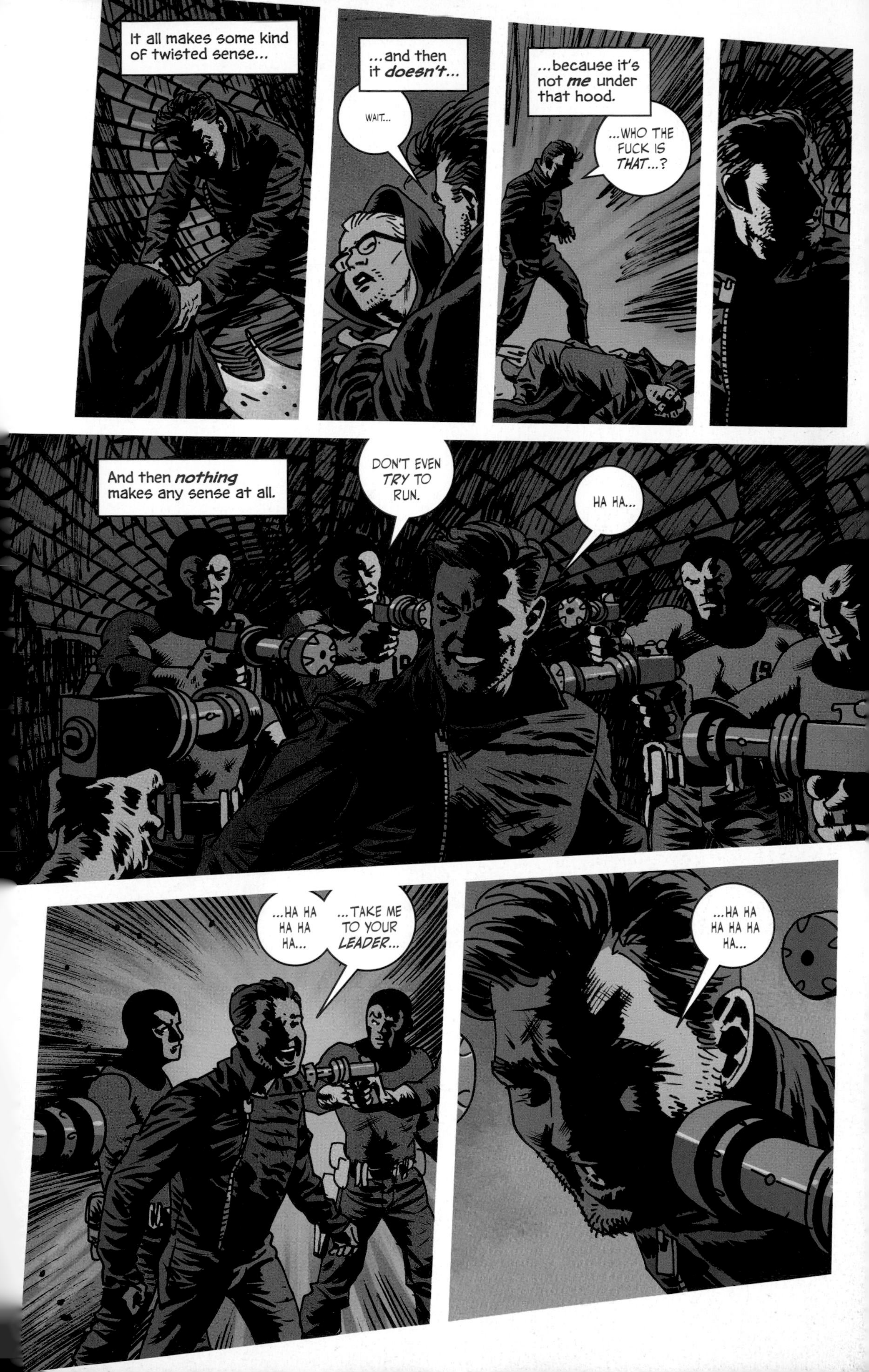
It all makes some kind of twisted sense...
...and then it *doesn't*...
WAIT...
...because it's not *me* under that hood.
...WHO THE FUCK IS *THAT*...?
And then *nothing* makes any sense at all.
DON'T EVEN *TRY* TO RUN.
HA HA...
...HA HA HA HA HA...
...TAKE ME TO YOUR *LEADER*...
...HA HA HA HA HA HA...

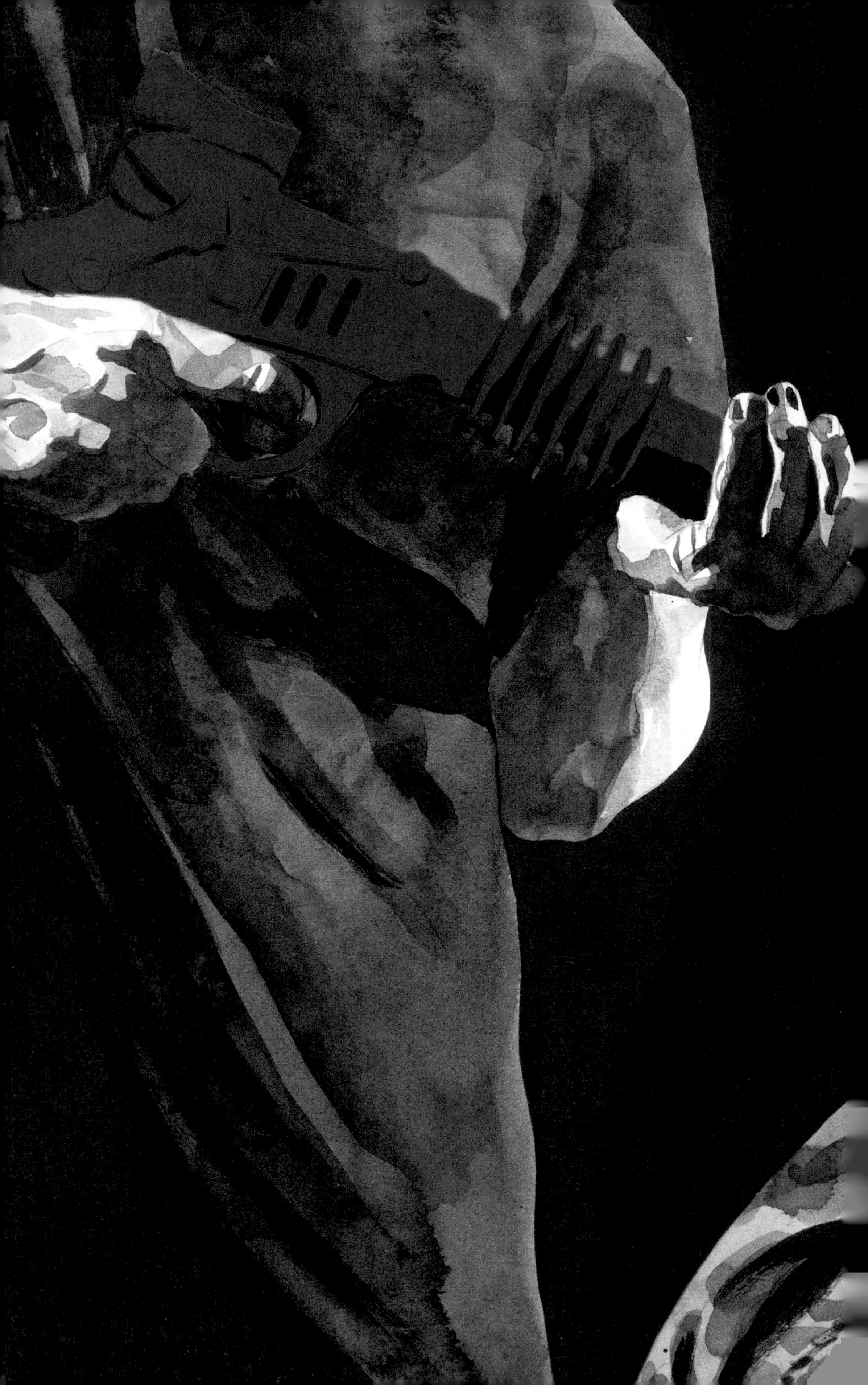

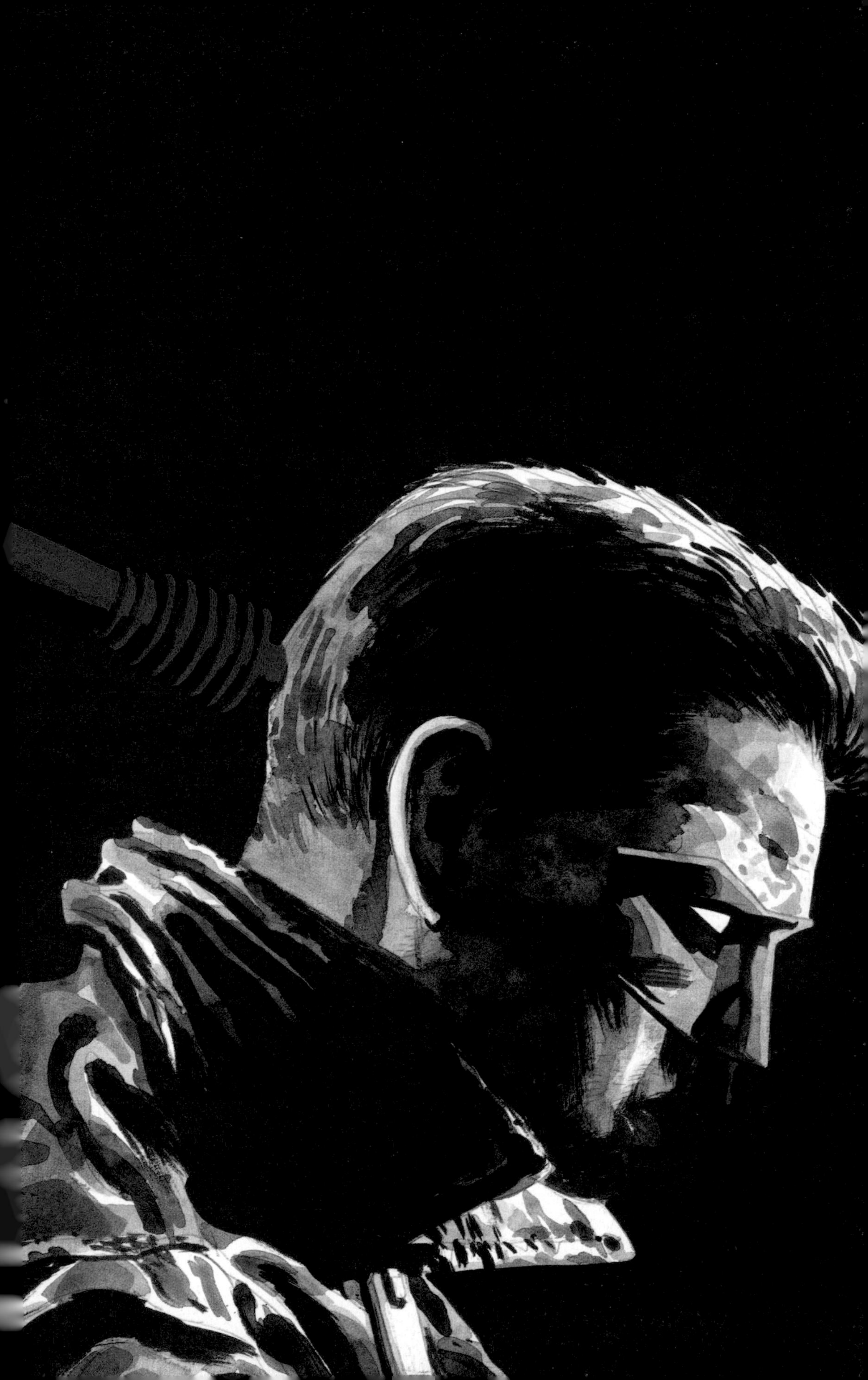

Chapter Five

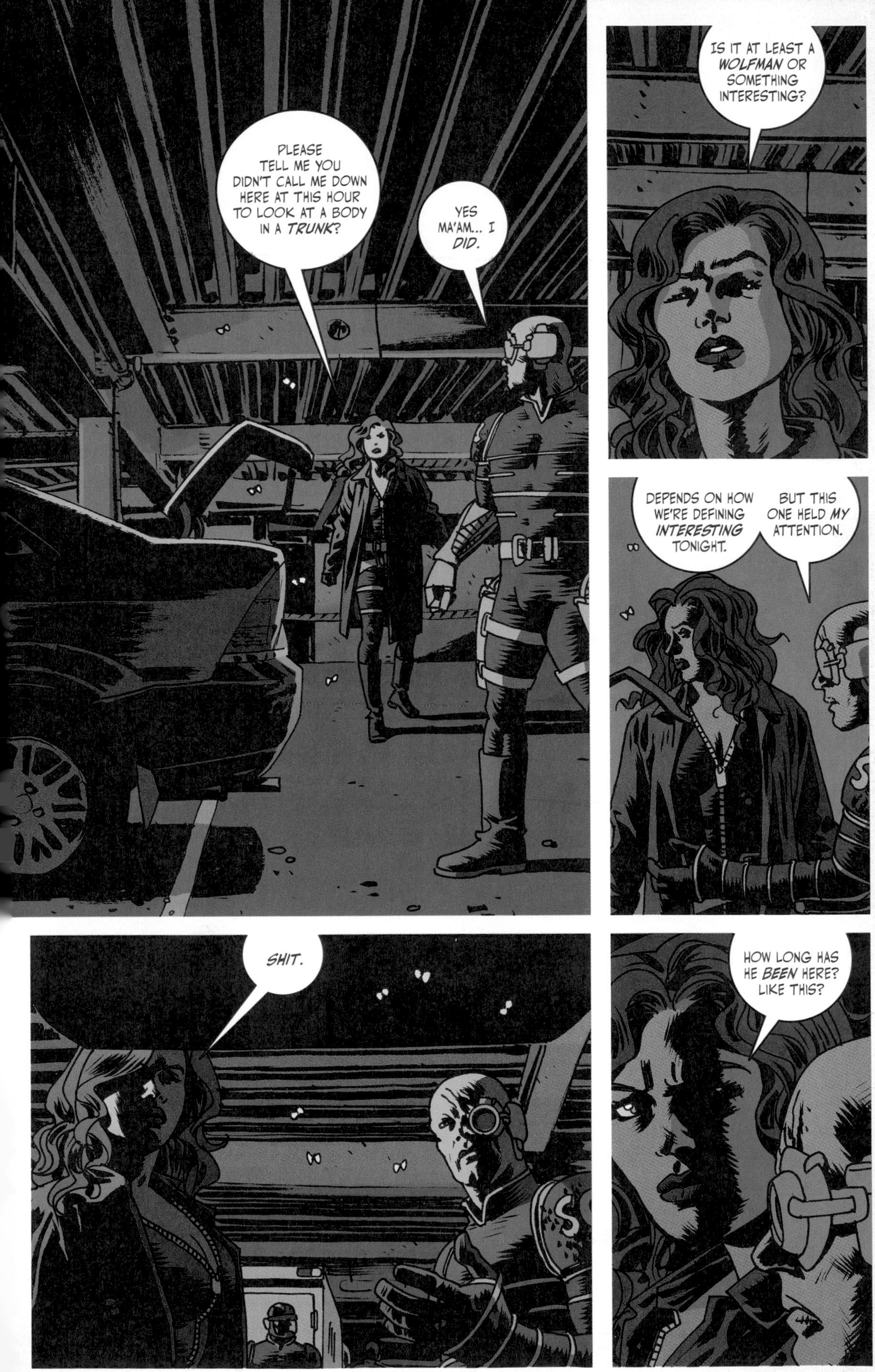
PLEASE TELL ME YOU DIDN'T CALL ME DOWN HERE AT THIS HOUR TO LOOK AT A BODY IN A *TRUNK*?
YES MA'AM... I *DID*.
IS IT AT LEAST A *WOLFMAN* OR SOMETHING INTERESTING?
DEPENDS ON HOW WE'RE DEFINING *INTERESTING* TONIGHT.
BUT THIS ONE HELD *MY* ATTENTION.
SHIT.
HOW LONG HAS HE *BEEN* HERE? LIKE THIS?

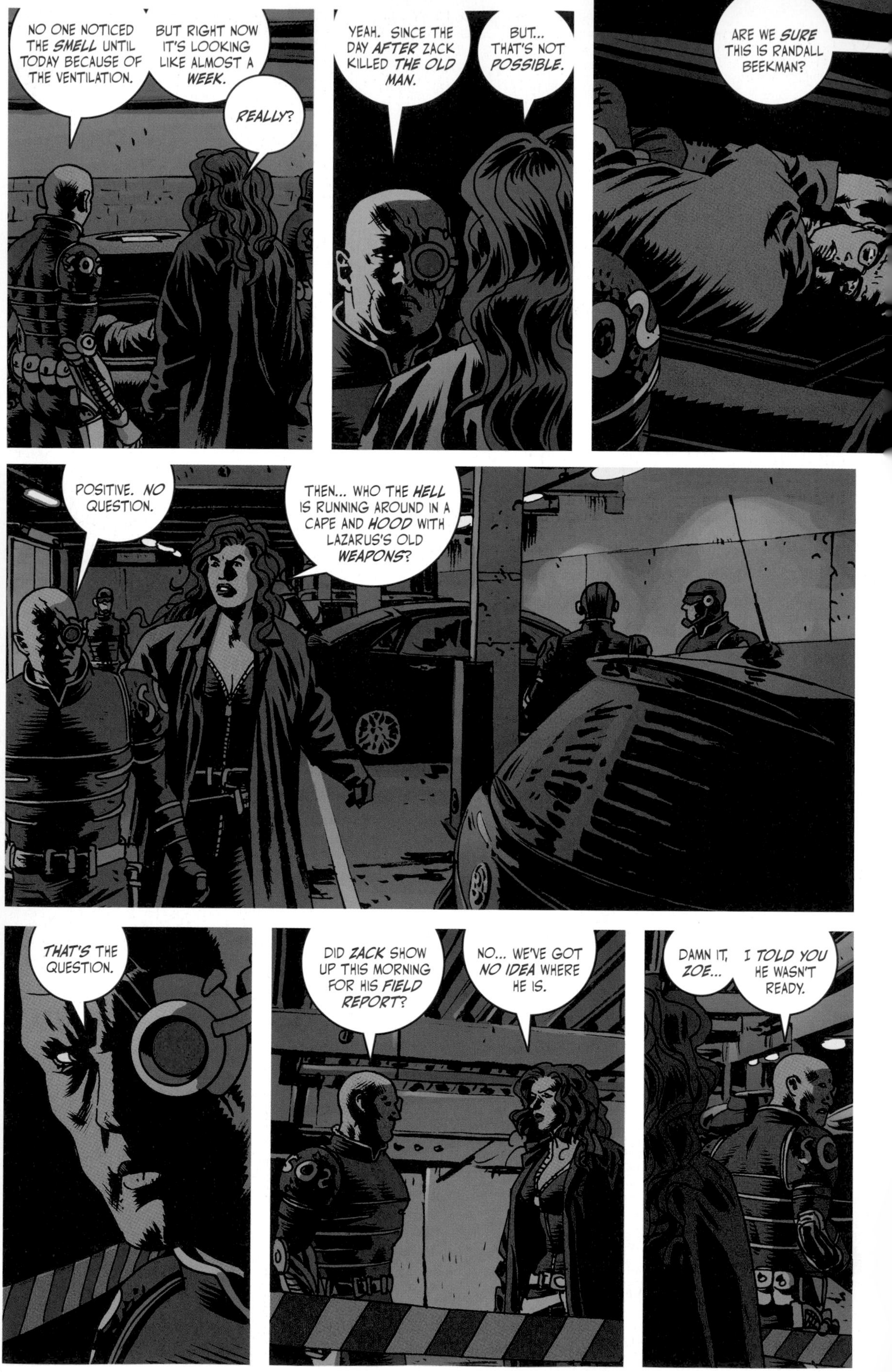
NO ONE NOTICED THE SMELL UNTIL TODAY BECAUSE OF THE VENTILATION.
BUT RIGHT NOW IT'S LOOKING LIKE ALMOST A WEEK.
REALLY?
YEAH. SINCE THE DAY AFTER ZACK KILLED THE OLD MAN.
BUT... THAT'S NOT POSSIBLE.
ARE WE SURE THIS IS RANDALL BEEKMAN?
POSITIVE. NO QUESTION.
THEN... WHO THE HELL IS RUNNING AROUND IN A CAPE AND HOOD WITH LAZARUS'S OLD WEAPONS?
THAT'S THE QUESTION.
DID ZACK SHOW UP THIS MORNING FOR HIS FIELD REPORT?
NO... WE'VE GOT NO IDEA WHERE HE IS.
DAMN IT, ZOE...
I TOLD YOU HE WASN'T READY.

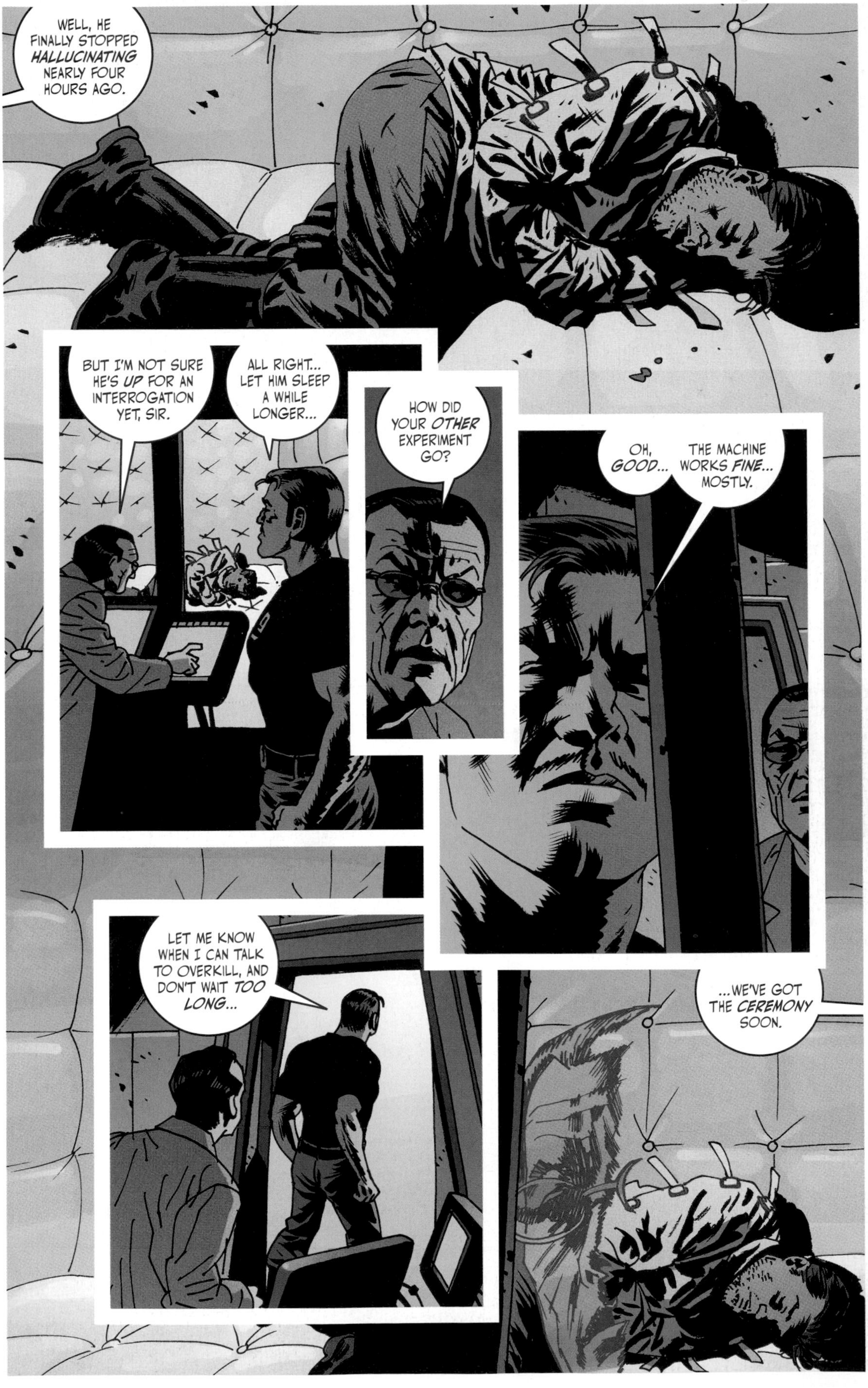
WELL, HE FINALLY STOPPED *HALLUCINATING* NEARLY FOUR HOURS AGO.
BUT I'M NOT SURE HE'S *UP* FOR AN INTERROGATION YET, SIR.
ALL RIGHT... LET HIM SLEEP A WHILE LONGER...
HOW DID YOUR *OTHER* EXPERIMENT GO?
OH, *GOOD*...
THE MACHINE WORKS *FINE*... MOSTLY.
LET ME KNOW WHEN I CAN TALK TO OVERKILL, AND DON'T WAIT *TOO LONG*...
...WE'VE GOT THE *CEREMONY* SOON.

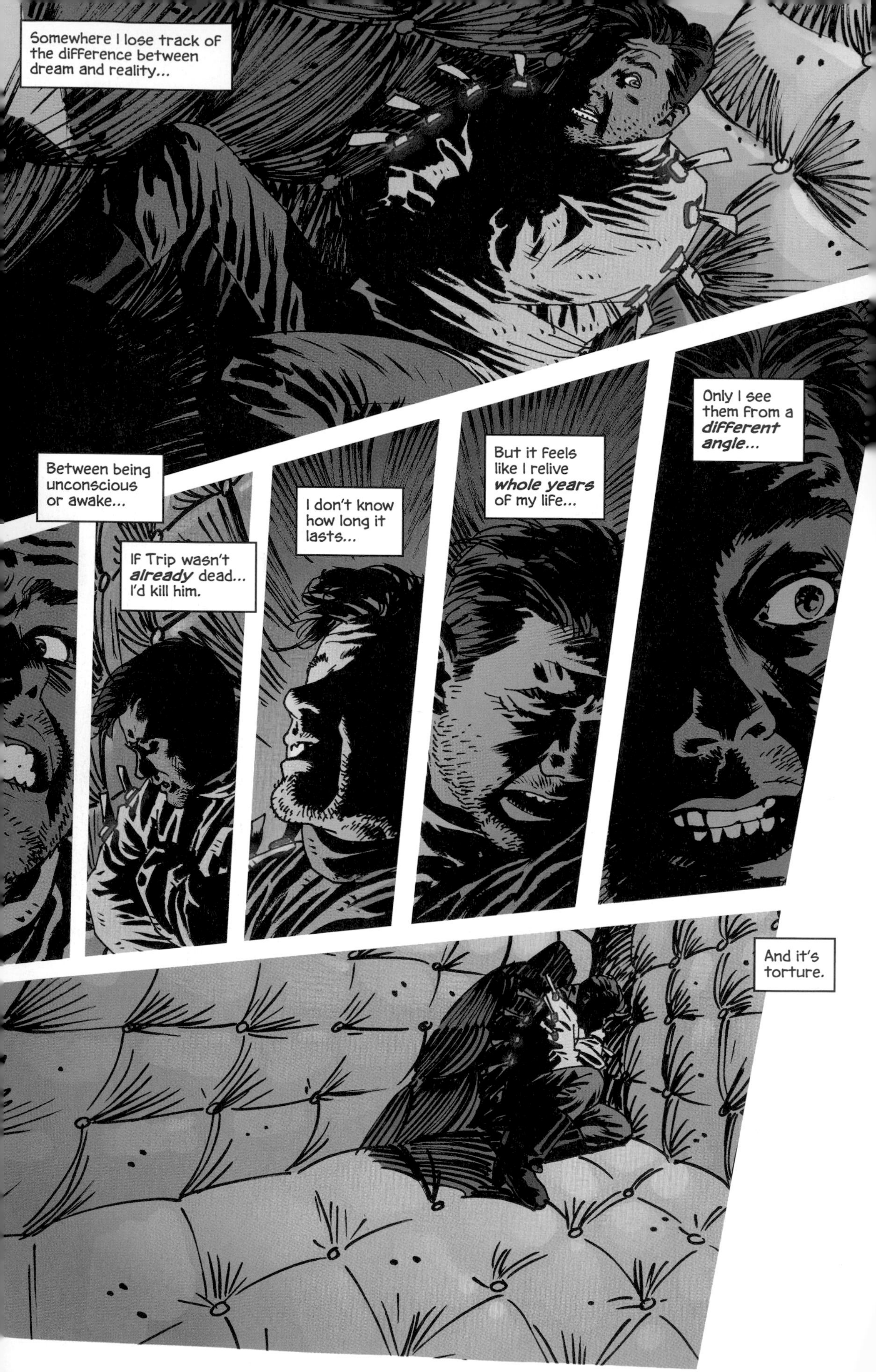
Somewhere I lose track of the difference between dream and reality...
Between being unconscious or awake...
If Trip wasn't *already* dead... I'd kill him.
I don't know how long it lasts...
But it feels like I relive *whole years* of my life...
Only I see them from a *different angle*...
And it's torture.

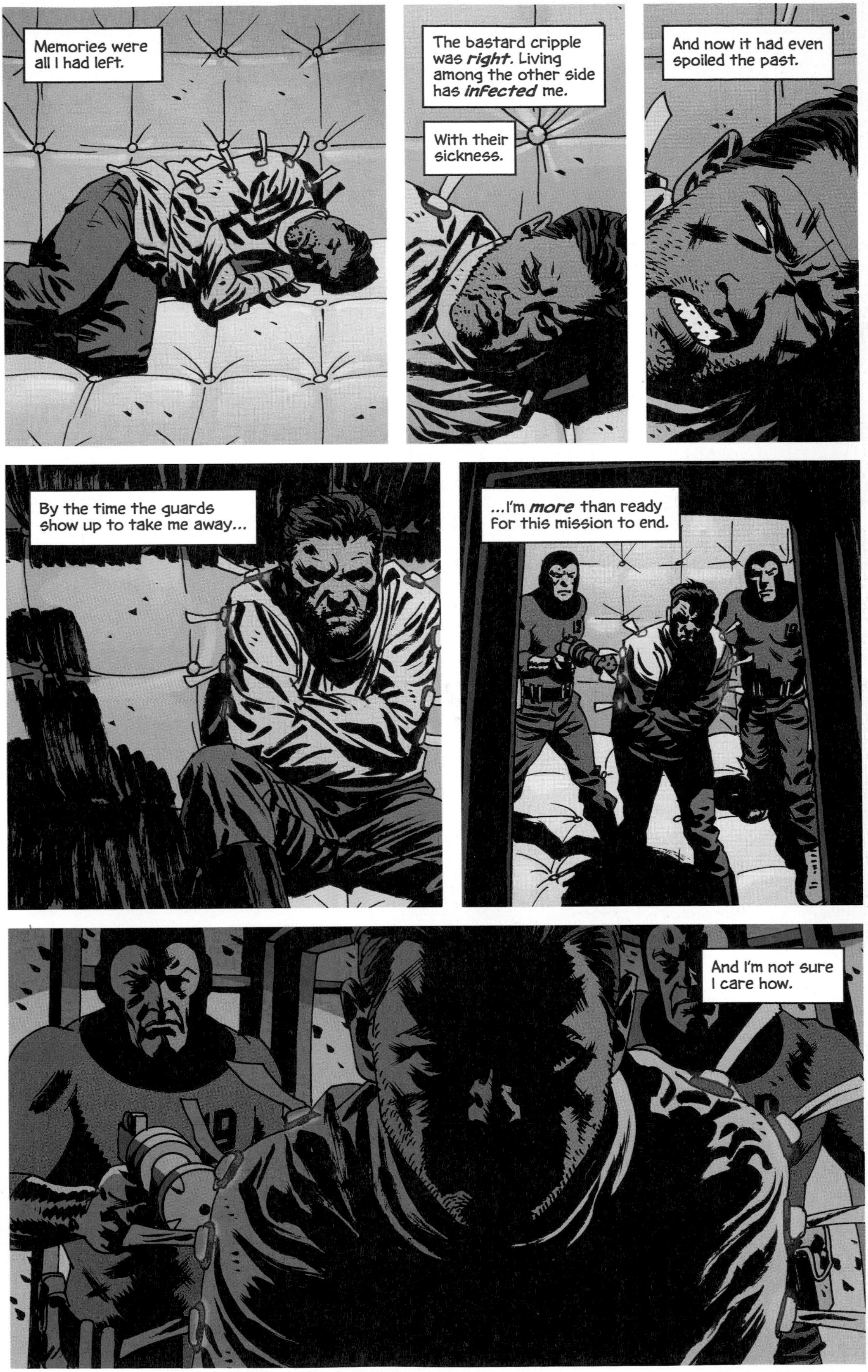
Memories were all I had left.
The bastard cripple was *right*. Living among the other side has *infected* me.
With their sickness.
And now it had even spoiled the past.
By the time the guards show up to take me away...
...I'm *more* than ready for this mission to end.
And I'm not sure I care how.

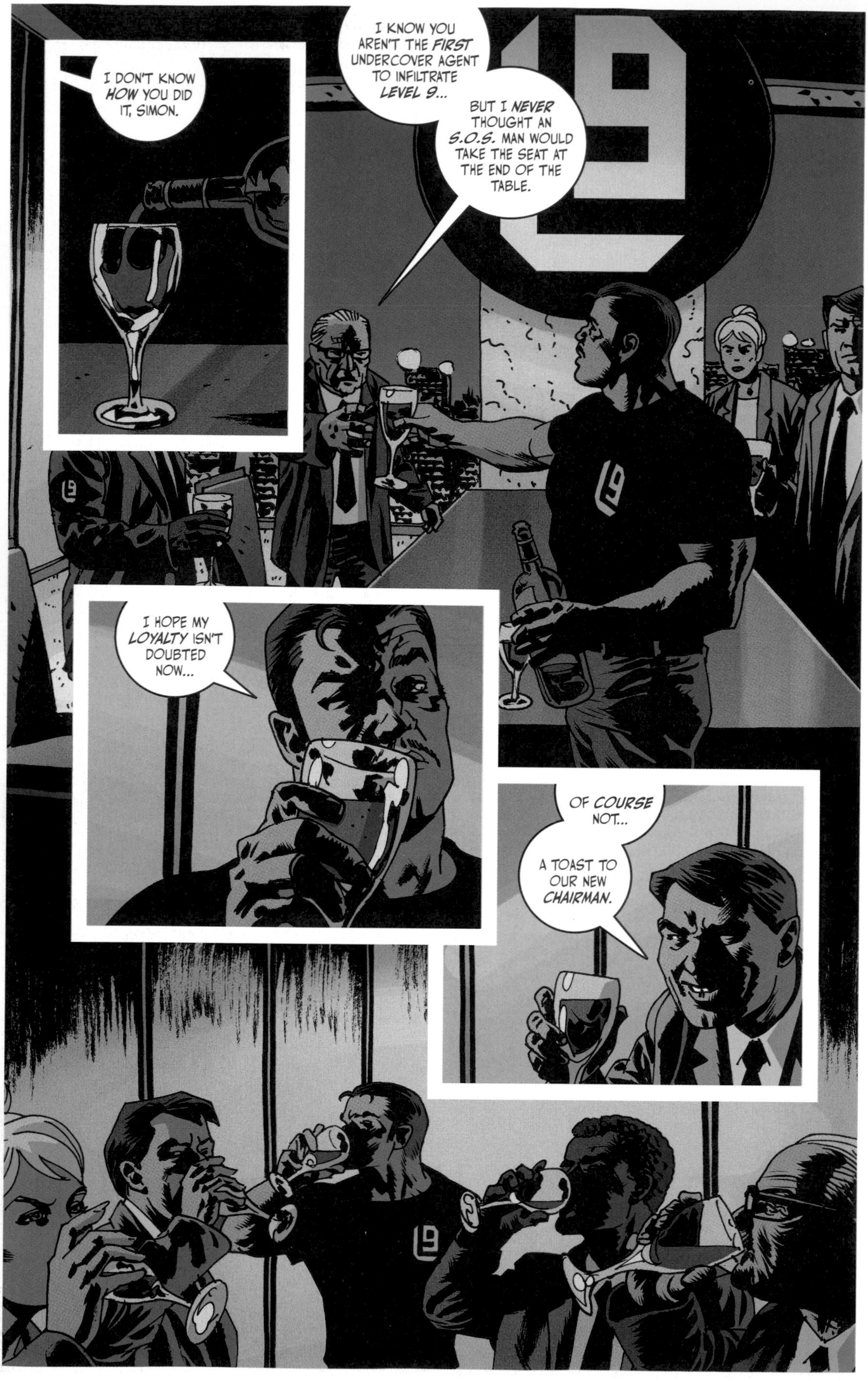
I DON'T KNOW HOW YOU DID IT, SIMON.
I KNOW YOU AREN'T THE FIRST UNDERCOVER AGENT TO INFILTRATE LEVEL 9...
BUT I NEVER THOUGHT AN S.O.S. MAN WOULD TAKE THE SEAT AT THE END OF THE TABLE.
I HOPE MY LOYALTY ISN'T DOUBTED NOW...
OF COURSE NOT...
A TOAST TO OUR NEW CHAIRMAN.

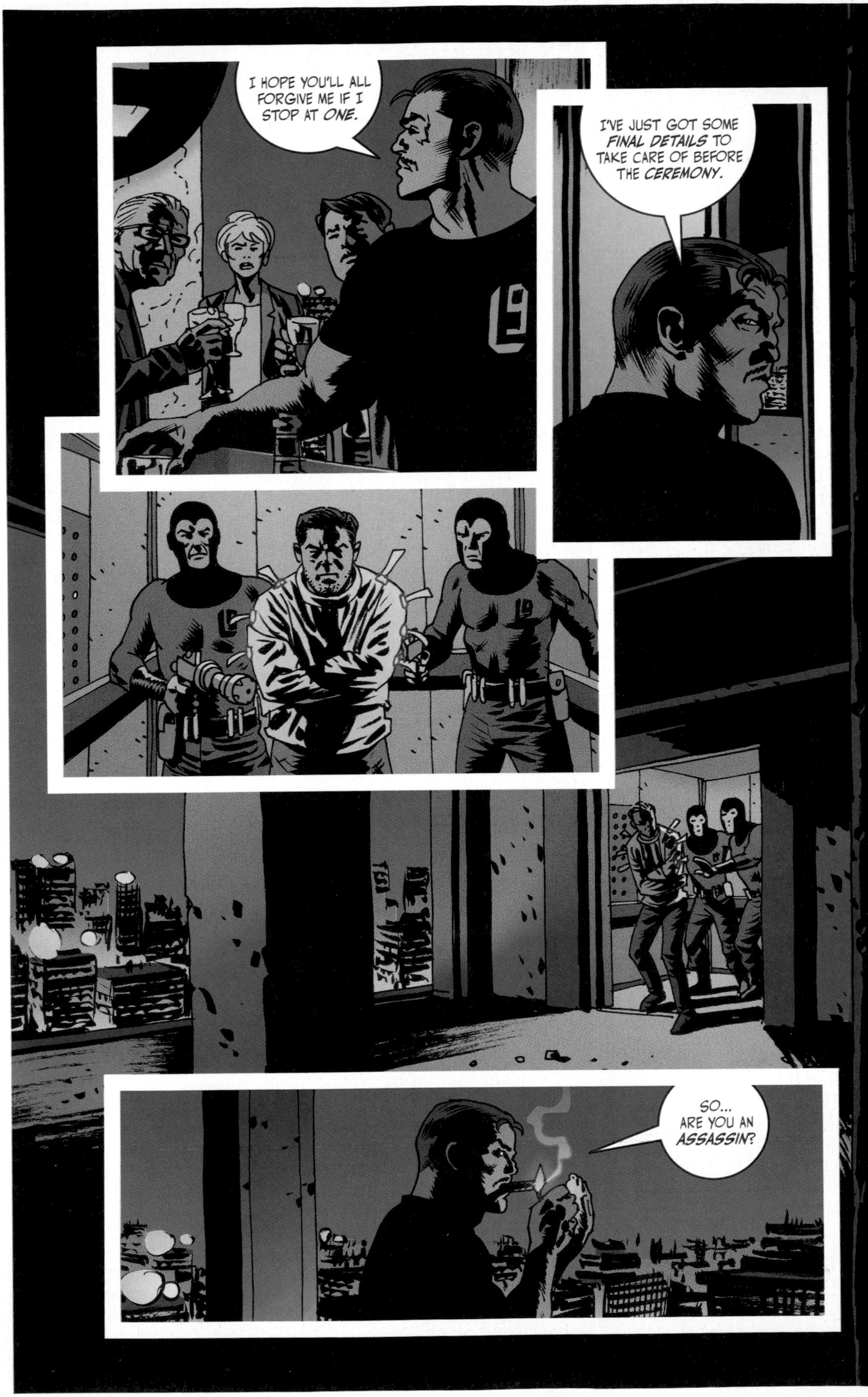
I HOPE YOU'LL ALL FORGIVE ME IF I STOP AT ONE.
I'VE JUST GOT SOME FINAL DETAILS TO TAKE CARE OF BEFORE THE CEREMONY.
SO... ARE YOU AN ASSASSIN?

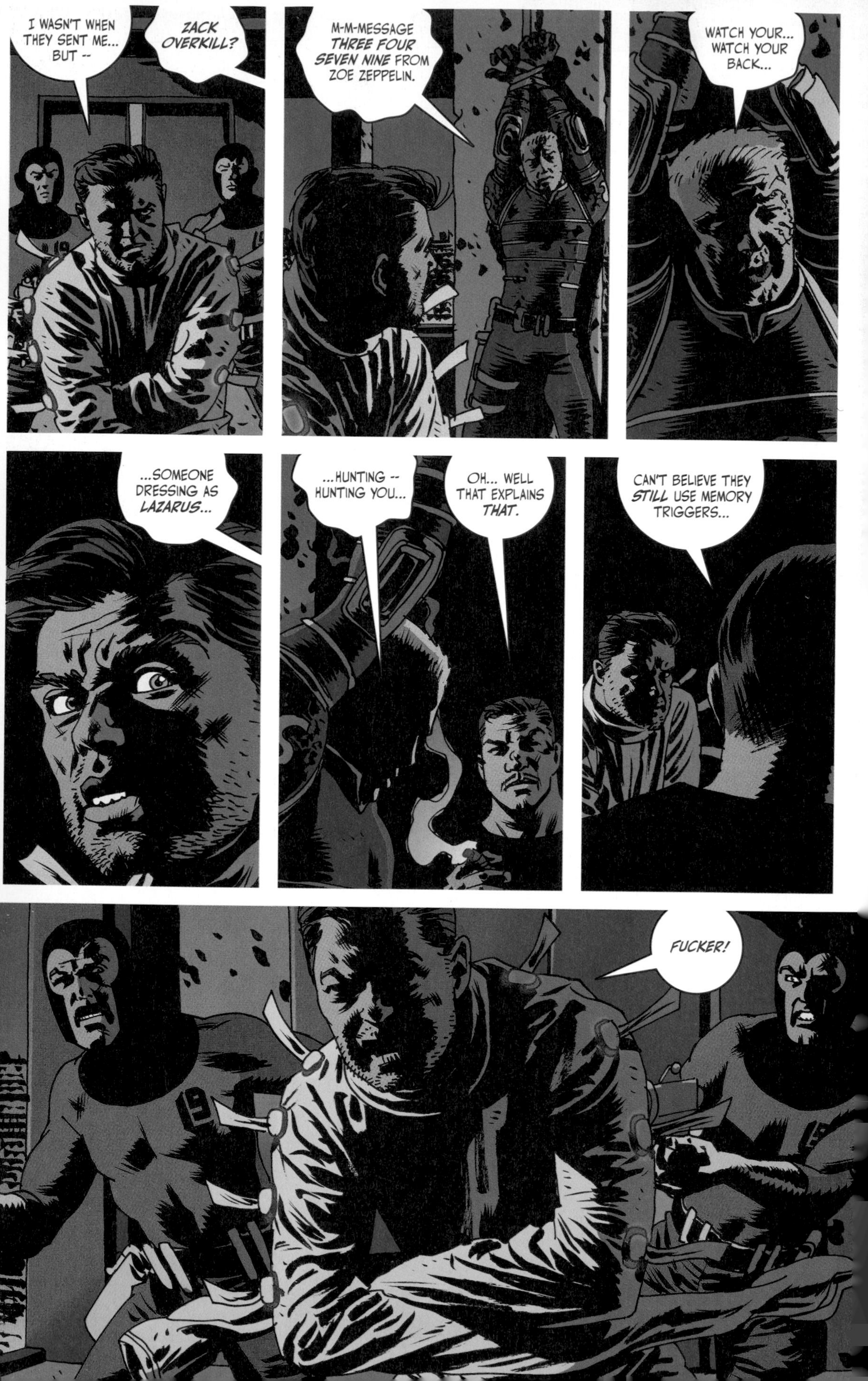
I WASN'T WHEN THEY SENT ME... BUT --
ZACK OVERKILL?
M-M-MESSAGE THREE FOUR SEVEN NINE FROM ZOE ZEPPELIN.
WATCH YOUR... WATCH YOUR BACK...
...SOMEONE DRESSING AS LAZARUS...
...HUNTING -- HUNTING YOU...
OH... WELL THAT EXPLAINS THAT.
CAN'T BELIEVE THEY STILL USE MEMORY TRIGGERS...
FUCKER!

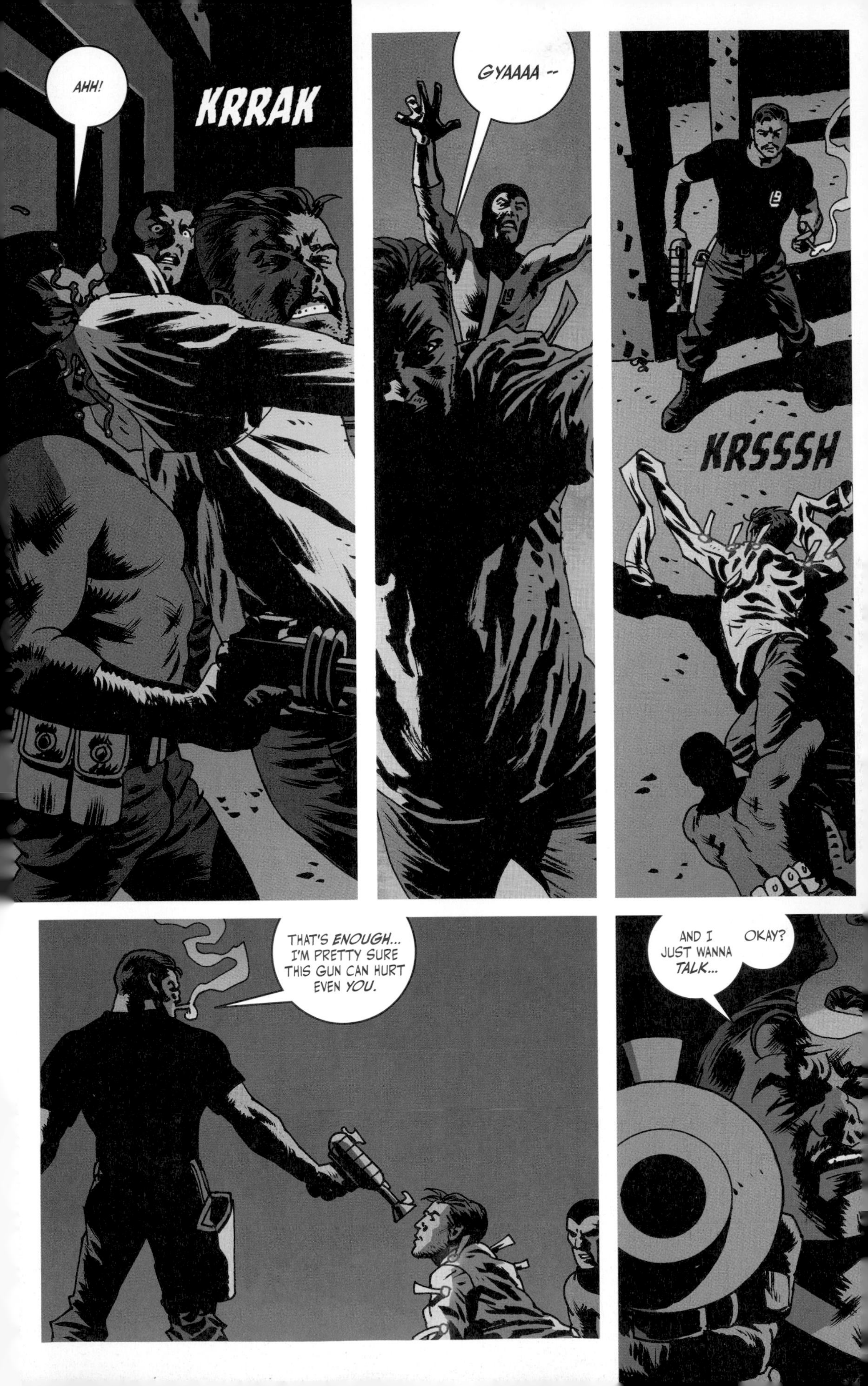
AHH!
KRRAK
GYAAAA --
KRSSSH
THAT'S ENOUGH... I'M PRETTY SURE THIS GUN CAN HURT EVEN YOU.
AND I JUST WANNA TALK...
OKAY?

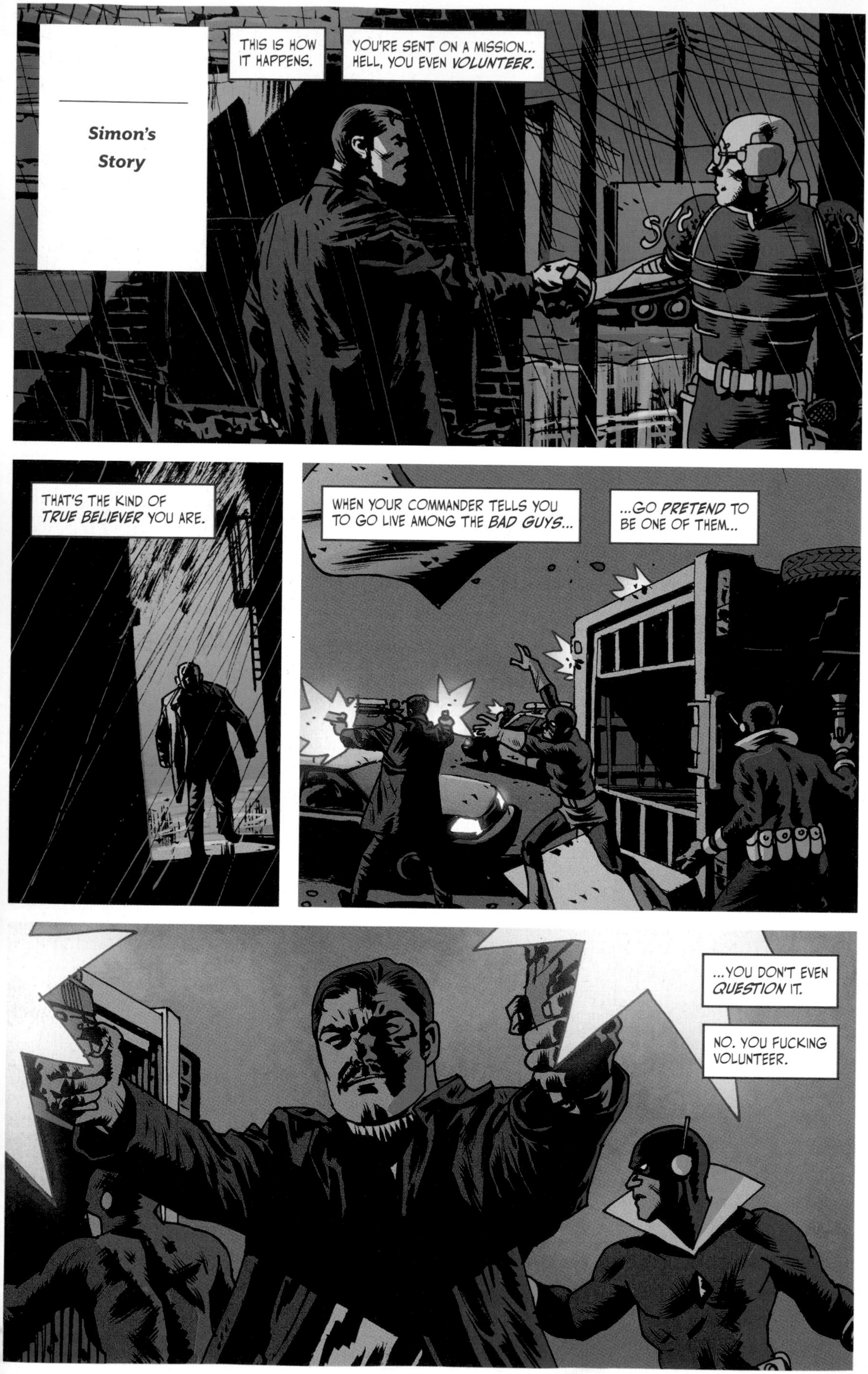
Simon's Story
THIS IS HOW IT HAPPENS.
YOU'RE SENT ON A MISSION... HELL, YOU EVEN *VOLUNTEER*.
THAT'S THE KIND OF *TRUE BELIEVER* YOU ARE.
WHEN YOUR COMMANDER TELLS YOU TO GO LIVE AMONG THE *BAD GUYS*...
...GO *PRETEND* TO BE ONE OF THEM...
...YOU DON'T EVEN *QUESTION* IT.
NO. YOU FUCKING VOLUNTEER.

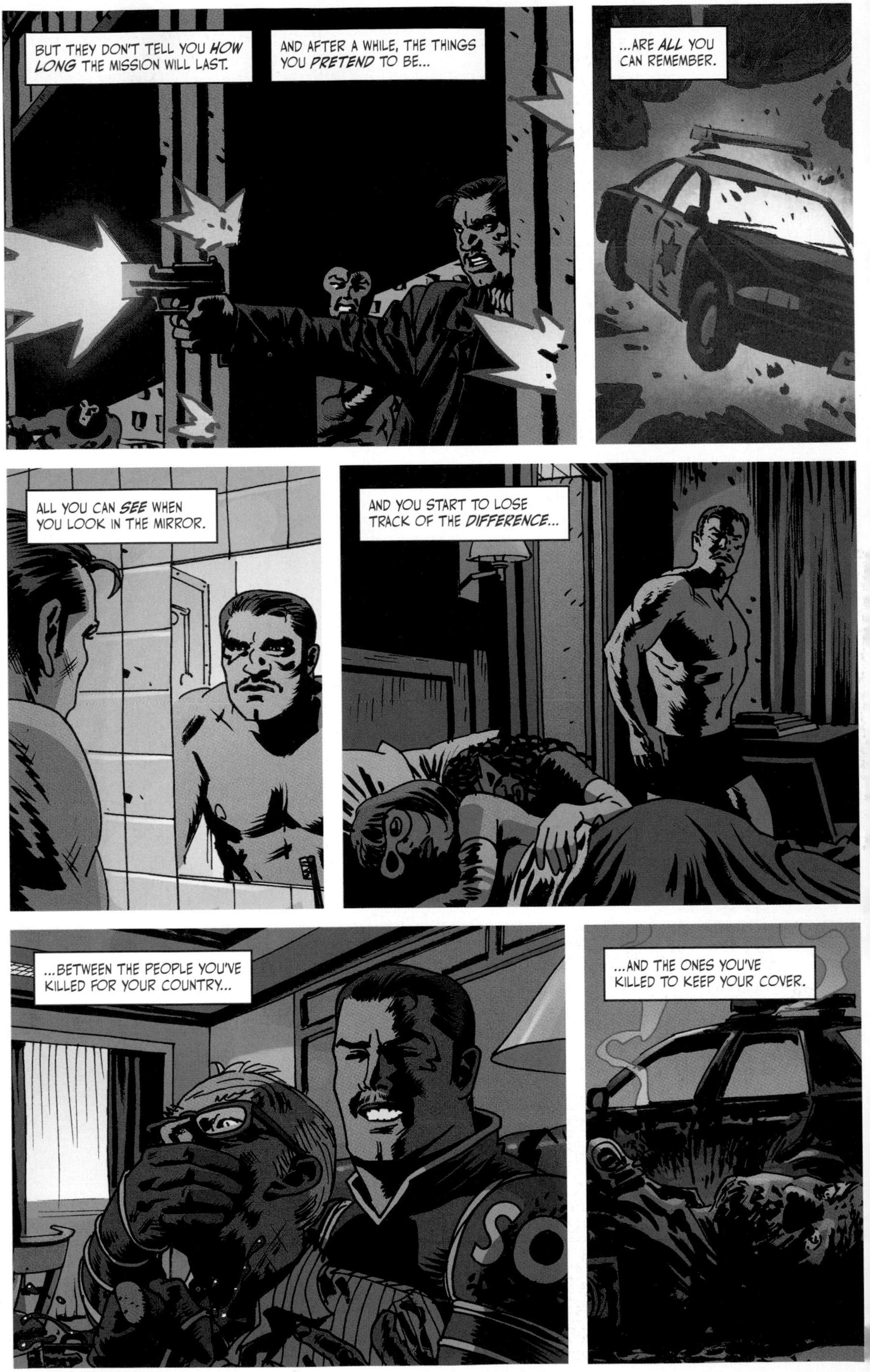
BUT THEY DON'T TELL YOU HOW LONG THE MISSION WILL LAST.
AND AFTER A WHILE, THE THINGS YOU PRETEND TO BE...
...ARE ALL YOU CAN REMEMBER.
ALL YOU CAN SEE WHEN YOU LOOK IN THE MIRROR.
AND YOU START TO LOSE TRACK OF THE DIFFERENCE...
...BETWEEN THE PEOPLE YOU'VE KILLED FOR YOUR COUNTRY...
...AND THE ONES YOU'VE KILLED TO KEEP YOUR COVER.

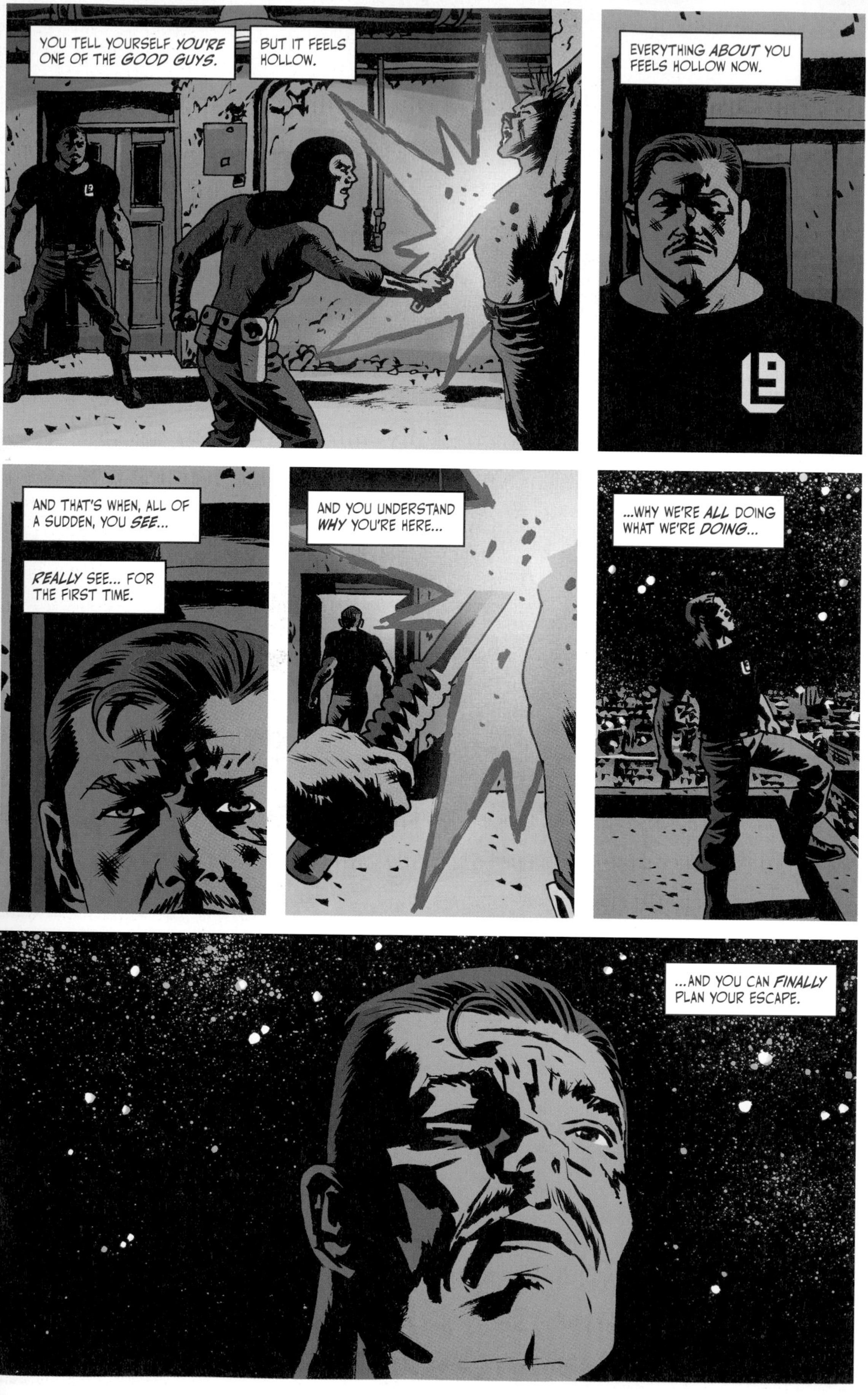
YOU TELL YOURSELF YOU'RE ONE OF THE GOOD GUYS.
BUT IT FEELS HOLLOW.
EVERYTHING ABOUT YOU FEELS HOLLOW NOW.
AND THAT'S WHEN, ALL OF A SUDDEN, YOU SEE...
REALLY SEE... FOR THE FIRST TIME.
AND YOU UNDERSTAND WHY YOU'RE HERE...
...WHY WE'RE ALL DOING WHAT WE'RE DOING...
...AND YOU CAN FINALLY PLAN YOUR ESCAPE.

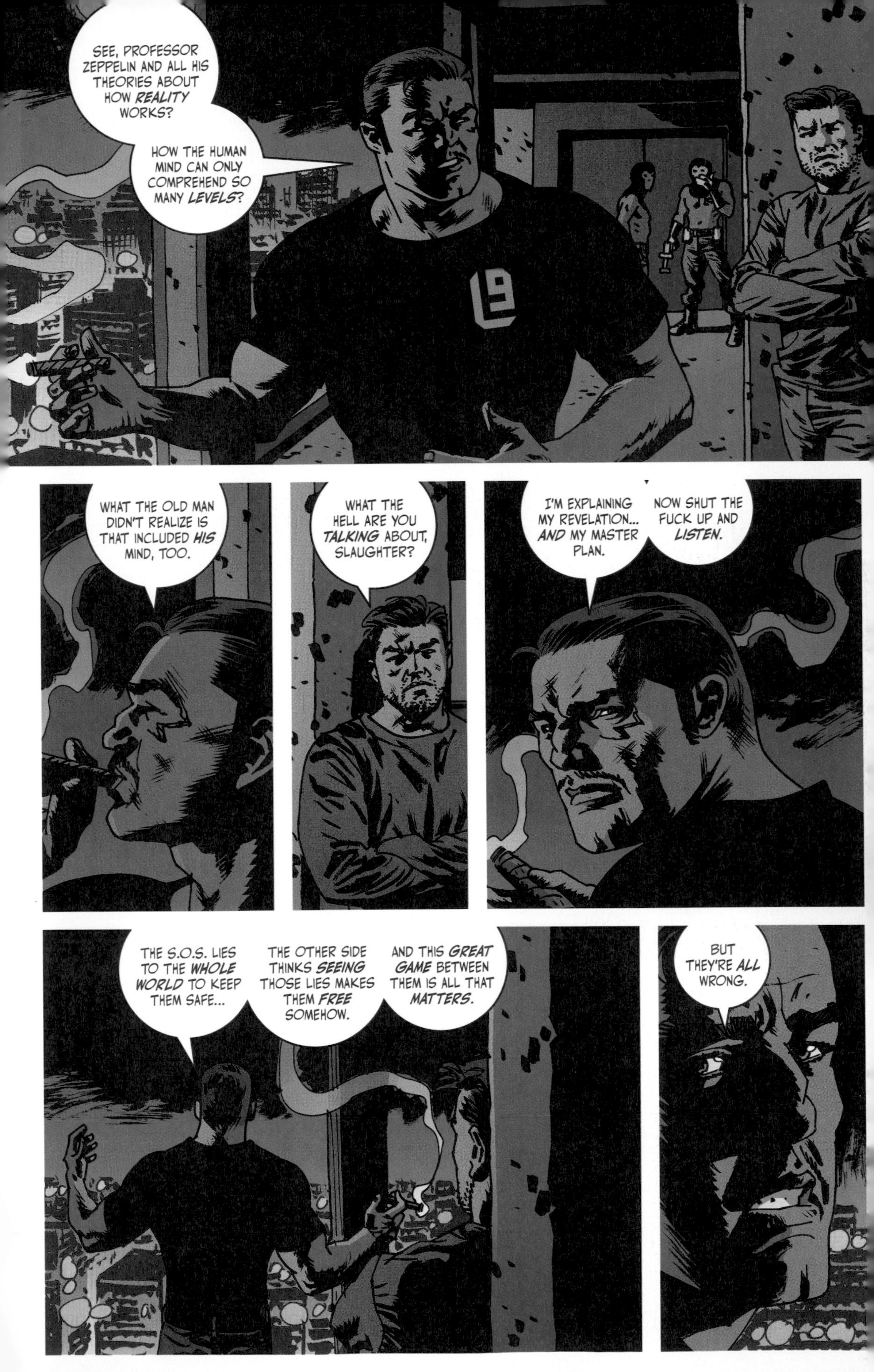
SEE, PROFESSOR ZEPPELIN AND ALL HIS THEORIES ABOUT HOW *REALITY* WORKS?
HOW THE HUMAN MIND CAN ONLY COMPREHEND SO MANY *LEVELS*?
WHAT THE OLD MAN DIDN'T REALIZE IS THAT INCLUDED *HIS* MIND, TOO.
WHAT THE HELL ARE YOU *TALKING* ABOUT, SLAUGHTER?
I'M EXPLAINING MY REVELATION... *AND* MY MASTER PLAN.
NOW SHUT THE FUCK UP AND *LISTEN*.
THE S.O.S. LIES TO THE *WHOLE WORLD* TO KEEP THEM SAFE...
THE OTHER SIDE THINKS *SEEING* THOSE LIES MAKES THEM *FREE* SOMEHOW.
AND THIS *GREAT GAME* BETWEEN THEM IS ALL THAT *MATTERS*.
BUT THEY'RE *ALL* WRONG.

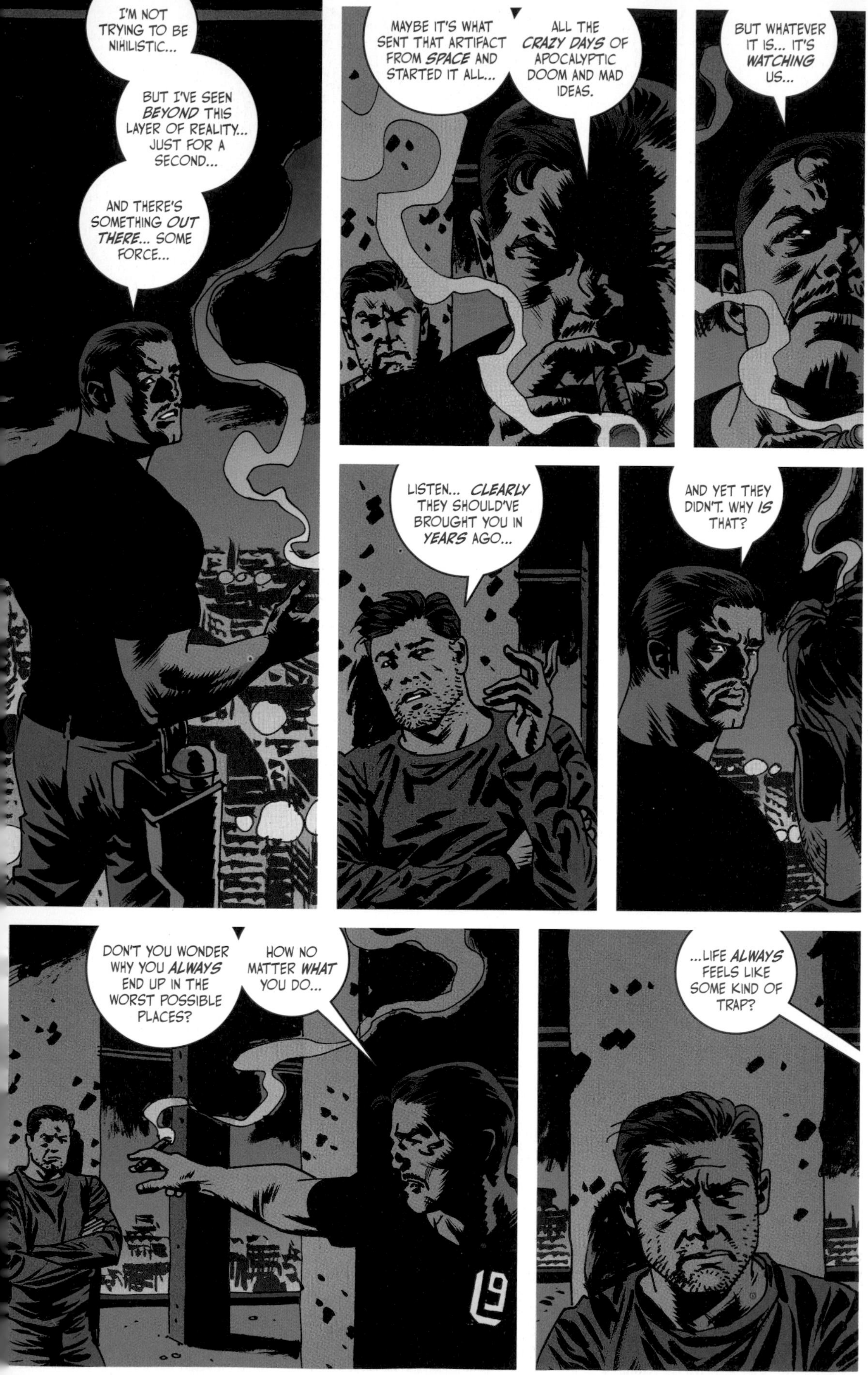
I'M NOT TRYING TO BE NIHILISTIC...
BUT I'VE SEEN *BEYOND* THIS LAYER OF REALITY... JUST FOR A SECOND...
AND THERE'S SOMETHING *OUT THERE*... SOME FORCE...
MAYBE IT'S WHAT SENT THAT ARTIFACT FROM *SPACE* AND STARTED IT ALL...
ALL THE *CRAZY DAYS* OF APOCALYPTIC DOOM AND MAD IDEAS.
BUT WHATEVER IT IS... IT'S *WATCHING* US...
LISTEN... *CLEARLY* THEY SHOULD'VE BROUGHT YOU IN *YEARS* AGO...
AND YET THEY DIDN'T. WHY *IS* THAT?
DON'T YOU WONDER WHY YOU *ALWAYS* END UP IN THE WORST POSSIBLE PLACES?
HOW NO MATTER *WHAT* YOU DO...
...LIFE *ALWAYS* FEELS LIKE SOME KIND OF TRAP?

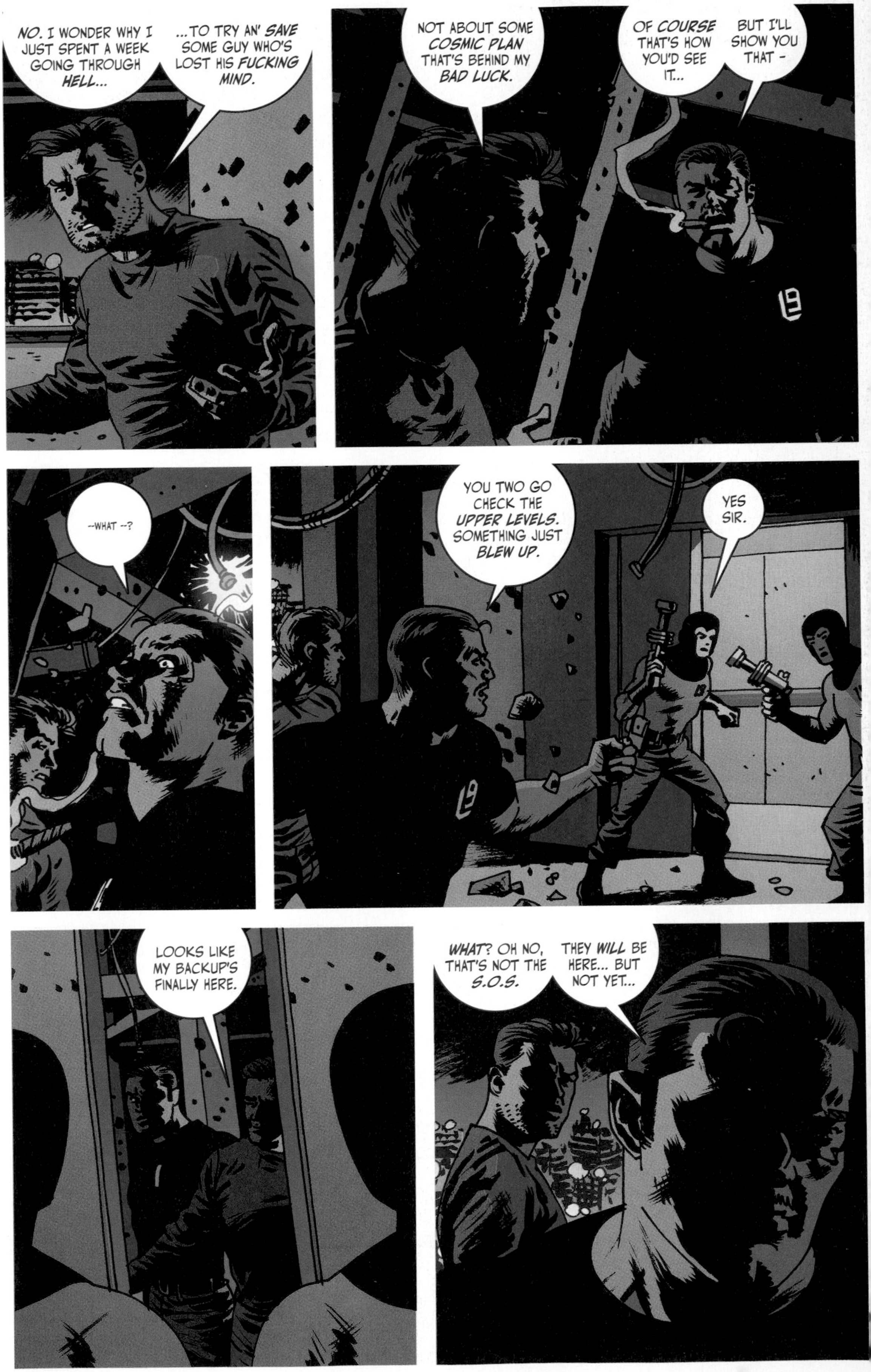
NO. I WONDER WHY I JUST SPENT A WEEK GOING THROUGH HELL...
...TO TRY AN' SAVE SOME GUY WHO'S LOST HIS FUCKING MIND.
NOT ABOUT SOME COSMIC PLAN THAT'S BEHIND MY BAD LUCK.
OF COURSE THAT'S HOW YOU'D SEE IT...
BUT I'LL SHOW YOU THAT -
--WHAT --?
YOU TWO GO CHECK THE UPPER LEVELS. SOMETHING JUST BLEW UP.
YES SIR.
LOOKS LIKE MY BACKUP'S FINALLY HERE.
WHAT? OH NO, THAT'S NOT THE S.O.S.
THEY WILL BE HERE... BUT NOT YET...

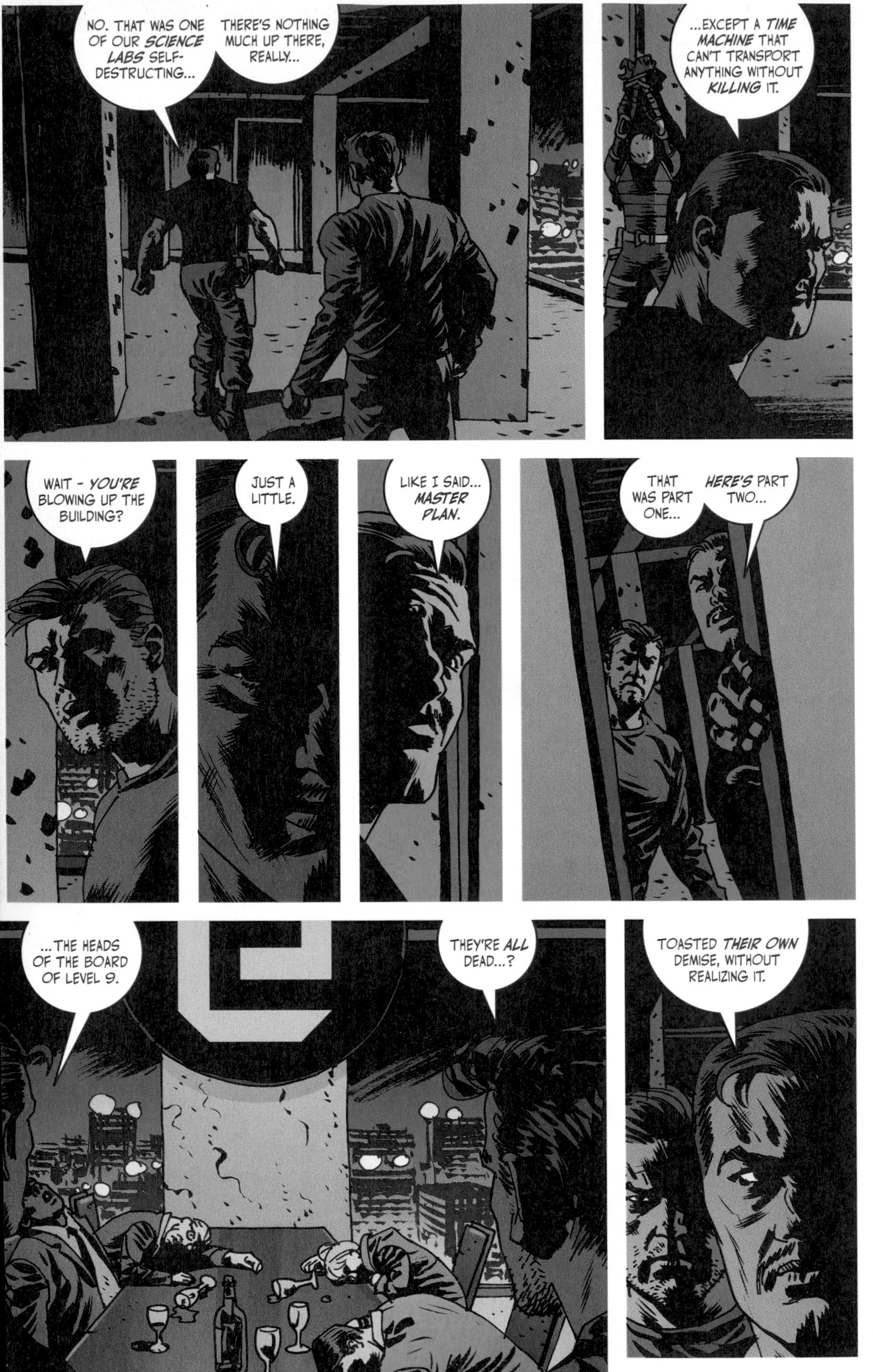
NO. THAT WAS ONE OF OUR *SCIENCE LABS* SELF-DESTRUCTING...
THERE'S NOTHING MUCH UP THERE, REALLY...
...EXCEPT A *TIME MACHINE* THAT CAN'T TRANSPORT ANYTHING WITHOUT *KILLING* IT.
WAIT - *YOU'RE* BLOWING UP THE BUILDING?
JUST A LITTLE.
LIKE I SAID... *MASTER PLAN.*
THAT WAS PART ONE...
HERE'S PART TWO...
...THE HEADS OF THE BOARD OF LEVEL 9.
THEY'RE *ALL* DEAD...?
TOASTED *THEIR OWN* DEMISE, WITHOUT REALIZING IT.

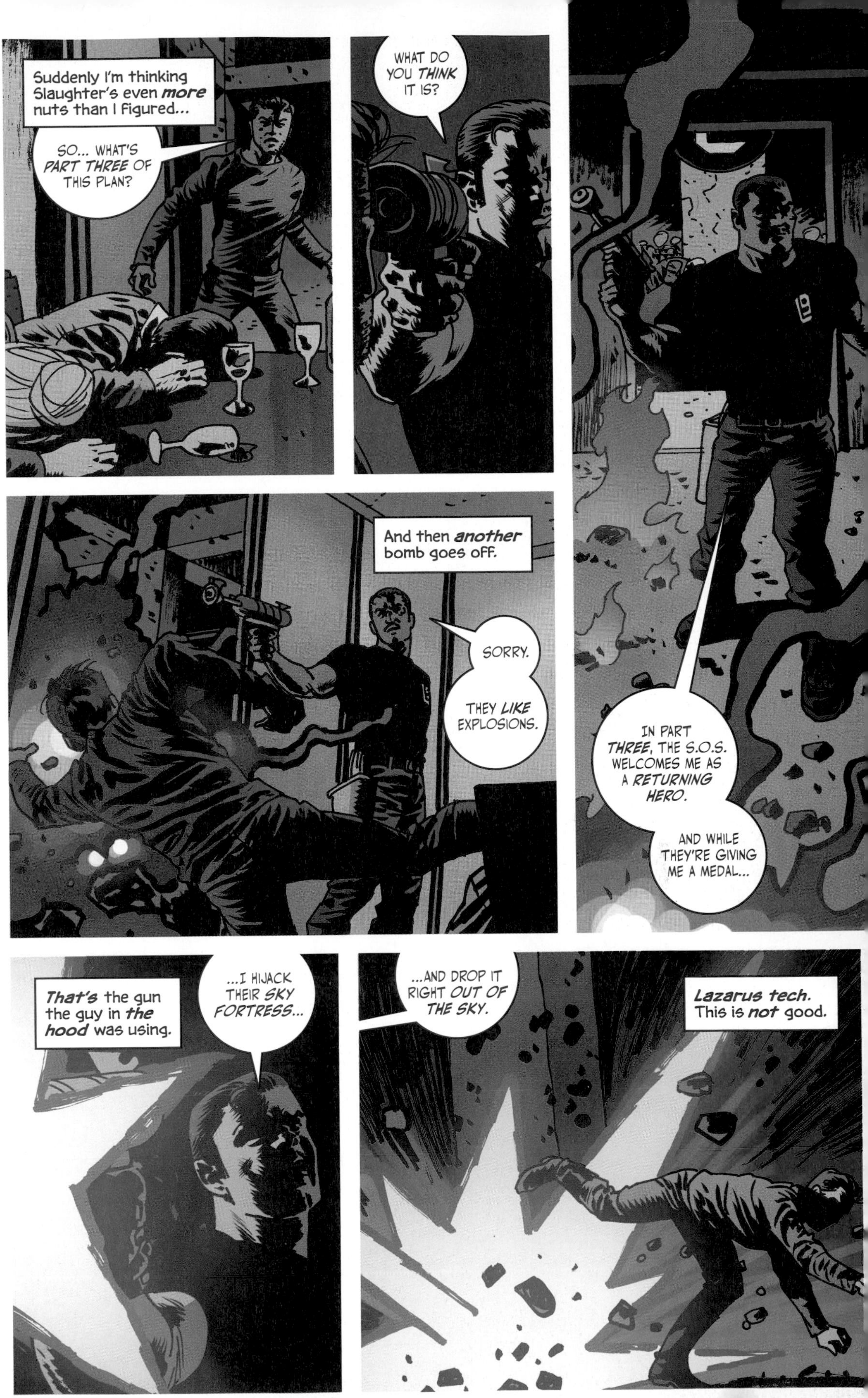
Suddenly I'm thinking Slaughter's even *more* nuts than I figured...
SO... WHAT'S *PART THREE* OF THIS PLAN?
WHAT DO YOU *THINK* IT IS?
And then *another* bomb goes off.
SORRY.
THEY *LIKE* EXPLOSIONS.
IN PART *THREE*, THE S.O.S. WELCOMES ME AS A *RETURNING HERO*.
AND WHILE THEY'RE GIVING ME A MEDAL...
That's the gun the guy in *the hood* was using.
...I HIJACK THEIR *SKY FORTRESS*...
...AND DROP IT RIGHT *OUT OF THE SKY*.
Lazarus tech. This is *not* good.

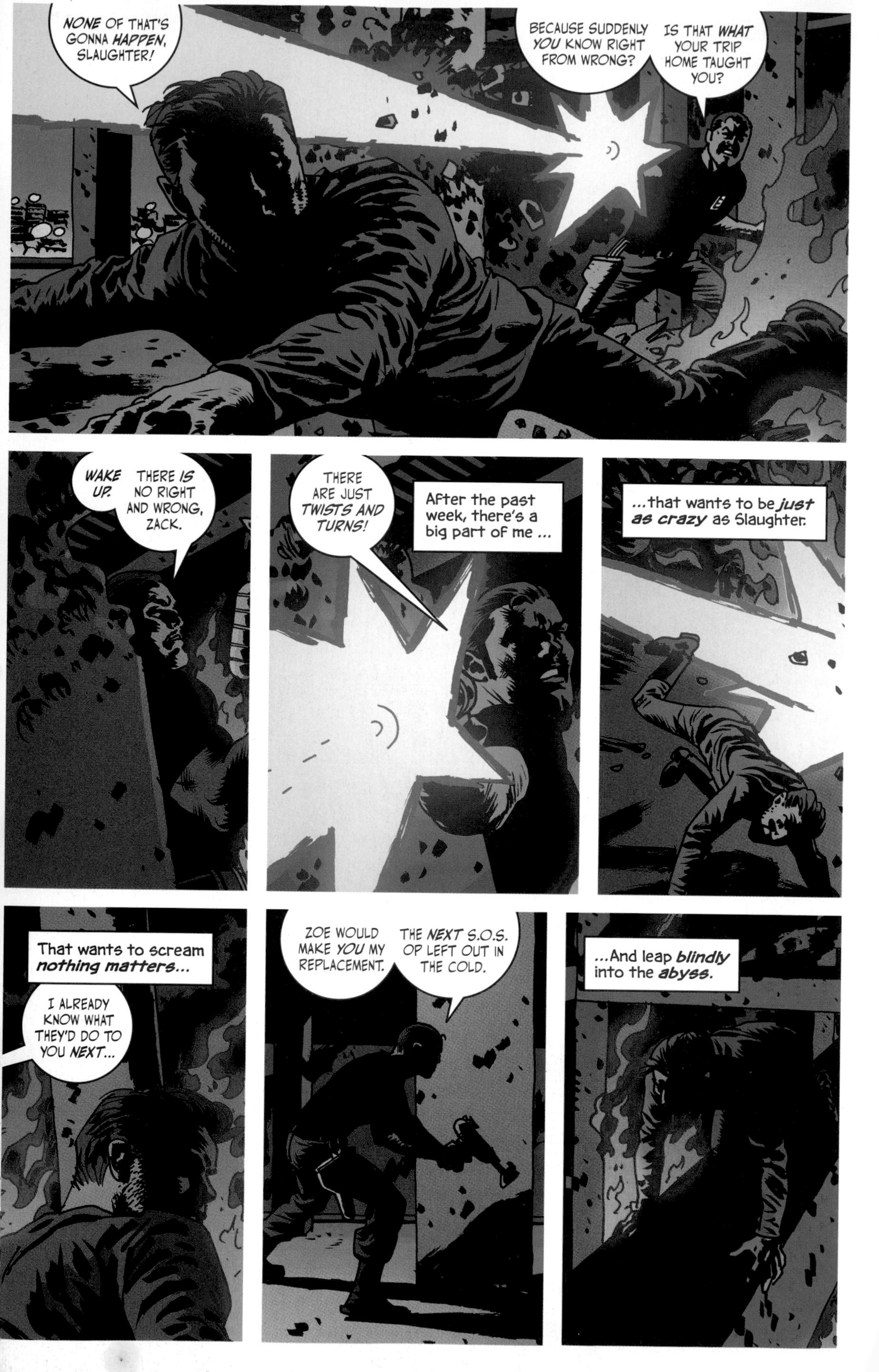
NONE OF THAT'S GONNA HAPPEN, SLAUGHTER!
BECAUSE SUDDENLY YOU KNOW RIGHT FROM WRONG?
IS THAT WHAT YOUR TRIP HOME TAUGHT YOU?
WAKE UP.
THERE IS NO RIGHT AND WRONG, ZACK.
THERE ARE JUST TWISTS AND TURNS!
After the past week, there's a big part of me ...
...that wants to be just as crazy as Slaughter.
That wants to scream nothing matters...
I ALREADY KNOW WHAT THEY'D DO TO YOU NEXT...
ZOE WOULD MAKE YOU MY REPLACEMENT.
THE NEXT S.O.S. OP LEFT OUT IN THE COLD.
...And leap blindly into the abyss.

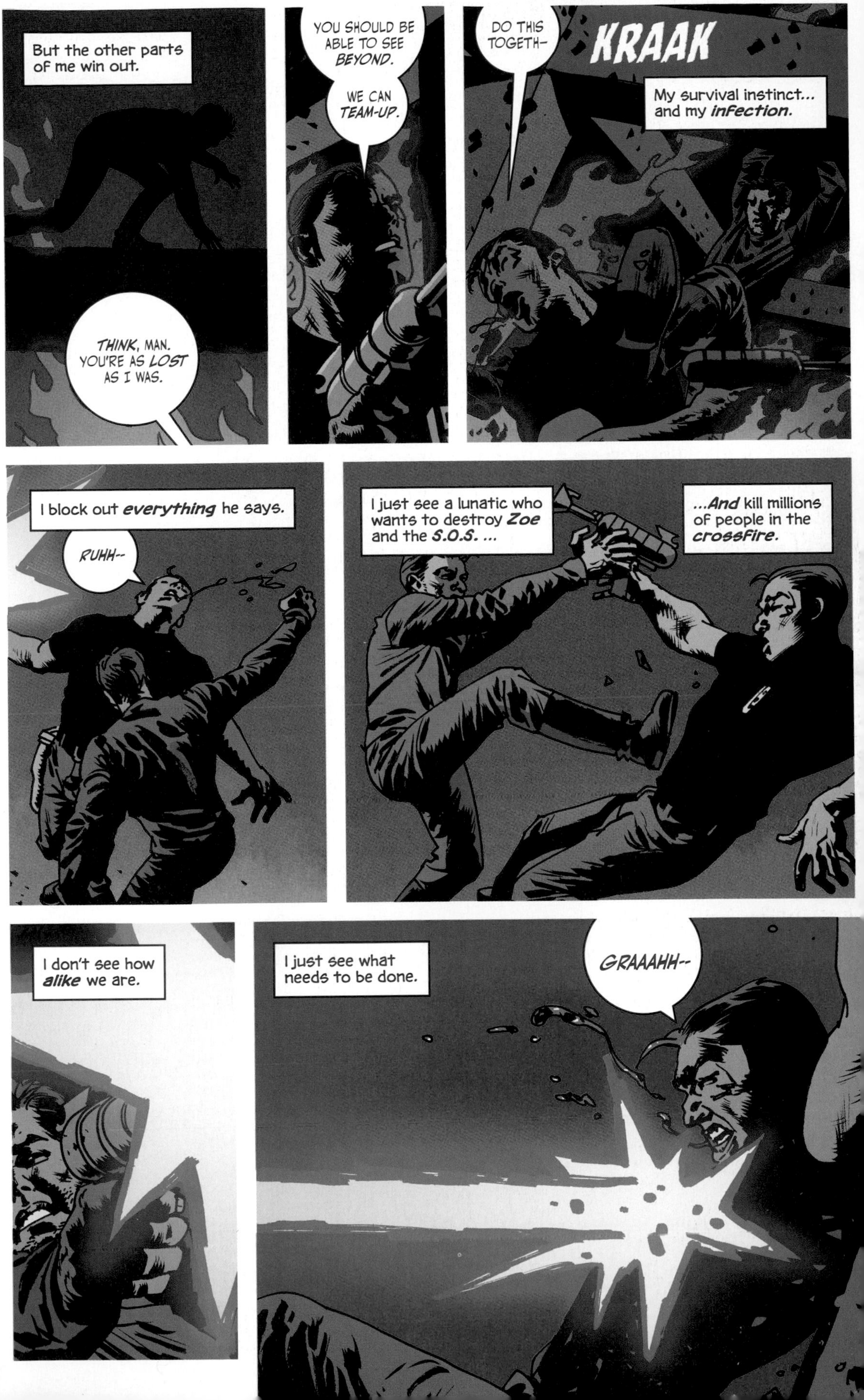
But the other parts of me win out.
THINK, MAN. YOU'RE AS LOST AS I WAS.
YOU SHOULD BE ABLE TO SEE BEYOND.
WE CAN TEAM-UP.
DO THIS TOGETH–
KRAAK
My survival instinct... and my infection.
I block out everything he says.
RUHH--
I just see a lunatic who wants to destroy Zoe and the S.O.S. ...
...And kill millions of people in the crossfire.
I don't see how alike we are.
I just see what needs to be done.
GRAAAHH--

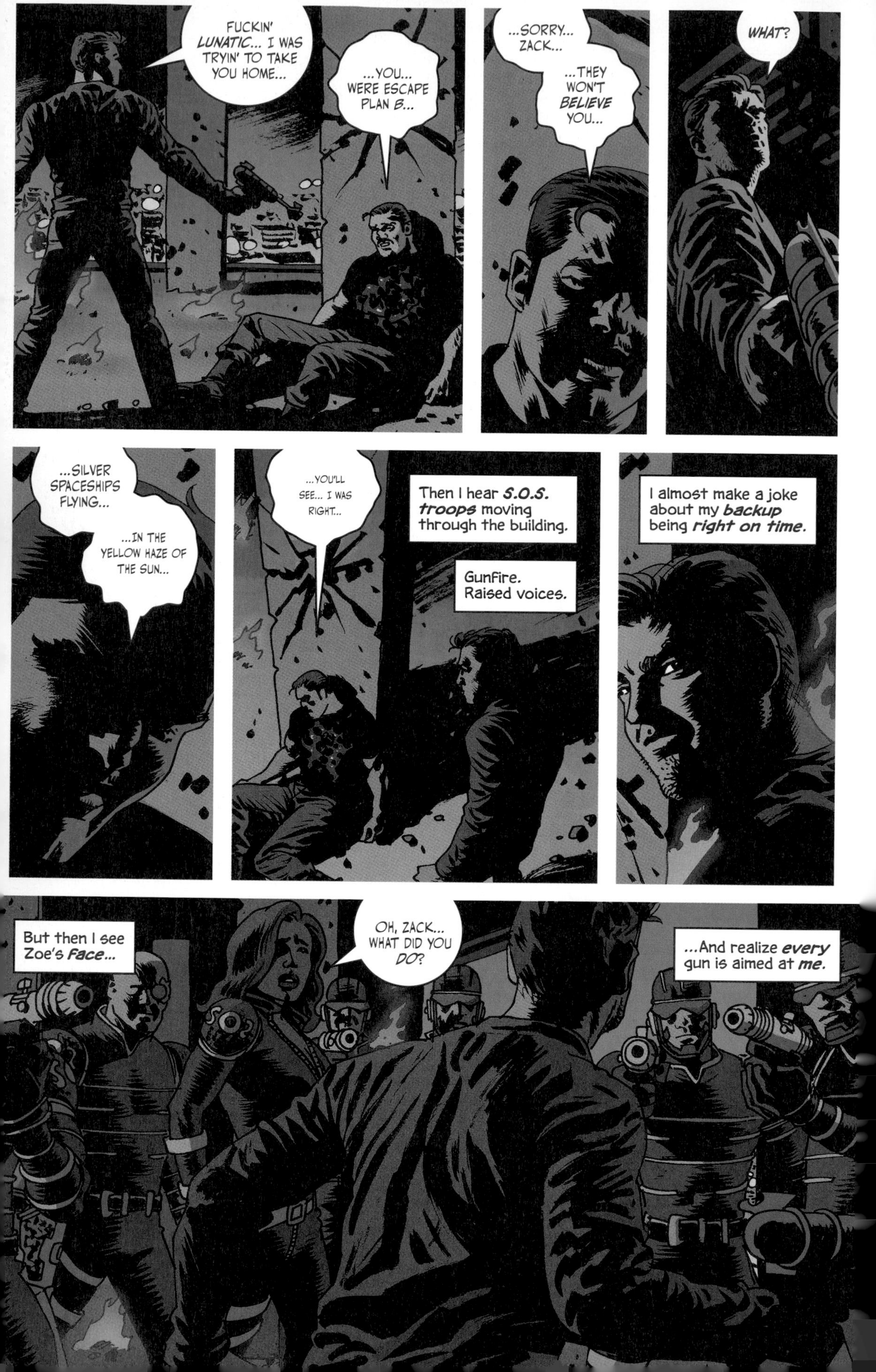
FUCKIN' LUNATIC... I WAS TRYIN' TO TAKE YOU HOME...
...YOU... WERE ESCAPE PLAN B...
...SORRY... ZACK...
...THEY WON'T BELIEVE YOU...
WHAT?
...SILVER SPACESHIPS FLYING...
...IN THE YELLOW HAZE OF THE SUN...
...YOU'LL SEE... I WAS RIGHT...
Then I hear S.O.S. troops moving through the building.
Gunfire. Raised voices.
I almost make a joke about my backup being right on time.
But then I see Zoe's face...
OH, ZACK... WHAT DID YOU DO?
...And realize every gun is aimed at me.

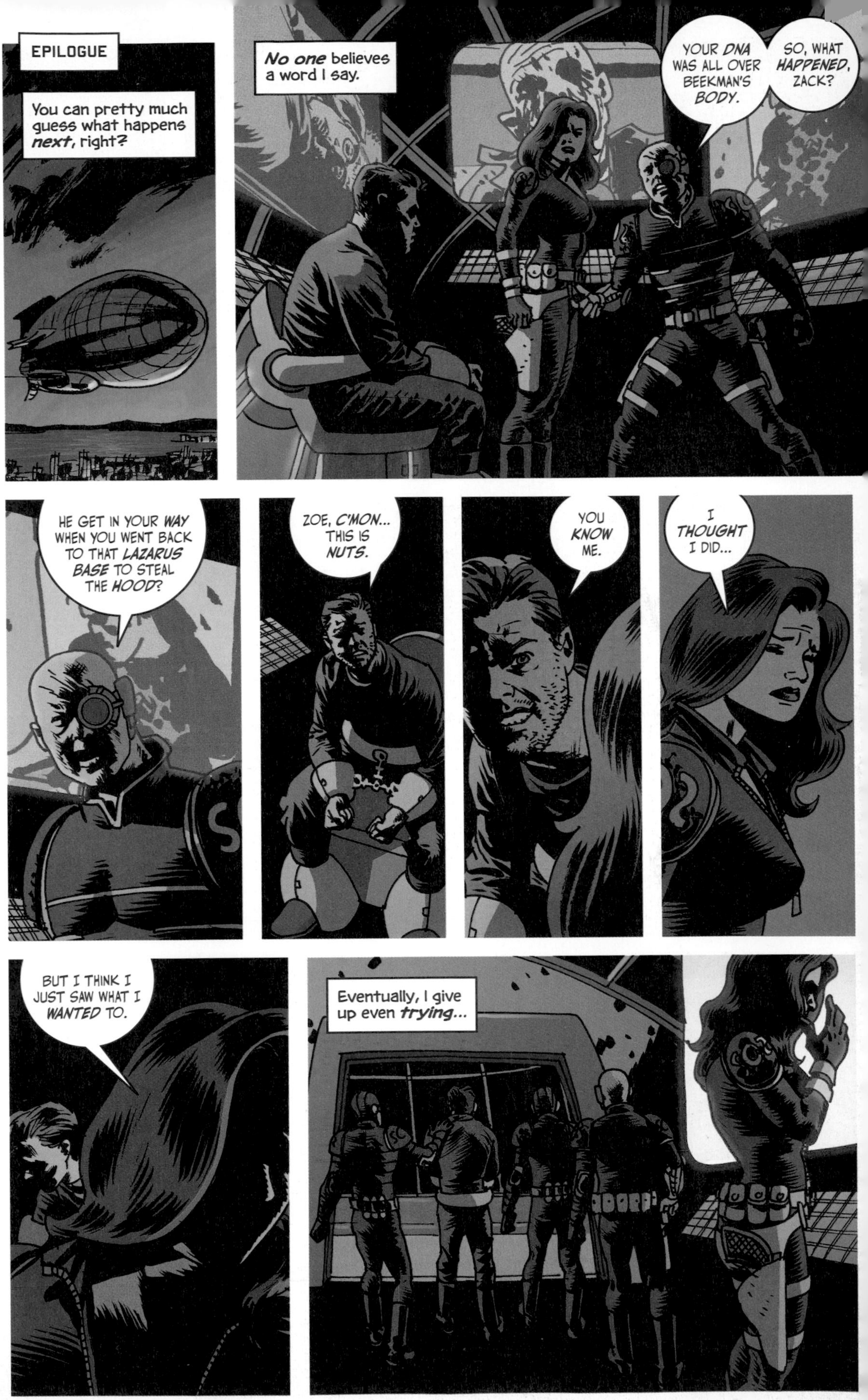
EPILOGUE
You can pretty much guess what happens next, right?
No one believes a word I say.
YOUR DNA WAS ALL OVER BEEKMAN'S BODY.
SO, WHAT HAPPENED, ZACK?
HE GET IN YOUR WAY WHEN YOU WENT BACK TO THAT LAZARUS BASE TO STEAL THE HOOD?
ZOE, C'MON... THIS IS NUTS.
YOU KNOW ME.
I THOUGHT I DID...
BUT I THINK I JUST SAW WHAT I WANTED TO.
Eventually, I give up even trying...

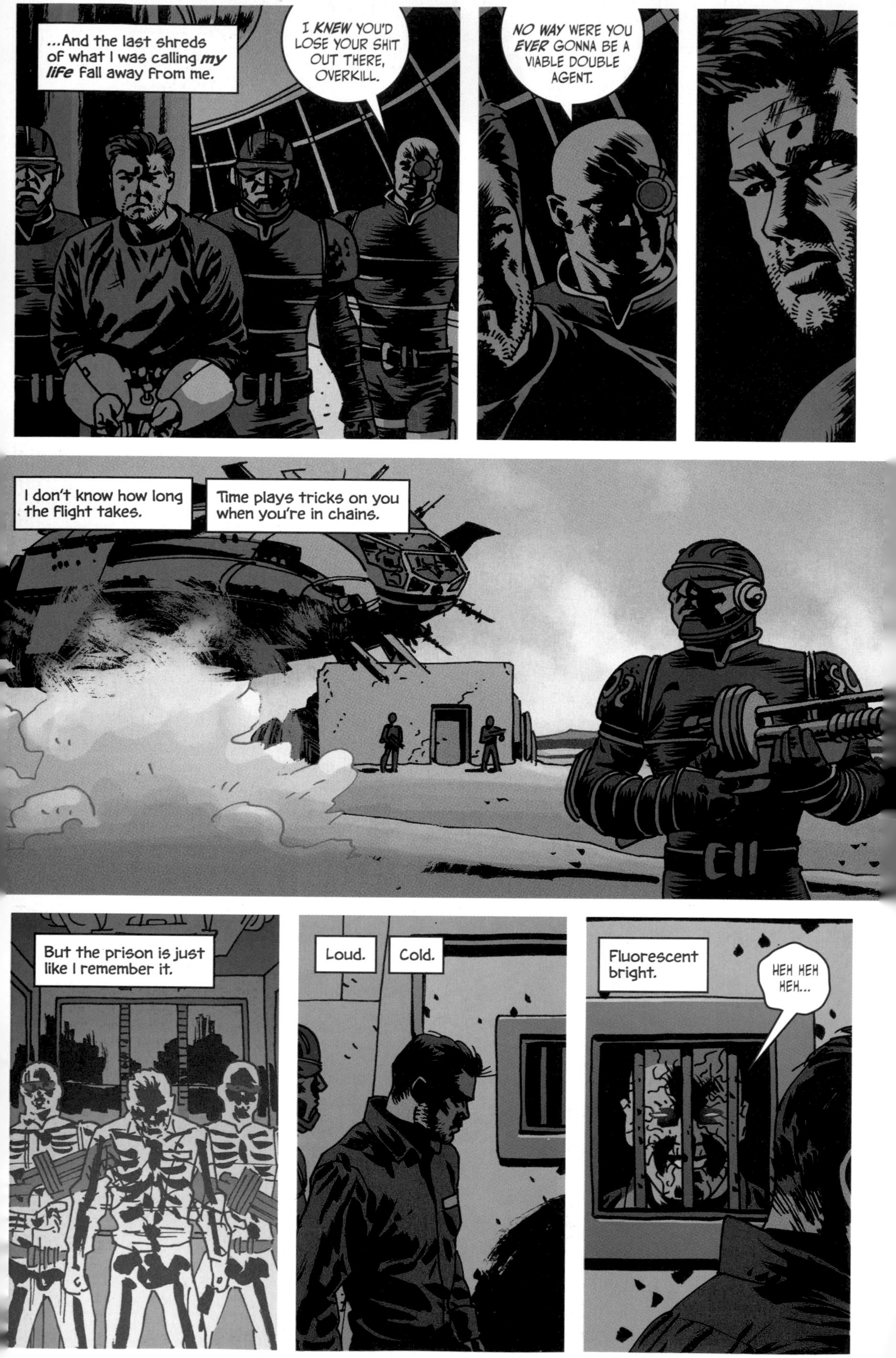
...And the last shreds of what I was calling *my life* fall away from me.
I *KNEW* YOU'D LOSE YOUR SHIT OUT THERE, OVERKILL.
NO WAY WERE YOU *EVER* GONNA BE A VIABLE DOUBLE AGENT.
I don't know how long the flight takes.
Time plays tricks on you when you're in chains.
But the prison is just like I remember it.
Loud.
Cold.
Fluorescent bright.
HEH HEH HEH...

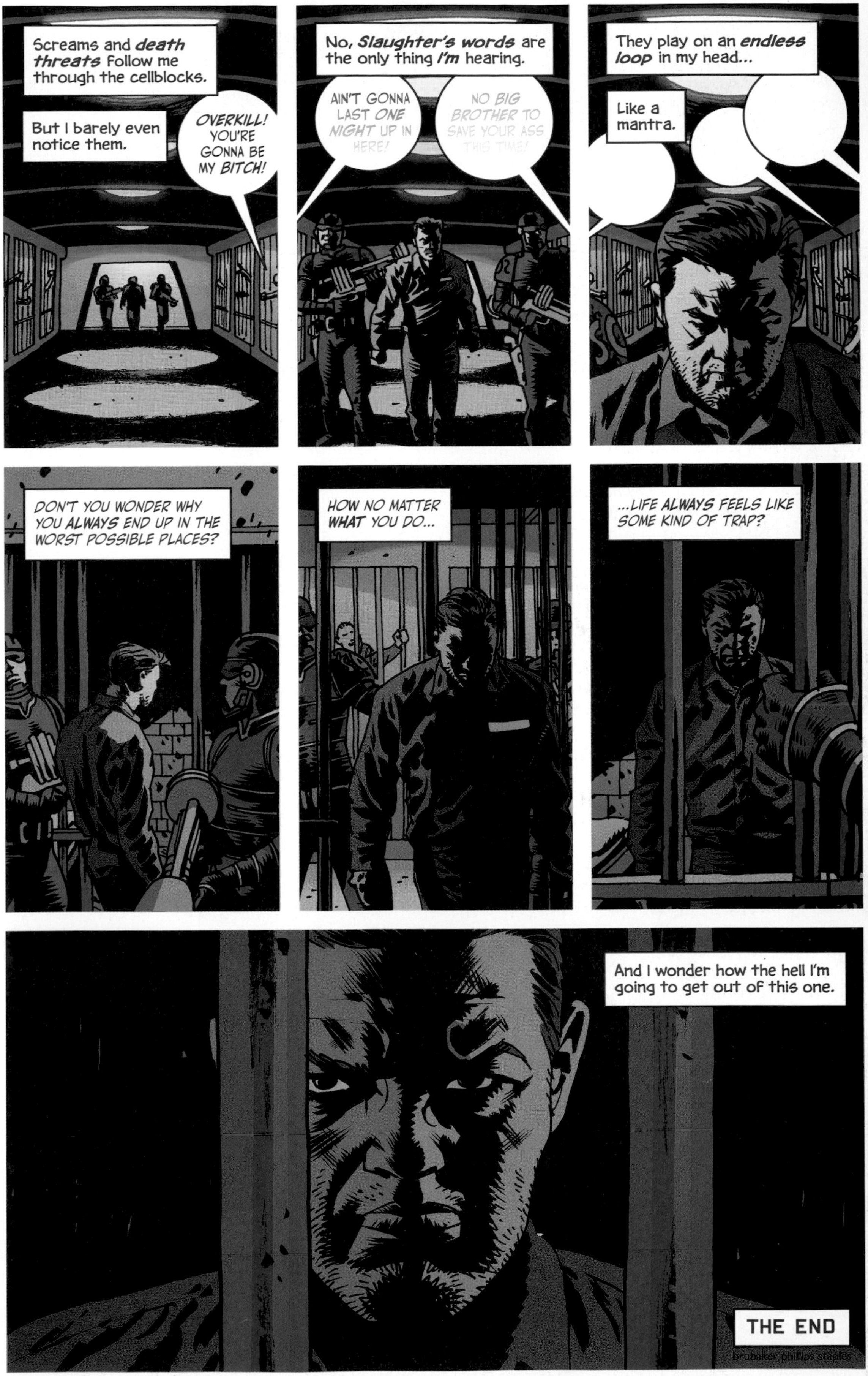

Screams and *death threats* follow me through the cellblocks.
But I barely even notice them.
OVERKILL! YOU'RE GONNA BE MY *BITCH!*
No, *Slaughter's words* are the only thing *I'm* hearing.
AIN'T GONNA LAST *ONE NIGHT* UP IN HERE!
NO *BIG BROTHER* TO SAVE YOUR ASS THIS TIME!
They play on an *endless loop* in my head...
Like a mantra.
DON'T YOU WONDER WHY YOU **ALWAYS** END UP IN THE WORST POSSIBLE PLACES?
HOW NO MATTER **WHAT** YOU DO...
...LIFE **ALWAYS** FEELS LIKE SOME KIND OF TRAP?
And I wonder how the hell I'm going to get out of this one.
THE END
brubaker phillips staples

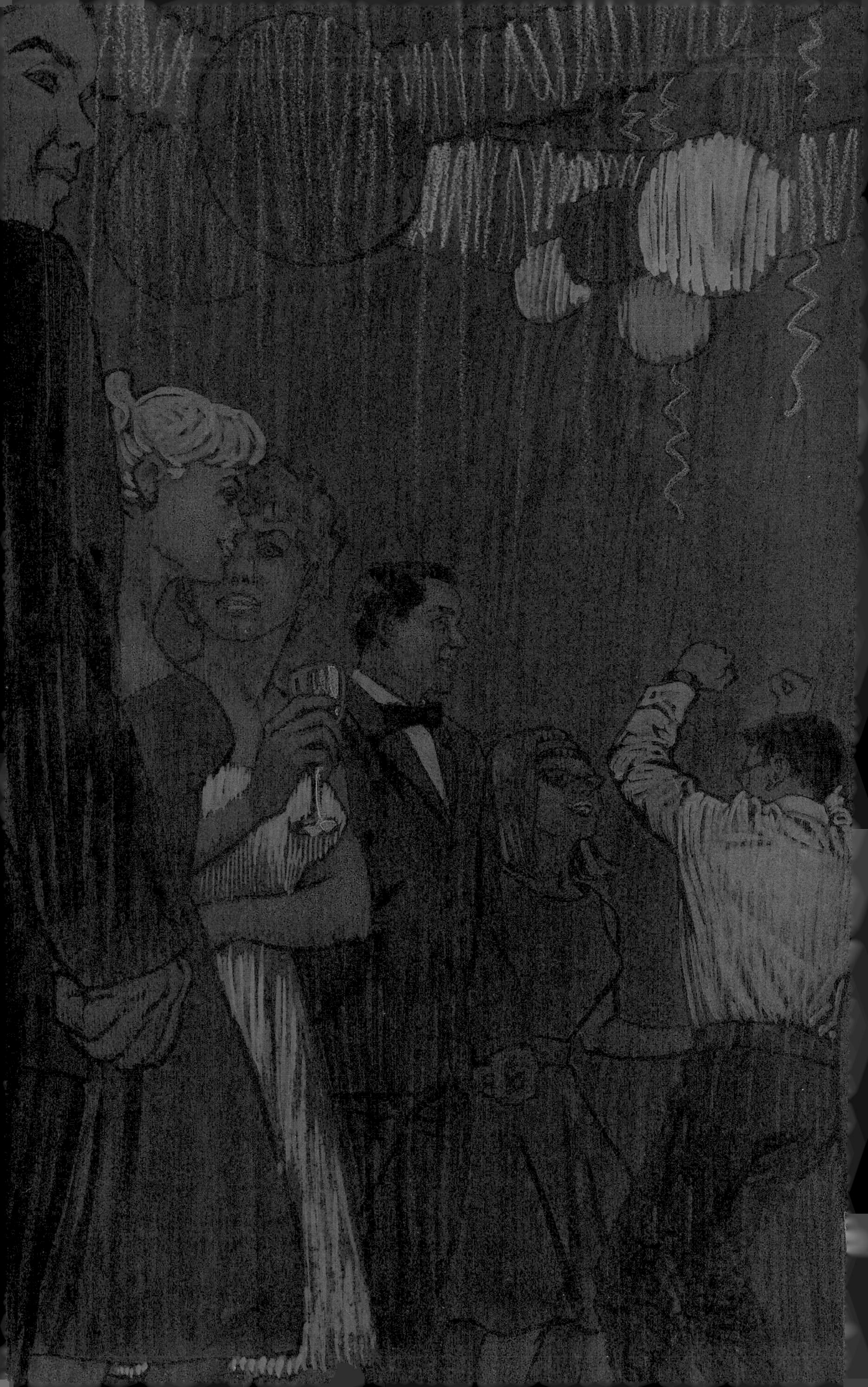

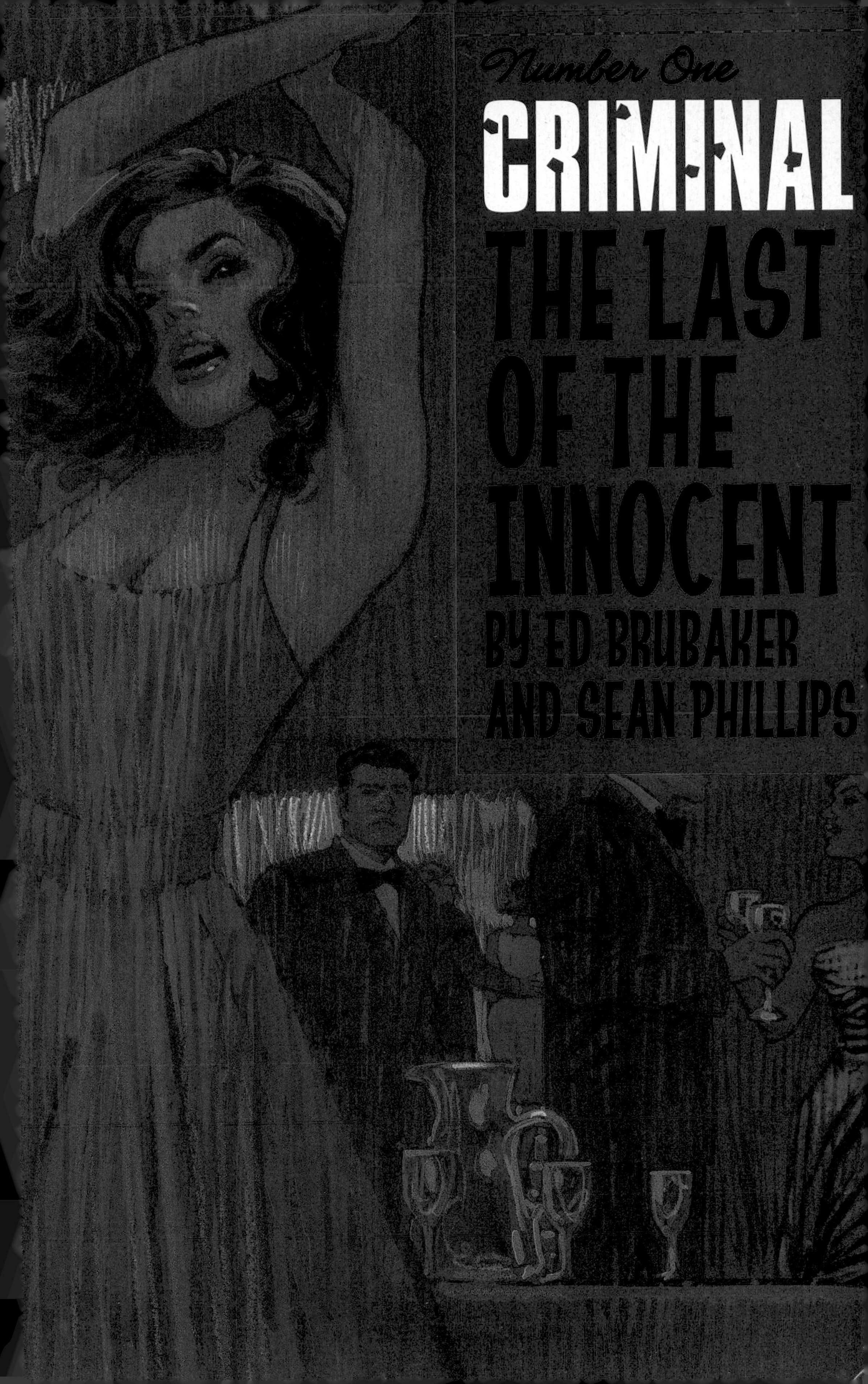
Number One
CRIMINAL
THE LAST OF THE INNOCENT
BY ED BRUBAKER
AND SEAN PHILLIPS

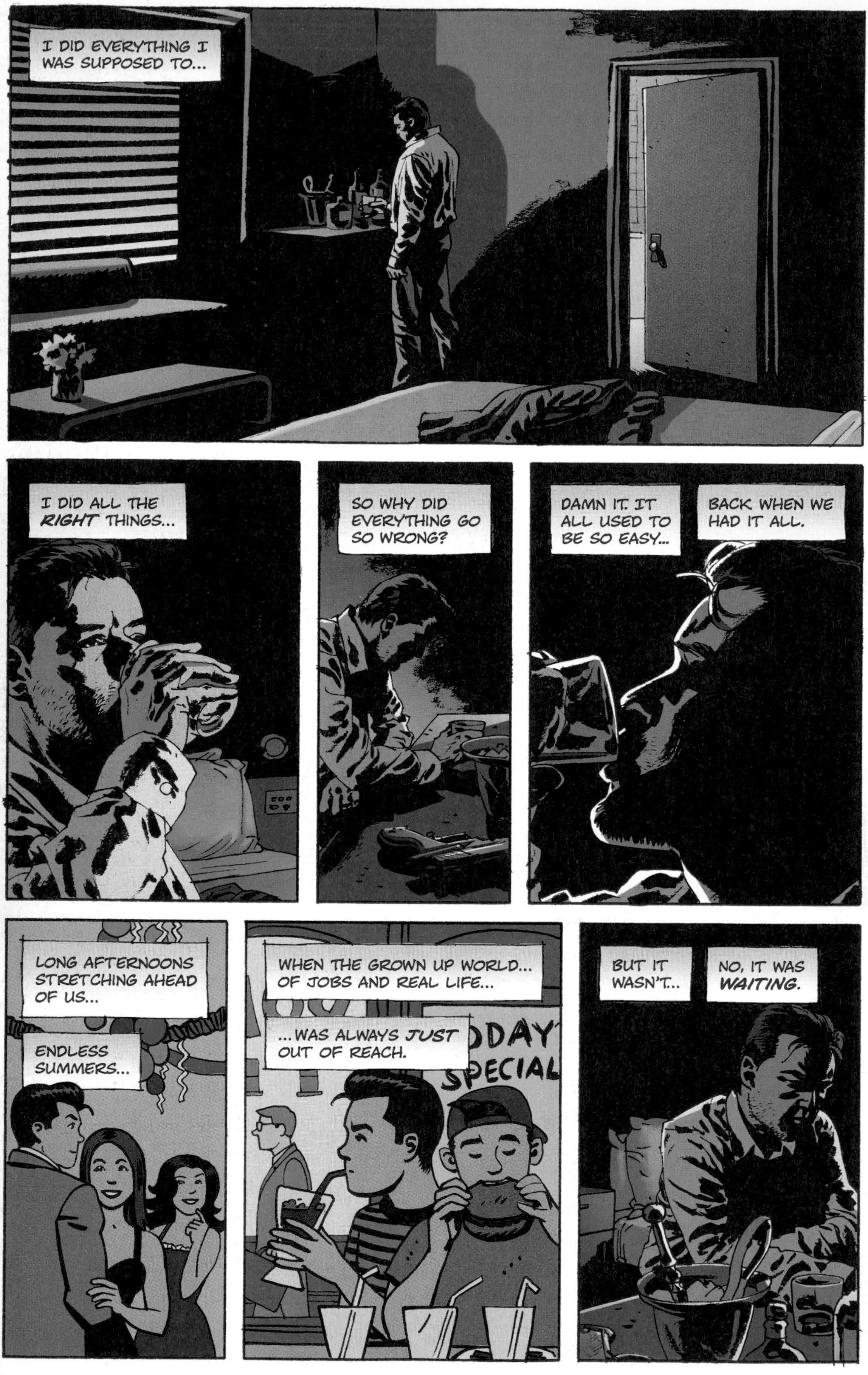
I DID EVERYTHING I WAS SUPPOSED TO...
I DID ALL THE *RIGHT* THINGS...
SO WHY DID EVERYTHING GO SO WRONG?
DAMN IT. IT ALL USED TO BE SO EASY...
BACK WHEN WE HAD IT ALL.
LONG AFTERNOONS STRETCHING AHEAD OF US...
ENDLESS SUMMERS...
WHEN THE GROWN UP WORLD... OF JOBS AND REAL LIFE...
...WAS ALWAYS *JUST* OUT OF REACH.
BUT IT WASN'T...
NO, IT WAS *WAITING*.

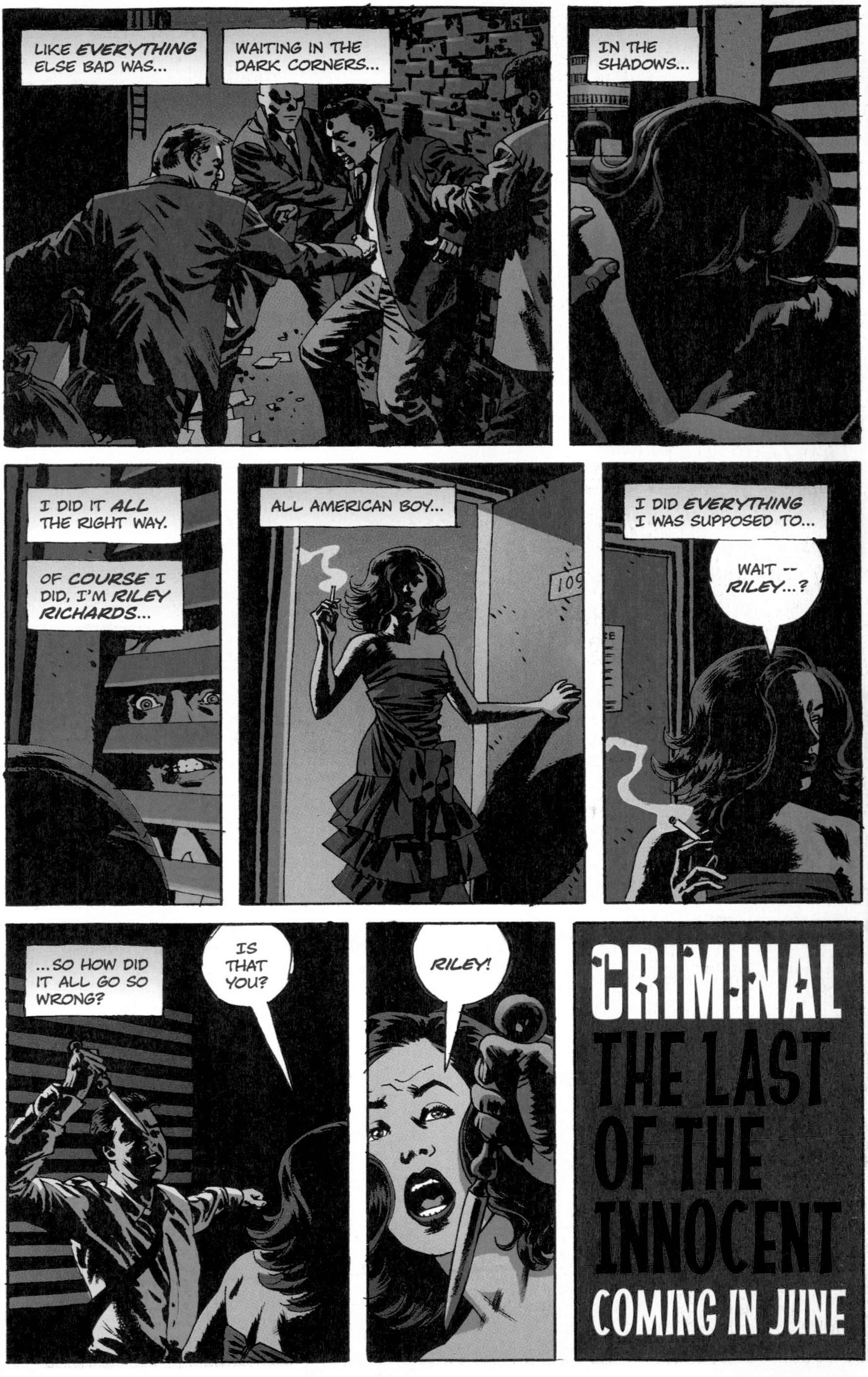
LIKE EVERYTHING ELSE BAD WAS...
WAITING IN THE DARK CORNERS...
IN THE SHADOWS...
I DID IT ALL THE RIGHT WAY.
OF COURSE I DID, I'M RILEY RICHARDS...
ALL AMERICAN BOY...
I DID EVERYTHING I WAS SUPPOSED TO...
WAIT -- RILEY...?
...SO HOW DID IT ALL GO SO WRONG?
IS THAT YOU?
RILEY!
CRIMINAL
THE LAST OF THE INNOCENT
COMING IN JUNE

Bibliography

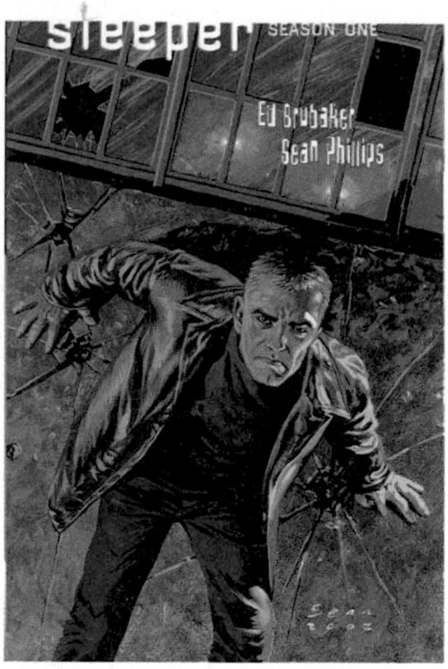
sleeper SEASON ONE
Ed Brubaker
Sean Phillips

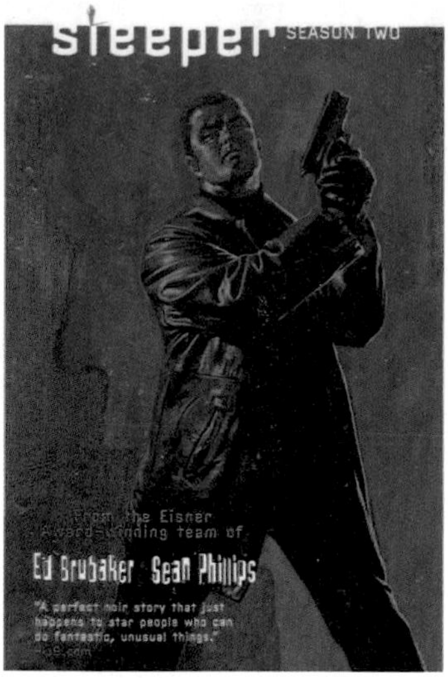
sleeper SEASON TWO
Ed Brubaker Sean Phillips
"A perfect noir story that just happens to star people who can do fantastic, unusual things."

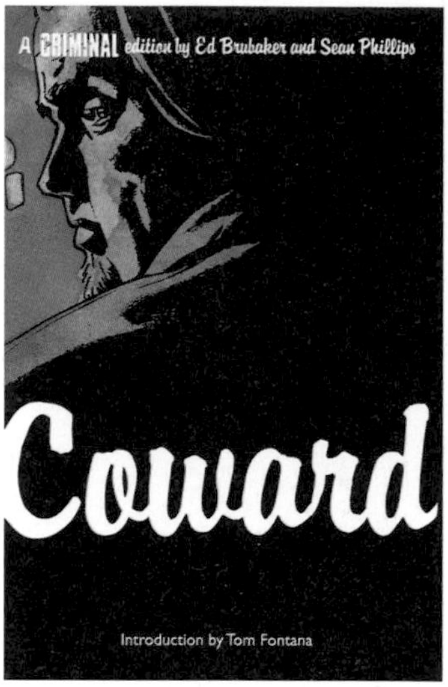
A CRIMINAL edition by Ed Brubaker and Sean Phillips
Coward
Introduction by Tom Fontana

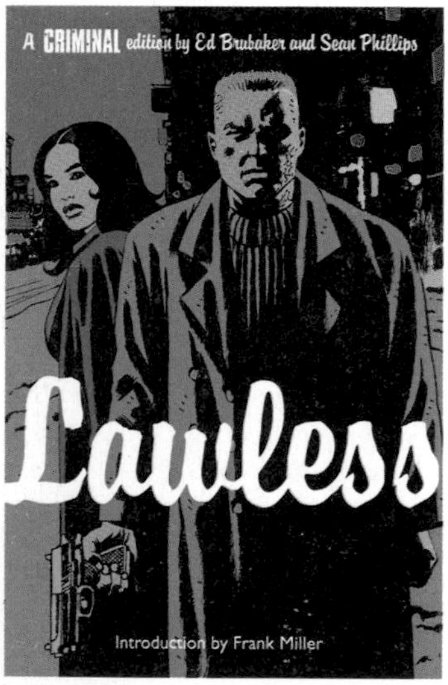
A CRIMINAL edition by Ed Brubaker and Sean Phillips
Lawless
Introduction by Frank Miller

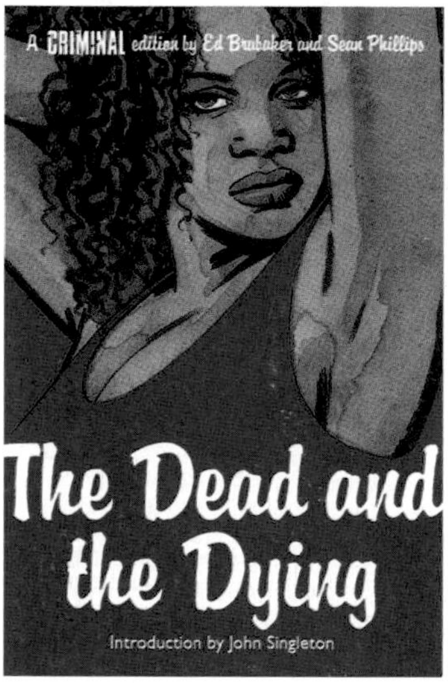
A CRIMINAL edition by Ed Brubaker and Sean Phillips
The Dead and the Dying
Introduction by John Singleton

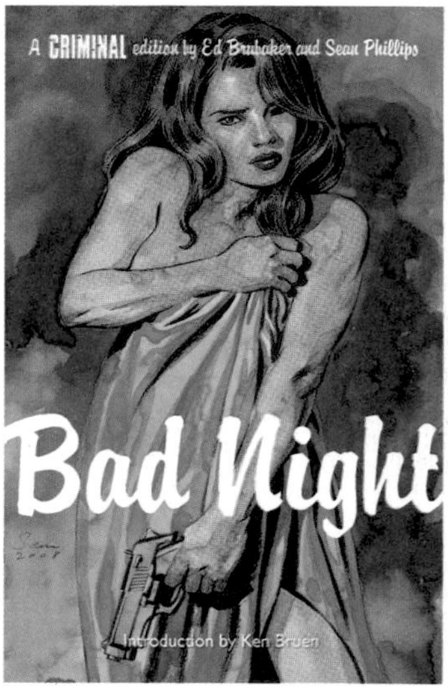
A CRIMINAL edition by Ed Brubaker and Sean Phillips
Bad Night
Introduction by Ken Bruen

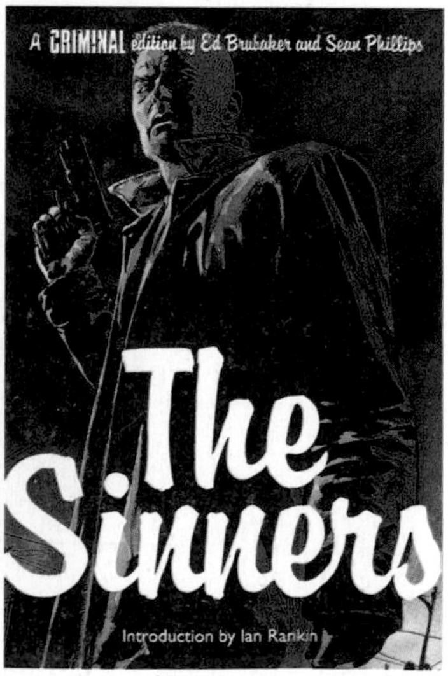
A CRIMINAL edition by Ed Brubaker and Sean Phillips
The Sinners
Introduction by Ian Rankin

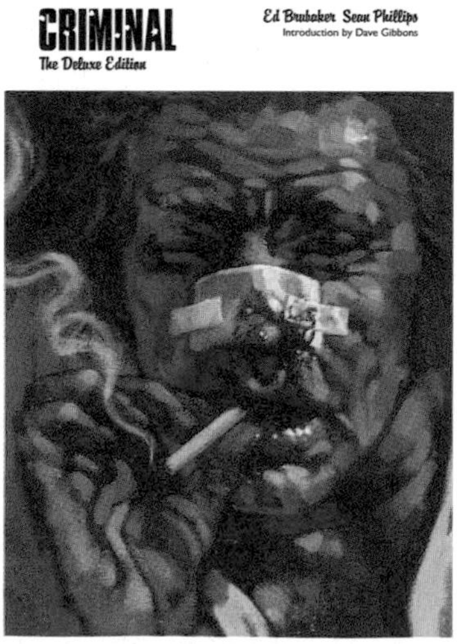
CRIMINAL
The Deluxe Edition
Ed Brubaker Sean Phillips
Introduction by Dave Gibbons

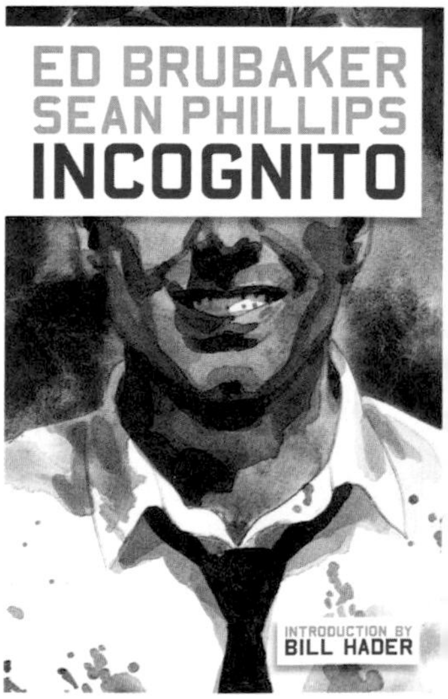
ED BRUBAKER
SEAN PHILLIPS
INCOGNITO
INTRODUCTION BY
BILL HADER